T0330422

Measuring More than Money

Measuring More than Money

The Social Economics of Job Quality

Rafael Muñoz de Bustillo

University of Salamanca, Spain

Enrique Fernández-Macías

University of Salamanca, Spain

José-Ignacio Antón

University of Salamanca, Spain

Fernando Esteve

Autónoma-University of Madrid, Spain

Edward Elgar

Cheltenham, UK • Northampton, MA, USA

Published by
Edward Elgar Publishing Limited
The Lypiatts
15 Lansdown Road
Cheltenham
Glos GL50 2JA
UK

Edward Elgar Publishing, Inc.
William Pratt House
9 Dewey Court
Northampton
Massachusetts 01060
USA

A catalogue record for this book
is available from the British Library

Library of Congress Control Number: 2011925752

MIX
Paper from
responsible sources
FSC® C018575

ISBN 978 1 84980 359 5

Typeset by Servis Filmsetting Ltd, Stockport, Cheshire
Printed and bound by MPG Books Group, UK

Contents

Acknowledgements

We thank the insightful comments on earlier drafts of this book from Kea Tijdens, Mark Smith, John Hurley and Ricardo Rodríguez. The funding provided by the Junta de Castilla y León (research project SA008A10-1) and the European Parliament (IP/A/EMPL/FWC/2007-017/C1-SC3) is gratefully acknowledged. Finally, we express our gratitude to the ILO for granting us permission to use the photos on the cover of the book, part of its splendid photo collection of the world of work.

1. Introduction

1.1. AIMS AND STRUCTURE OF THIS BOOK

The aim of this book is threefold. The first is to discuss the different options available for the construction of an indicator of job quality for comparative purposes, and their implications. The second is to provide an overview of existing indicators of job quality, their development and on-going work at national and international level. The third is to present our own proposal of an index of job quality applicable to the European context that can offer a rigorous evaluation of job quality in Europe.

To be able first to evaluate the different available indicators or systems of indicators of job quality, and later to develop our own Job Quality Index (JQI), it is necessary to have a clear idea of the different steps that have to be taken in the process of constructing such an indicator. The obvious starting point is the discussion of the pertinence and value of constructing an indicator of job quality. The process of building an indicator is long and costly, both in time and resources; therefore, the first task to be accomplished is to present a convincing justification of the need for yet another economic and social indicator. In the second part of this introduction we present a list of reasons that justify the increasing social and political concern about this issue, as reflected in the programmes of international organizations such as the ILO (International Labour Organization) (Decent Work Agenda) and the European Union (the 'more and better jobs' motto of the European Employment Strategy).

The next step is to define what is meant by 'job quality' and operationalize the concept. This phase is especially complex as job quality is clearly a multidimensional concept affected by the subjectivity of the observer: different people might consider different things when defining or evaluating job quality. Furthermore, the same job might be perceived differently depending on what specific dimension of its quality is considered. Chapter 2 of the book, which can probably be considered its backbone, discusses the different approaches that can be followed in the process of selecting the dimensions of work and employment relevant for job quality. In order to do so, we discuss the virtues and shortcomings of following a purely subjective approach based on job satisfaction, a two-step mixed approach based on the self-selection and weighting of the relevant dimensions by the workers themselves, and a third and last approach based on the review of existing theoretical perspectives on job quality, drawing on the economic and sociological traditions.

With that frame of reference, Chapter 3 addresses a set of methodological choices that have to be made prior to the process of selection of the dimensions to be included in the index. This review includes the question of its periodicity, the option of favouring a system of indicators as opposed to an aggregate indicator, the utilization of individual or aggregate data, etc. A separate section is devoted to the analysis of how to deal with those interventions from the public sector affecting job quality through the provision to workers (or citizens in general) of specific social services.

With this theoretical (Chapter 2) and methodological (Chapter 3) background, Chapter 4 reviews around 20 different proposed indices of job quality. The aim of this chapter is to discuss, in a homogeneous framework, the characteristics, strengths and shortcomings of the most important pre-existing indicators. Chapter 5, drawing again on previous chapters, introduces our own proposal of a model-based Index of Job Quality, based on the aggregation of information on five different areas of work which the specialized literature identifies as having an important impact on workers' well-being (these areas are: pay, intrinsic quality of work, employment quality, health and safety and work-life balance). In Chapter 6, we put our proposal into practice, using it to study the distribution of job quality in Europe, at the country level and for specific categories of workers. Finally, in Chapter 7 we discuss the main conclusions we could draw from this exercise.

1.2. THE IMPORTANCE OF HAVING A RELIABLE INDICATOR OF JOB QUALITY

It is important to make two things clear from the very beginning. It is our understanding that any job quality indicator has to be strictly limited to those aspects of the job that have a clear and direct impact on the well-being of workers.[1] The concept of job quality is linked on the one hand with the characteristics of the work performed and its environment (which we can call the work dimension, including among other things the level of autonomy at work, as well as its social and physical environment), and on the other hand with the characteristics of the contractual conditions under which such job is performed (which we can call the employment dimension, and includes pay, contractual stability and development opportunities, among other things). This concept excludes issues which may be related to the well-being of workers but which are not characteristics of the jobs they perform (such as their psychological states, or the social support they have outside work), as well as concepts which concern the labour market rather than the characteristics of jobs people have (such as the level of unemployment).

It is also important to clarify from the very beginning the target groups of workers considered in our analysis of job quality. As it is known, from a statistical point of view there are two different kinds of workers: self-employed workers and employees. In 2009 in the EU27, 15 per cent of workers were not employees (including self-employed, employers and family workers), with a maximum of 30 per cent in Greece, and a minimum of 8 per cent in Estonia and Luxembourg. The equivalent for Japan was 13 per cent and 7 per cent for the US. Although there is some discussion about the renaissance of self-employment in the twenty-first century, the analysis of statistical data simply does not support such conclusion. Focusing in the EU15, only in Germany, the Netherlands and the UK has there been a clear increase in self-employment in the last quarter of a century (with an increase in the self-employment rate of 1.9, 3.6 and 3.1 percentage points respectively). In the rest of the EU countries (countries with a higher self-employment rate) the trend has been a reduction of the self-employment rate. The same is valid for Japan and the US. In principle, the self-employed have more latitude to specify their own working conditions, although there are important qualifications to take into account. Firstly, self-employment, or at least part of it, can be driven by competitive pressures to 'choose' undesired working conditions in order to remain in business. If this were the case there would not be much difference between self-employed and employed workers. Secondly, nowadays there is a lively debate about whether there is a growing (and relevant) percentage of self-employed who in fact are 'employees in disguise' (subordinate workers) as a result of the process of contracting-out of firms and their preference for civil law contracts rather than employment contracts. Once again, in this case the differences between employees and self-employees would become blurred. For these reasons, and because they constitute an important proportion of the working population whose conditions should also be monitored, we will include both employees and self-employed workers in our empirical analysis of job quality.

Measuring job quality, it is argued in the following pages, is a complex and difficult task, but no more complex than measuring other economic phenomena such as the price level, aggregate production or employment quantities. All of these variables, now routinely measured by the Consumer Price Index, the Gross Domestic Product or the Labour Force Surveys, respectively, were also in their origin theoretical concepts difficult to operationalize. Their conversion into largely unquestioned statistics was a long process of analyses, debates, compromises and decisions. To use a well-known example, in order to be considered as employed by the Labour Force Survey, it is enough to work for one hour the week prior to the interview, a condition which is certainly open to question, but nevertheless a convention that allows clearly separating the employed from the non employed. Furthermore, the generation of indicators of employment, unemployment and so on demands the utilization, on a quarterly basis, of a considerable amount of resources. Labour Force Surveys were created with that purpose; resources were allocated to such end because employment figures were considered to be of crucial importance to guide economic policy. Therefore neither the complexity of the objective nor the lack of proper statistics should be used as an excuse to consign to oblivion the development of an indicator of job quality. We are living in a quantitative world, where those variables that are not satisfactorily measured are frequently left out of the political arena.[2] It is not a coincidence that while the quantitative dimension of employment is at the forefront of the political debate, its qualitative dimension is seldom mentioned. Obviously, part of the different treatment can be explained by their different position in terms of priorities (especially in times of high and growing unemployment), but part of it can surely be related to the statistical 'invisibility' of job quality.

But why should we care about measuring job quality? Even though it may seem obvious that job quality is an important issue, there are a significant number of social scientists that consider job quality to be a 'non-problem' (especially in the field of economics, as it is discussed in the following chapter). And it is not unusual that in the political arena the question of job quality is considered as a diversion from the most important problem: the need to create more jobs. All these doubts and concerns cannot be simply dismissed, so this book must start by asking ourselves why we should care about job quality.

There are a number of reasons that justify the research on job quality and its monitoring for policy purposes. In the first place, the average European full-time worker spends almost 42 hours in his/her job (and the average part-time worker 20 hours). That means that the average full-timer works for a quarter of his/her available weekly time (the average part-time worker for one-eighth). It is obvious that whatever happens in that quarter of the weekly life of workers will have important implications for their well-being. Furthermore, there is abundant evidence showing that people do not only work to earn a living, proving that work is an important element of social and personal life in itself, an activity that is important for self-realization and social integration (Layard 2004).

Therefore the quality of working life is a key element of the quality of life. In this respect, the meta-analysis of Dolan et al. (2008) shows how both having work *per se* and some of the job characteristics (working hours, for example) have a clear positive impact on subjective well-being.

Second, the standard analysis of the labour market usually focuses on quantity, the number of jobs, and their correlate, the employment or unemployment rate. But jobs are a heterogeneous category. There are 'good' and 'bad' jobs, jobs come with different combinations of amenities and disamenities, different bundles of positive and negative attributes. In order to rightly evaluate an economy it is important to know the quality of the jobs created and destroyed in the process of creative destruction that sustains economic growth. As it is shown in detail in Chapter 2, mainstream economists frequently argue that there is no problem in adding good and bad jobs in a single employment measure because the market will homogenize the quality differences of jobs by paying higher wages to those jobs of lower quality. However, this position, as it is shown in that chapter (and in Chapter 6, we provide some further empirical evidence), is highly debatable. As long as we cannot rely on the existence of such a process of compensation, the question of job quality will deserve a specific treatment with specific indicators.

Third, in times of rapid changes in the labour market (globalization, accelerated technological change, etc.), considered by many (Sennet 2005; Coyle 2001) as the harbinger of a breed of new capitalism, widening the analysis of work to take into account changes in other dimensions, apart from employment numbers or the earning structure, can help us to understand the nature of such changes and disentangle myth from reality (Doogan 2009).

Fourth, having a good measure of job quality can contribute to our understanding of the existence of trade-off between quantity and quality of jobs, and to empirically prove the existence of different *employment regimes* in terms of quantity/quality trade-off. A similar approach is explored by Gallie (2007).

The fifth reason is that it would be useful to know in detail the level and components of job quality in each country, and their relation to job quantity, as a necessary step to detect best practices in the field of labour policy. In this respect, we consider that the construction of an index of job quality must be linked to a practical goal, a policy intention. Knowledge is positive *per se*, but it is much more fruitful if it contributes to the improvement of reality.

Six, quality refers to the characteristics of the types of goods and services known in economics as *luxury goods*, meaning that their demand grows faster than income. If that is the case, it is to be expected that, in the process of economic growth, workers' interest in job quality will grow. That also means that jobs which at present can be considered as average or good-quality jobs might turn, as time goes by, into 'bad' jobs, leading to a process of social dissatisfaction even in a context of high employment and stable conditions of work and employment.

Seven, perhaps being unemployed is the worst circumstance a worker can face in terms of economic life, and the best example of a failure in the functioning of the labour market. However, it should not be forgotten that in a normal economic situation, and even in a situation of crisis, the great majority of workers are employed, and, hence, an important part of their interest will be in how their jobs measure up in terms of quality: in other words, the task is not over even with full employment.

Finally, job quality is obviously an important consideration for workers when deciding whether to engage in employment. Therefore, increasing the attractiveness of jobs will lead to an increase in the labour force, something that will become a pressing necessity in the near future because of current demographic changes (demographic ageing).

In fact, the concern about job quality is not new. Governments have been regulating conditions affecting job quality (health and safety, extension of the work week, paid vacations, etc.) since the mid-nineteenth century. Although in some areas, such as health and safety, regulation has been preceded by abundant research (see Chapter 2), in most cases we can say that regulation has preceded knowledge about the impact of a given working condition on workers' well-being. Improving our knowledge about the dimensions of job quality and integrating what is known in a unified approach to job quality seems to be a task well worth doing.

As this book is being written, Europe is in the middle of an unprecedented economic crisis with negative economic growth and growing unemployment, especially in countries such as Spain, Greece and Ireland. This situation has an impact on the debate of job quality and on job quality itself. With growing unemployment, a shift of priority towards employment creation *per se* is to be expected, probably leaving quality (again) in a secondary place. Does it mean that monitoring and evaluating job quality is not relevant in a context of economic crisis? We believe it is not so, at least for three different reasons. First, a crisis is a period of sudden and rapid change in which it is more necessary than ever to monitor what is happening. We know very well, almost in real time, what is happening in terms of quantity of employment, but we know almost nothing about what is happening in terms of employment quality. This is in itself an important argument for developing a good indicator of job quality, especially in times of crisis. Second, the impact of the crisis on job quality is likely to be ambiguous. On the one hand, the worst jobs usually tend to be destroyed first. Such dynamics can lead to an apparent improvement of overall job quality (due to a composition effect). On the other hand, the rapid increase of unemployment weakens the relative position of workers vis-à-vis employers, forcing them to accept worse working and employment conditions, with a negative impact on job quality. It is crucial to be able to monitor this dual dynamics in order to be able to design effective employment and social policies to deal with the impact of the crisis. Last, but certainly not least, the issue of job quality is not a luxury that can be put in second place in tough economic times. It must be remembered that job quality is directly linked to productivity and economic growth and, thus, it cannot be put aside in the process of developing a suitable strategy to overcome an economic crisis. It would be terribly myopic to forget this in the current situation.

NOTES

1. We could define workers' well-being as a state of being healthy, self-fulfilled, secure, with enough resources so as to enjoy a decent life, and time to have a satisfactory private life. For a comprehensive analysis of the concept see McGillivray (2006).
2. In the words of Lord Kelvin:

> I often say that when you can measure what you are speaking about, and express it in numbers, you know something about it; but when you cannot measure it, when you cannot express it in numbers, your knowledge is of a meagre and unsatisfactory kind (from 'Electrical Units of Measurement', a lecture delivered at the Institution of Civil Engineers, London (3 May 1883), *Popular Lectures and Addresses* (1889), Vol. 1, 73).

2. What is a good job? Accounting for the different dimensions shaping job quality

2.1. THE DIFFERENT APPROACHES FOR MEASURING JOB QUALITY

Job quality is necessarily a multidimensional concept. The general or overall quality of a job is the sum of multiple aspects, affecting both the employment relationship and work itself, that have an impact on workers' well-being (Skalli *et al.* 2008). This multidimensional nature of job quality makes the development of a single index or a system of indicators more difficult, as before such development is necessary to define what aspects should be taken into consideration and their overall impact on job quality. In this first section, we discuss three different possible strategies to perform such a task. The first strategy starts from the recognition of the difficulty of properly identifying all the aspects affecting job quality and their relative importance, and proposes a shortcut for such a task based on the level of job satisfaction reported by workers in surveys. The second approach is based on the utilization of workers' surveys to directly select the elements of job quality considered important by individuals themselves. The third and last strategy takes a completely different approach to the issue of job quality, using the theoretical work of economists, sociologists and other social scientists on job quality as a route map to select the relevant dimensions of job quality.

2.1.1. Subjective Approach I: Job Satisfaction as an Indicator of the Quality of Jobs

The complexity of the task of defining job quality, even without considering the difficulties related with the measurement of the chosen variables, has led some researchers to favour an alternative approach based on job satisfaction levels reported by workers. The argument is the following: we are interested in measuring job quality because we want to know the impact of different job characteristics on the well-being of the worker.

Then, instead on focusing on the input (characteristics of jobs) we can centre our efforts on measuring the output, that is, the well-being of the worker at his or her job. Unfortunately, lacking a method to directly measure well-being, we have to turn to an indirect measure of well-being: hence the use of job satisfaction as a measure of job quality.

This strategy has several advantages. First of all, it allows the researcher to turn a multidimensional concept into a single indicator, which is easier to manage and interpret than a system of indicators. Secondly, this perspective takes into account the fact that there are differences in tastes and preferences in relation to what is a good job: instead of using a rigid framework of good and bad characteristics for every worker, in this approach it is the worker himself/herself who applies his/her own criteria about what is positive and negative about the job. For example, if someone likes working at night, or at weekends, then he or she will consider it a positive characteristic of the job and this will contribute to his or her well-being and satisfaction with it. In contrast, for someone concerned about the possibility of spending time with his or her family, working on weekends will probably be considered as a negative attribute. Thirdly, it avoids the need to measure and weigh up the different characteristics. Fourthly, when answering to a question on job satisfaction the worker will probably consider many attributes of his or her job, more characteristics than can ever be included in any multidimensional model of job quality. Lastly, the information can be gathered easily and at a low cost.

Unfortunately, this approach has also important limitations, which makes job satisfaction a less than suitable indicator of the quality of jobs, especially from a comparative perspective, notwithstanding the merits for other types of research.

The first criticism has to do with the low variability exhibited by job satisfaction from a cross-country perspective, that is, the differences in the average reported job satisfaction are small even between countries with very different levels of economic development, social protection and employment regulation, and they are often inconsistent with other indicators on the conditions of work and employment commonly used in the public debate. This argument can be illustrated using data from the 2005 *International Social Survey Program* (ISSP), which contains comparable information on work values for 32 countries and territories with very different cultural backgrounds and level of development. Focusing on the average job satisfaction across countries[1] (see Figure 2.1), several concerns inevitably arise. The first issue to note is the very high level of job satisfaction in general (the overall average, for the 32 countries of the ISSP sample, is 7.08 out of 10).[2] A second point to note is the small range of

Measuring more than money

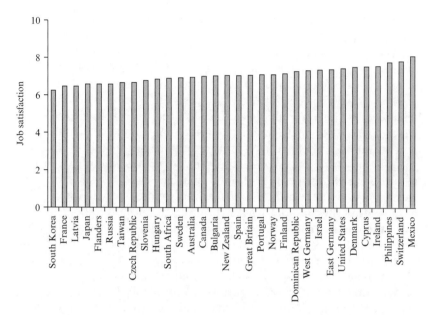

Source: Authors' analysis from *2005 International Social Survey Program* micro-data.

Figure 2.1   Job satisfaction across countries (2005)

variation in the average level of job satisfaction across countries: despite the disparity of countries included, this range only goes from 6.2 in South Korea to 8.1 in Mexico. The third issue is the ordering of countries: France is the second worst country in terms of job satisfaction, and Mexico the first, well above countries such as Denmark or Norway, for example. A quick comparison between this ranking of countries and any figures from the International Labour Organization's (ILO) Key Indicators of the Labour Market or Eurofound's Working Conditions Survey makes very clear that whatever this variable is capturing, it is certainly not (or not only) differences in job quality across countries.

There are different mechanisms that might account for both the relatively high level of job satisfaction and its little variability compared with the large differences in work and employment conditions existing across countries.

The first possibility is that the existence of compensating differentials (by which jobs would have different combinations of good and bad characteristics) tends to equalize the levels of overall satisfaction. Although, as we will see in section 2.1.2, this could explain the existence of similar levels of satisfaction for similar workers in jobs with different characteristics, it cannot explain the similar level of satisfaction of workers with different endowments (human capital, skills, etc).

The second – and probably most important – possible explanation is related to the existence of a process of adaptation in the expectations of workers to their objective conditions. For years, social psychologists have been studying psychological mechanisms (the best known theory in this respect is that of cognitive dissonance) that lead people to adapt their expectations and even their perceptions of the environment to its actual conditions (Festinger 1957). This behaviour could be interpreted as a strategy of emotional survival as it is very difficult to maintain a conception of the world (or in this case, of work) that is too discordant with reality. There is abundant literature beyond social psychology that shows the importance of endogenous determinants of satisfaction: for instance, recent literature on subjective well-being emphasizes the differential ability of people to cope and adapt on happiness (Diener *et al.* 1999; Oswald and Powdthavee 2008) or, particularly in the case of labour market studies, there is a relevant body of evidence suggesting that reported job satisfaction is affected by colleagues' payoffs (Clark and Oswald 1996; Zizzo and Oswald 2001; Brown *et al.* 2008).

The third mechanism is related to the existence of processes by which people change jobs until the new objective conditions adapt to expectations: if a person has a job that does not fit his/her expectations and is not able to change such expectations and adapt them to the facts of the jobs then he/she will probably end up leaving it. In fact, one of the key conclusions of recent research on job satisfaction is that it is a good predictor of turnover intent (Freeman 1978; Clark *et al.* 1999; Lambert *et al.* 2001).

The existence of a cognitive process of adaptation of expectations to reality is especially problematic for the goal of using job satisfaction as an indicator of the quality of jobs, because it implies that there are endogenous factors that interfere (to the point of breaking it up) the link between the conditions of work and employment and the evaluation that workers do of them when answering the question on job satisfaction. Obviously, this interpretation does not mean that there is no information in the figures of job satisfaction, or that such information is useless. What it means is that the information of job satisfaction cannot be used as an unambiguous indicator of the quality of the job performed (Muñoz de Bustillo and Fernández-Macías 2005).

But so far we have only discussed the differences in the average levels in job satisfaction across countries. Maybe job satisfaction does not make a good indicator of job quality for comparative purposes, but it can still work as an indicator of job quality at the individual level. Does job satisfaction correlate with other usual indicators of job quality at the level of individual workers? There is an abundant literature, especially in social psychology, which attempts to relate job satisfaction with different qualitative aspects of the job, such as autonomy and stress (Spector 1997), usefulness of the work performed (Mangione and Quinn 1975), supervisory support and job insecurity (Clark, 2005; Cornelissen 2006), etc. These studies have usually found a significant degree of correlation between these characteristics of the job and job satisfaction. But most of these studies have a problem which casts doubt on the validity of their results. In the vast majority of cases, the indicators of the qualitative aspects of work used are based on subjective evaluations made by the workers themselves, which are very likely to be affected by their job satisfaction. Thus, the correlation found between these indicators and job satisfaction does not necessarily involve a causal relation, but may just reflect the fact that they are different ways of measuring the same thing. In order to avoid this problem it is convenient to use indicators of job quality which are not 'contaminated' by the worker's subjectivity. When indicators that are less problematic in this sense are used, such as wage, sector, size of firm or job stability (Clark and Oswald 1996; Brown and McIntosh 1998; García Mainar 1999), the correlations with job satisfaction are usually very low and the results not very conclusive. Indeed, different studies often find contradictory relationships between a specific job attribute and job satisfaction. Spector (1997), in an extensive review of the literature on the determinants of job satisfaction, found a pronounced inconsistency among the results of different studies on wages, workload and organization of working time. A similar conclusion is presented by Muñoz de Bustillo and Fernández-Macías from a detailed analysis of the differences of job satisfaction among Spanish workers. In their own words: 'the variability of job satisfaction is surprisingly low and [. . .] the little variability there is bears practically no relation to any relevant social or economic variable' (Muñoz de Bustillo and Fernández Macías 2005, p. 670). For instance, the difference between the stated satisfaction of temporary and permanent workers in Spain is less than 0.5 in a scale of 1 to 10 (6.7 *versus* 7.2), despite the large gap in the conditions of work and employment of both categories of workers (Spain is often considered as one of the most extreme cases of labour market dualism).

The influence of cultural norms and values on workers' responses to the question of job satisfaction casts further doubts on its direct use as an indicator of the quality of jobs. As it has been showed repeatedly, the results of the surveys on subjective perception of well-being cannot be taken as raw facts without taking into account that they are tainted by different cultural and social attitudes or mediations.[3] Perception and responses to questions about job satisfaction are also dependent on the prevailing attitudes of workers about how the response ought to be when judging their working conditions.

For instance, the growing presence of the *positive thinking* approach in popular psychology can have an important impact on the stated levels of job satisfaction (making them generally higher and more homogeneous). The main tenet of this approach can be summarized as follows: when confronted with any kind of problem, having a positive and optimistic answer is always the first and most important step in its solution (Ehrenreich 2009). People who are negative or critical with their conditions can be ostracized because their negative/critical attitudes is considered as a sort of psychic contaminant, an impediment that stands in the way of the realization of the projects of the positive people.

As Barbara Ehrenreich has showed in her lucid recent account of the positive thinking mentality: 'positive thinking has made itself useful as an apology for the cruder aspects of the market economy. If optimism is the key to material success, and if you can achieve an optimistic outlook through the discipline of positive thinking, there is no excuse for failure' (Ehrenreich 2009, p. 8). When people convince themselves that all things are possible through an effort of mind, reality, however hard it might be, does not matter. 'This was a useful message for employees, who by the turn of the twenty-first century were being required to work longer hours for fewer benefits and diminishing job security' (Ehrenreich 2009, p. 12).

And it happens that 'a positive outlook is not always entirely voluntary: those who do not reach out to embrace the ideology of positive thinking may find it imposed on them. Workplaces make conscious efforts to instill a positive outlook with employers bringing motivational speakers or distributing free copies of self help books like the 2001 paperback mega-best-seller *Who Moved My Cheese?*, which counsels an uncomplaining response to lay-offs' (Ehrenreich 2009, pp. 47–8). In this kind of social environment, a worker who acts in a "negative" way, being critical of labour conditions, can find him or herself being rejected not only by employers but also by their fellow workers. As Ehrenreich says, 'when the gurus advise dropping "negative" people they are also issuing a warning: smile and be agreeable, go with the flow or prepare to be ostracized' (Ehrenreich 2009, p. 57).

It is difficult or impossible to ascertain the real weight of this ideology of 'be positive or perish' on the answers on job satisfaction surveys, but the importance in the growing service economy of interpersonal skills, emotional intelligence and the like to construct a professional life, must put a note of caution on the reliability of the responses to any surveys in which people are asked to express a critical opinion on job characteristics. As the cult of cheerfulness is more and more entrenched, people cannot allow themselves not just to express a negative opinion, but even to think 'negatively'.

Summing up, although job satisfaction might be related to job quality, there are many other variables not related with job quality (dissonance, relative thinking, adaptable expectation, cultural norms, etc.) affecting the reported level of job satisfaction. From this perspective, this variable is ill-suited as an output or 'catch-all' measure of job quality.[4]

2.1.2. Subjective Approach II: Asking Workers About What Makes a Good Job

An alternative method of taking into account the subjective evaluation of workers, but which allows the introduction of objective measures of job quality, is to ask workers about what type of job attributes they consider important when defining what is a good job (or when choosing a job), and then use those answers to evaluate the objective attributes of jobs. One advantage of such type of approach is that many surveys on quality of working life include questions about the desirability of specific job attributes. This sort of strategy is followed by Jencks *et al.* (1988) for the United States, and Vinopal (2009) for the Czech Republic, for instance: the former authors develop an Index of Job Desirability for the United States weighting each characteristic according to the importance given to them by workers themselves, drawing from an ad hoc survey.

2.1.2.1. Workers' opinions
Regarding workers' views on what makes a good job, it is convenient to have a look at international surveys that comprise comparable data on the issue. In this respect, Table 2.1 includes the answers given in the ISSP to the question 'how important do you personally think it is in a job . . .' the following list of job attributes: high income, opportunities of advancement, job security, an interesting job, a job that is useful to society, a job that helps other people, a job in which you can work independently and a job that allows to decide their times or days of work. The analysis involves 32 countries from different geographical areas and quite different levels of economic development, including 17 European countries or territories. The figures corresponding to the 17 EU countries present in the sample are reproduced in Figure 2.2, together with the data of Japan and the US for comparison. There are several things worth mentioning from looking at this figure:

(a) First of all, in Europe, Japan and the US, having a high income is not the most valued attribute of a good job. Although Europeans give high income more importance than workers from the US or Japan, still only 35 per cent consider this attribute important or very important (much

Table 2.1   What makes a good job?

	Job security	An inter-esting job	Useful to society	High income	Oppor-tunities of advance-ment	Auton-omy	Help other people	Allowed to decide the times or days of work
Australia	58.8	50.0	52.6	14.8	24.8	25.2	24.8	14.8
Bulgaria	79.1	54.3	45.3	78.2	54.8	39.9	37.5	39.6
Canada	56.1	59.8	45.6	18.3	29.8	31.7	31.4	20.6
Cyprus	47.4	25.4	54.8	46.8	20.0	20.9	16.6	16.4
Czech Republic	58.0	33.2	49.7	31.3	14.6	18.8	15.7	14.0
Denmark	31.9	58.8	44.5	9.6	6.3	44.7	26.2	18.1
Dominican Rep.	34.8	38.5	56.8	49.1	46.7	32.9	37.9	30.4
East Germany	74.1	49.6	49.3	28.5	19.3	40.9	29.4	13.9
Finland	53.6	50.4	40.7	20.3	10.2	22.6	15.2	20.7
Flanders	54.1	40.8	48.0	17.6	22.5	25.4	20.0	21.9
France	63.2	66.3	46.4	22.6	22.7	23.0	19.1	21.1
Great Britain	51.9	52.4	45.6	17.5	24.9	20.6	22.2	14.3
Hungary	72.5	29.5	50.7	42.9	24.2	27.9	23.3	15.9
Ireland	55.9	57.4	47.1	27.1	40.9	31.5	39.1	23.7
Israel	80.2	79.7	29.6	66.5	67.7	54.9	59.9	39.4
Japan	34.6	23.1	56.1	23.2	4.7	8.0	14.7	10.7
Latvia	62.4	44.9	52.3	65.5	28.5	25.6	19.8	28.4
Mexico	75.3	57.3	39.7	60.3	68.0	46.9	48.9	40.6
New Zealand	43.6	57.2	48.9	17.7	27.3	29.1	27.2	18.9
Norway	51.2	49.9	47.0	10.8	8.4	23.4	15.9	18.4
Philippines	61.3	40.0	49.8	66.3	50.2	37.8	35.4	26.6
Portugal	62.4	50.5	47.8	42.7	45.4	32.7	40.0	24.9
Russia	53.0	46.3	45.1	65.4	32.1	25.7	24.1	21.1
Slovenia	54.2	46.0	55.7	41.5	27.7	35.9	31.9	26.2
South Africa	72.2	52.9	43.2	59.5	51.6	39.9	47.3	31.0
South Korea	60.0	55.2	49.3	42.8	48.1	24.5	31.2	23.0
Spain	69.3	48.8	41.6	61.0	44.0	38.1	37.4	36.8
Sweden	57.9	51.0	44.2	17.7	11.7	31.3	23.7	20.9
Switzerland	58.9	60.3	63.4	7.6	12.8	42.8	26.3	23.0
Taiwan	50.5	32.9	64.0	21.0	20.0	9.0	16.5	19.6

Table 2.1   (continued)

	Job security	An interesting job	Useful to society	High income	Opportunities of advancement	Autonomy	Help other people	Allowed to decide the times or days of work
United States	62.8	56.8	42.5	30.3	42.5	34.3	43.3	17.6
West Germany	64.8	46.7	52.0	15.4	16.8	38.0	21.1	14.4
EU 9	56.5	52.3	45.8	25.2	24.5	30.8	26.4	21.7
EU 27	58.7	47.3	47.9	34.9	26.0	29.8	25.6	22.3
High income	57.7	49.7	48.0	31.1	26.4	30.3	27.2	21.7
Medium/ low income	58.2	46.2	49.7	52.1	45.2	31.0	34.5	27.5
Mean	58.3	48.9	48.4	35.6	30.3	30.8	28.8	22.7
Total	58.1	49.1	48.5	36.4	31.8	30.7	29.7	23.3

Note: In the Survey, East and West Germany are analysed separately. In Belgium, there are only data from Flanders.

Source: Authors' analysis from *2005 International Social Survey Program* micro-data.

less than job security, usefulness to society or that it is an interesting job).[5] Even when viewed in the long run (as opportunities for advancement, supposedly also in terms of wages), only a fourth of those interviewed consider the pay dimension as important or very important.

(b) The most valued attribute in the US and EU (and the second most appreciated feature in Japan) is job security.

(c) Workers are also quite concerned about the nature of the job, whether it is interesting and useful to society.

(d) In contrast with the growing literature on work-life balance and autonomy at work, the importance given by workers to these two aspects seems secondary to the other attributes already mentioned (29.8 and 22.3 per cent in the EU)

Focusing now on the difference in importance given across countries to the different attributes, it is evident that, for many of the features, there is quite an agreement between countries about their relative importance – although there are some important differences, such as the low importance

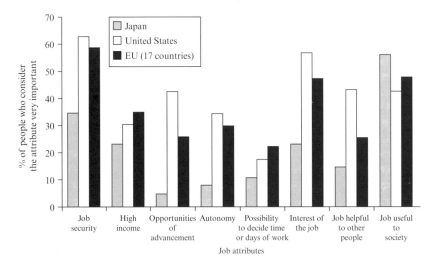

Source: Authors' analysis from *2005 International Social Survey Program* micro-data.

Figure 2.2 What makes a good job in the European Union (17 countries), Japan and USA (2005)

given in Denmark to job security, or the very low importance given in the same country to high income compared to the weight given to income in Bulgaria. The coefficient of variation, a measure of relative dispersion, of the importance given to the different attributes in the 17 EU countries and territories of the sample is presented in Figure 2.3. With the exception of the issues related to present and future income, with relatively high dispersion in the valuation given to them among the countries of the sample, the rest of the attributes exhibit a relatively low degree of dispersion, particularly, in the case of having an interesting and a useful or secure job, which are highly valued attributes everywhere.

Furthermore, the dispersion of the values given to having a high income can be largely explained by the differences in income levels of the countries comprised in the sample. The existence of such relation becomes evident if one explores the relationship between the importance conceded to having a high wage and the GDP per capita across countries (Figure 2.4). As can be seen, despite a few exceptions, there is a robust inverse statistical relationship between the level of per capita income and the relevance given to a high wage as an attribute of a good job. The same pattern holds when we restrict the analysis to high income countries (GDP per capita near or above PPP US$20,000 for 2005); in fact, the statistical fit is even better ($R^2 = 0.64$).

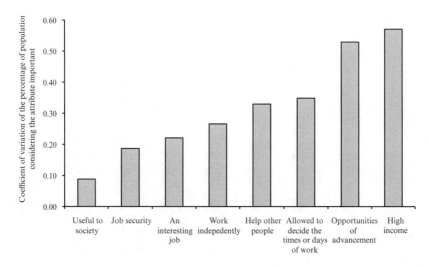

Source: Authors' analysis from *2005 International Social Survey Program* micro-data.

Figure 2.3   Dispersion of importance given to different job attributes in 17 EU countries or territories

This inverse relationship between the importance given to high wages and the level of GDP per capita is coherent with the results obtained in the literature dealing with the economic determinants of happiness, known as Happiness Economics. According to such body of research (Easterlin 1974; Oswald 1997; Layard 2005), there is growing evidence of the existence of an income threshold beyond which the positive relation between income and happiness weakens. This idea is used in the construction of the Human Development Index (HDI), where the impact of per capita GDP on the income component of the index is lower the higher is the level of income. In both cases, the argument is that once people reach a certain minimum level of material well-being, their level of welfare becomes more and more dependent on non-material things.[6]

However, as shown in Figure 2.5, there seems to be no apparent relation between the appreciation for job security and the level of income. Whatever makes people more sensitive to job security is independent of the level of per capita income of the country. This feature suggests the existence of other elements, probably related – among other things – with the regulation and functioning of the labour market, that are important in explaining the appreciation of job security. In this respect, it is impossible not to mention the very low score of Denmark and Japan, two countries with opposite models of labour market regulation. Job security in Japan

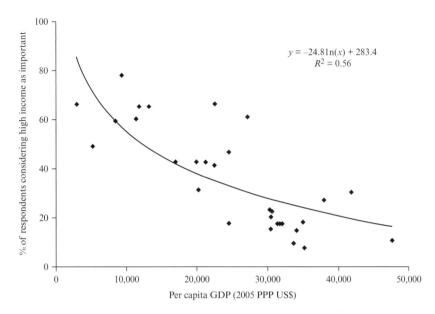

$$y = -24.81\text{n}(x) + 283.4$$
$$R^2 = 0.56$$

Source: Authors' analysis from *2005 International Social Survey Program* micro-data and World Bank Development Indicators.

Figure 2.4 Relationship between per capita GDP and importance given by workers to high income (2005)

might not be considered important by workers as they might take it for granted thanks to the model of 'a job for life' that still characterizes the Nippon economy, if only for the core labour force (Chatani 2008). In Denmark, the reason probably lies in the existence of the well known flexi-security model, a combination of high job mobility with low employment protection and a generous system of unemployment benefits and active labour market policies (Bredgaard, *et al.* 2005). This combination is likely to have transformed the work *ethos* of the Danish society making security in the job an almost irrelevant attribute of a good job.

Nevertheless, this high degree of coincidence in the importance given to different job attributes does not mean that there is a high homogeneity across countries. Looking at the average, maximum and minimum values given to the different attributes in a sample including European countries, the US and Japan, it becomes evident that there exist substantial differences, particularly, but not only, in wages and opportunities for advancement (Figure 2.6). These differences point to one of the major challenges to be faced when trying to operationalize the very broad concept of job

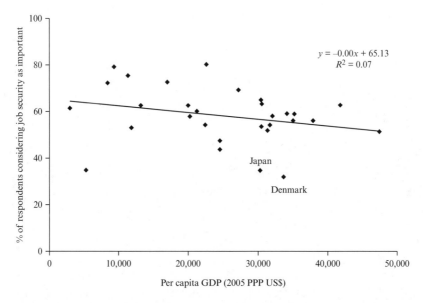

Source: Authors' analysis from *2005 International Social Survey Program* micro-data and World Bank Development Indicators.

Figure 2.5   *Relationship between per capita GDP and importance given to job security (2005)*

quality in the real world. These obstacles relate to the existence of structural and cultural differences that might make the characteristics of the job that affect the well-being of the worker different across countries. Even job security, which in the previous analysis was shown to be the most widely agreed important attribute of a good job, does not seem to be considered such an important attribute for the workers of Denmark and Japan, as mentioned earlier. Also the role of wages, by all accounts a valuable attribute of job quality, differs considerably across states and territories. The implications of such differences for the construction of a job quality index will be discussed in the next chapter.

The information provided by this type of analysis about which attributes are considered by workers when defining a 'good' job point to the existence of multiple determining factors behind the understanding of this concept. Therefore, these results can be considered as empirical evidence showing that, from this subjective perspective, job quality is a multidimensional concept. Another interesting outcome is the relevance given to job security and the subordinated role played by wages, if only among high income countries. This secondary role played by wages is also evident in the high

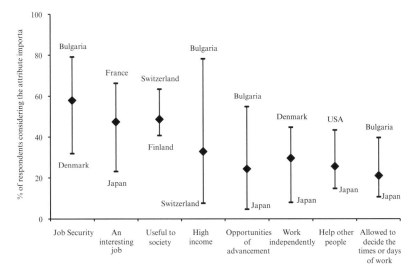

Source: Authors' analysis from *2005 International Social Survey Program* micro-data.

Figure 2.6 *Differences in importance given to different job attributes in Europe, US and Japan*

percentage of workers in the vast majority of countries that declare they would enjoy having a paid job even if they did not need the money (Figure 2.7). Lastly, although there are some remarkable similarities in the ranking of the different attributes considered, they cannot be interpreted in terms of all countries adhering to a single norm in terms of the importance and ordering of the different attributes.

A final question that we can address with these data on workers' views of the relevance of different job characteristics is whether there is some kind of taxonomy of preferences on job quality across Europe.[7] In order to deal with this task, we perform a cluster analysis, which allows us to group a set of countries according to the empirical similarities in a range of workers' opinions on the importance of different job attributes. Six groups of countries arise from the cluster analysis, whose results are presented in Figure 2.8 and Table 2.2. Firstly, the results of such analysis yields three clusters composed of only one country, Portugal, Ireland and Denmark. While in Portugal, features like income and security attract great attention, in Denmark 'non-materialist' attributes are dominant. This probably reflects the poor performance of the Portuguese labour market and economy during the last decade, contrasting with the Danish recent record of full employment. Ireland shows values not far from

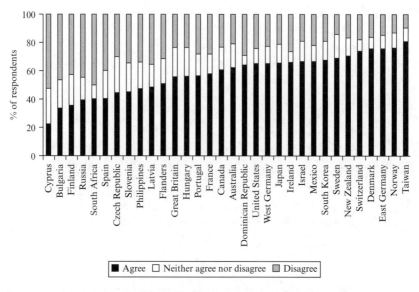

Source: Authors' analysis from *2005 International Social Survey Program* micro-data.

Figure 2.7   Workers' agreement on the willingness to have a job even if they do not need the money (2005)

Portugal except regarding income, probably reflecting the big economic push experienced by Irish wages since the early nineties. Secondly, we have two clusters (3 and 4) composed by Eastern Countries, Spain and Cyprus. These groups are primarily characterized by the great importance assigned to job security and flexible working times and the interest of the job. A final and residual cluster, comprising the remaining nine countries, seems to agglutinate countries where wages are not a big concern, but where job security is perceived as essential. The rest of the dimensions, apart from the interest of the job, receive only very secondary attention. Though the results from the analysis might not offer a clear picture, this exercise illustrates how countries can be grouped into 'regions' in terms of the relative importance given to the same dimensions of job quality.

2.1.2.2.   Desired versus actual job characteristics

It could be argued, though, that people might render important precisely the specific attributes of their current jobs. Two different reasons could lead to such outcome. First, it could be that workers select precisely the kind of job that best suits their preferences (that is, their idea of a good

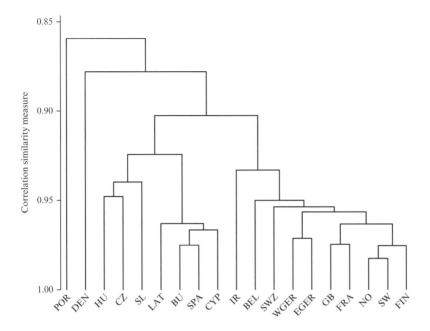

Source: Authors' analysis from *2005 International Social Survey Program* micro-data

Figure 2.8   *Dendogram for cluster analysis of job characteristics that are very important according to national citizens in selected countries of Europe (2005)*

job). The existence of a perfect or quasi-perfect match between jobs characteristics and desired attributes could lead to such result. Second, alternatively, workers might learn to appreciate the specific characteristics of their jobs, in a process of psychological adaptation to reduce cognitive dissonance by which those desired attributes lacking in the job are underplayed and those characteristics present in the job overvalued. This process, making virtue from necessity, would be functional to the psychological well-being of the worker. In the latter case, it would be wrong to arrive at conclusions about the attributes of a good job by just looking at the opinion of workers about the issue.[8]

    In order to test this question, we explore the correlation between the characteristics of the jobs actually held by workers and the attributes of a good job in their opinion. The results, calculated at country level for the whole sample, show a very low correlation between the actual and desired characteristics, especially when focusing on high income and opportunities for advancement and job security, probably the less

Table 2.2 Cluster analysis of job characteristics that are very important according to national citizens in selected countries of Europe (2005)

No. of cluster	Countries	Average proportion of people considering a job attribute very important							
		Job security	High income	Opportunities of advancement	Interesting job	Work independently	Help to other people	Useful to society	Flexible time of work
1	Portugal	62.4	42.7	45.4	50.5	32.7	40.0	45.2	24.9
2	Denmark	31.9	9.6	6.3	58.8	44.7	26.2	21.4	18.1
3	Czech Republic, Hungary, Slovenia	61.6	38.6	22.2	36.2	27.5	23.6	23.9	18.7
4	Bulgaria, Cyprus, Latvia, Spain	64.6	62.9	36.8	43.4	31.1	27.8	29.5	30.3
5	Ireland	55.9	27.1	40.9	57.4	31.5	39.1	42.4	23.7
6	Belgium (Flanders), Finland, France, United Kingdom, Sweden, Switzerland, West Germany, Norway	58.9	17.6	16.6	51.9	29.8	21.4	19.2	18.7

Note: The number of clusters has been selected using the Calinski-Harabasz criterion.

Source: Authors' analysis from 2005 *International Social Survey Program* micro-data.

'subjective' of the bundle of characteristics considered (Figure 2.9). The average correlation for the 32 countries and territories for job security is only 0.089 (with a maximum for Ireland of 0.230 and a minimum for the former East Germany of −0.020), and the results are even lower for high income, with an average correlation of 0.049. When we focus on the attributes (probably more 'ethereal') related to the capacity to work independently, helping other people or being useful to society, the correlation rises, but even then the average correlation lies in the vicinity of 0.20. Furthermore, there is no country and no attribute with a correlation higher than 0.34. The results remain relatively similar even when the model controls for gender, age and household income.[9] One can safely conclude that in this case there is not a process of reduction of cognitive dissonance by which workers only answer with respect to the attributes of their own jobs, nor a process of good matching by which workers end up working in jobs characterized by exactly those qualities they value (with a good fit of desired and actual characteristics). These results can be interpreted in terms of the existence of a shared set of attributes of what is a good job unrelated to the specific circumstances of the worker (in terms of characteristics of their jobs). This, in turn, would support the utilization of this type of information in the construction of a list of characteristics of good jobs.

2.1.2.3. Gender, age and desired job attributes

We finish this section addressing how social and demographic characteristics of people might influence their views on desired job attributes. It is possible that, even if there were a common ideal job shared by all countries, the same is not true in terms of different groups of workers. For instance, if women, young workers or older men had different ideas about what makes a good job then the construction of a set of indicators reflecting job quality will turn into a chimera, as each group would have a different ideal type. The response to this question is again based on the ISSP database, which is exploited in order to analyse the effect of gender, age and educational level on the probability of considering a certain job attribute as very important. Although, in order to make the reading easier, the detailed results of this exercise are confined to the appendix, the main lessons obtained from them are summarized here. Firstly, there are several cases where these socio-demographic characteristics have no effect on the responses; for example, this applies especially to variables such as interest of the job or the possibility of helping society. A second and remarkable feature is the significant difference between the sexes in the valuation of some job attributes, such as the interest of the job or the flexibility of working time. Third, even in those cases where the

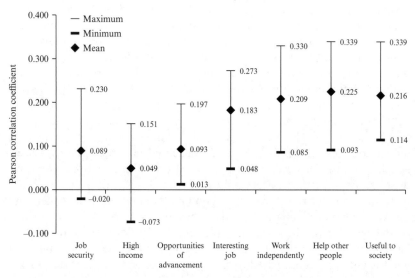

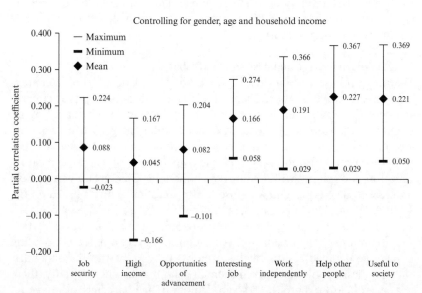

Source: Authors' analysis from *2005 International Social Survey Program* micro-data.

*Figure 2.9   Correlation between the importance given to a job
characteristic and actual presence of job characteristic in
current job (EU countries) (2005)*

effects by gender are in the same direction, the magnitude of such influence varies largely across countries. For example, an additional year of schooling means a 0.6 per cent decrease in the valuation of job security in Spain, and almost 2 per cent in France. The same happens with age and the valuation of earning a high wage. There are also some dimensions of quality of working life, like the interest of the job, the possibility of working independently or being useful to society, that are considered very important mainly by people with high educational attainment. This fact is probably related to some extent with the lower valuation of purely monetary aspects of the job as long as some minimum levels are attained. It could reflect, in some sense, the decreasing positive effect of income on subjective well-being. In other words, it is quite likely that the valuation of job attributes is intrinsically related to high or low levels of job quality in other dimensions.

In sum, the valuation of job attributes is variable across basic sociodemographic characteristics of workers and, in addition, across countries. The non-negligible divergences found across the different national cases (see Table 2.3 for an example) suggests that building a job quality indicator for each country would be not only quite tedious but also would probably reduce the transparency of the measure.

Before finishing this section, we must explicitly evaluate the advantages and disadvantages of this second type of subjective approach. Firstly, it gives workers themselves a voice in the definition of what makes a good job. It seems reasonable to think that they should have some idea about what are the most important attributes of a good job. In the second place, it is very flexible (as long as there is the possibility of including such question in a survey): it facilitates adapting the model of job quality to national specificities (the model can vary according to the answers in the different countries) or even to historical changes in what is considered to be a good job (since the model can also vary over time). One last advantage of such type of approach is that most surveys on the quality of working life include questions about the desirability of specific job attributes. Nevertheless, one should bear in mind the main limitations of this strategy as well, especially if it is used as the only basis for the development of a model of job quality. Firstly, it requires presenting workers a predefined set of options (attributes of jobs to be ranked): the identification of the elements to be included in this list can be almost as difficult as the model of job quality itself, and leaving out important elements would severely limit the modelling of job quality (for instance, the set of items listed in the ISSP questionnaire is clearly very narrow and lacks important issues such as the social environment, physical demands or skills development). Second, if the model varies

Table 2.3   Impact of being female on the importance attached to job, security, high wage, opportunities of advancement and control overtime (2005)

	Positive effect	Negative effect	No effect
Job security	Norway, Sweden, Czech Republic, France, Denmark, Finland	West Germany, Ireland, Great Britain	US, Hungary, Slovakia, Bulgaria, Japan, Spain, Latvia, Cyprus, Portugal, Belgium, East Germany
High income		Germany, Great Britain, Bulgaria, France, Cyprus, Latvia, Denmark	US, Hungary, Ireland, Norway, Sweden, Czech Republic, Slovakia, Romania
Opportunities of advancement	Norway, Latvia	West Germany, Great Britain, Ireland, Japan, France, Cyprus, Denmark, Finland, Japan, Slovakia	US, Hungary, Sweden, Czech Republic, Bulgaria, Spain, Romania, Portugal, Belgium
Control over working time	Sweden, France	Hungary, Ireland, Norway, Cyprus, Portugal	Germany, Great Britain, US, Czech Republic, Slovakia, Bulgaria, Romania, Japan, Spain, Latvia, Denmark, Belgium, Finland

Source: Authors' analysis from *2005 International Social Survey Program* micro-data. See appendix for details.

across countries or moments in time, the comparability can be seriously affected compromising the usefulness of the whole effort. Third, workers' opinions can be conditioned – in any direction – by their current jobs. And finally, just because people say something is important (without any proper contextualization or understanding of the reasons behind those answers) might not be enough justification for its inclusion into a definition of job quality. In our view, therefore, this approach can certainly be very useful for informing the definition of job quality, but it cannot be its sole basis.

2.2. SELECTING THE ATTRIBUTES OF A GOOD JOB: THE ECONOMIC AND SOCIOLOGICAL TRADITION

An alternative to using surveys on desired job attributes to select the dimensions of job quality and to determine their relative importance is to identify such dimensions on the basis of the existing literature about the impact of job attributes on workers' well-being. This approach is not totally incompatible with the subjective approach presented in the previous section, as the opinion of the workers can be one of the elements taken into consideration in the process of choosing the different possible dimensions of job quality. In fact, both approaches are clearly linked. When the researchers are designing a questionnaire addressing the attributes that make up a good job, the possible answers are not randomly selected, nor are the respondents offered an endless list of attributes; the possible choices are selected having in mind – either explicitly or implicitly – a model of job quality based on previous research in the area.

As we will see along this chapter, the economic tradition (reviewed in section 2.2.1) is rich in approaches, although the dominant school tends to focus on only one factor: wages. The sociological tradition, reviewed in section 2.2.2, opens the analysis to include the intrinsic qualities of work, such as skills and autonomy, as well as the contractual conditions of employment, health and safety and work-life balance.

2.2.1. Quality of Work: The Economic Perspective

Economics, as usual, does not provide a single perspective about the question of job quality, its measure, evaluation and importance in the design of labour policy. This diversity of perspectives should not provoke any surprise or be, once again, the basis of jokes about the well-known proverbial incapacity of economists to present concrete and definitive answers to social and economic problems. On the contrary, such variety of approaches is precisely what should be expected in accordance with the theoretical complexity and practical importance of the subject. No other outcome could be expected in view of the relevance that economic life has to the individual's welfare or happiness. Consequently, it is evident that the quality of labour's experience, as affected by the operation and characteristics of a given economic system, should be a central element when evaluating its general economic efficiency.

2.2.1.1.   The orthodox view: job quality as a Becker-Lancaster good

In *The Importance of Being Ernest*, one of Oscar Wilde's most felicitous plays, is the following dialogue between Jack, a young dandy, and Lady Bracknell, a high society woman:

> *Lady Bracknell*: [. . .] Do you smoke?
> *Jack*: Well, yes, I must admit I smoke.
> *Lady Bracknell*: I am glad to hear it. A man should always have an occupation of some kind. There are far too many idle men in London as it is. How old are you?
> *Jack*: Twenty-nine.

This scene still produces, more than a century later, the same satiric/social criticism effect that Wilde looked for. The reason is that everybody, except old aristocrat ladies who can allow themselves to live outside the real world, without working or having no connection with any labour activity, knows too well that working is an occupation completely different, even opposite, to smoking or any other leisure or consuming activities.

However, as it happens, not just old aristocrat ladies but most economists share Lady Bracknell's point of view, which is now the standard or orthodox position of mainstream labour economics after the works of Gary Becker and Kelvin Lancaster. This perspective is useful because it allows dealing with the issue of job quality in a simple way.

According to the traditional economic perspective, individuals are forced to work as an undesirable consequence of not having enough money for enjoying a leisurely life: they have to choose between income and leisure, the two basic economic goods that enter into their preference orderings. From such perspective people will renounce to some of their leisure, i.e., will work, only if they get some compensation, an income, for it. As leisure is thought as an economic good, its opposite – working – had necessarily to be an economic *bad*.

In contrast, the perspective inaugurated by Gary Becker and Kelvin Lancaster argues that what people do is to distribute their disposable time in each period among different activities: market activities and nonmarket activities; each one combining time with goods. In nonmarket or consuming activities, individuals combine time and consumer goods understood as inputs to a kind of production function, a 'domestic production function', to get, as a final product, the 'things' (recreation, eating, sleep, childrearing, housekeeping, travelling, and the like) or *characteristics* or *attributes* (using the terminology of Lancaster 1966) that really satisfy their wants, desires and necessities. These 'things' would enter as the arguments of their utility functions. From this perspective, individuals, actually, do not consume goods as meat, fish, cigarettes, vegetables, bread or wine, cars or bicycles, or houses: what they do is consuming vitamins, calories, proteins, flavour or nicotine in domestic activities or productions like eating, travelling, smoking and housing. Engaging in these activities, people combine or process the goods that they have with their own time, providing themselves with satisfaction: from this perspective, this is analogous to the labour activities performed by people within the production function of firms.

Market activities or labour activities, unlike consumption activities, provide economic (monetary and in-kind) earnings to individuals. But they have in common that both activities require the use of time and 'goods' to realize them. These 'goods' are the attributes or characteristics of the jobs the individuals can do. They are the conditions of work in a broad sense.

The difference between market/labour activities and consumption/non-market activities is that the output of the labour activities enters the utility function of the individual in two ways: indirectly, since working provides the individual with a monetary reward to purchase the goods that enter in the consuming activities, but also directly, in so far as the labour activity in itself 'produces' utility or disutility to the individual.

Each individual worker can be conceived as endowed with a given stock of human capital, innate or acquired, which he or she can hire to employers for its use in the production activities of firms, in exchange for a remuneration. This reward would be the value of its marginal productivity, and in equilibrium, it would be the same in each of the different occupations in which such human capital could be employed. Each individual worker decides, in a process known as occupational choice, where his/her human capital will be used, i.e., what job or jobs he will do given his own preferences and the characteristics of the different jobs open to him.

(A)   Quality of job in the mainstream view: the theory of compensating wage differentials.

The first economic approach to the question of job quality goes back to the eighteenth century, to the very beginnings of scientific economic thought. In *An Enquiry into the Nature and Causes of Wealth of Nations*, Chapter X, Book I, Adam Smith, the founding father of economics, put forward an argument that, in more recent times, was to become known as the *theory of compensating (wage) differentials.* In Smith's own words:

> The wages of labour vary with the ease or hardship, the cleanliness or dirtiness, the honourableness or dishonourableness of the employment. Thus in most places, take the year round, a journeyman taylor earns less than a journeyman weaver. His work is much easier. A journeyman weaver earns less than a journeyman smith. His work is not always easier, but it is much

cleanlier. A journeyman blacksmith, though an artificer, seldom earns so much in twelve hours as a collier, who is only a labourer, does in eight. His work is not quite so dirty, is less dangerous, and is carried on in day-light, and above ground. Honour makes a great part of the reward of all honourable professions. In point of pecuniary gain, all things considered, they are generally under-recompensed, as I shall endeavour to show by and by. Disgrace has the contrary effect. The trade of a butcher is a brutal and an odious business; but it is in most places more profitable than the greater part of common trades. The most detestable of all employments, that of public executioner, is, in proportion to the quantity of work done, better paid than any common trade whatever. (Smith [1776] 1976, p. 117)

Paradoxically, the theory of compensating (wage) differentials, 'the fundamental long-run market equilibrium construct in labor economics' in the words of Rosen (1986, p. 641), is a non-starter from a job quality perspective because it can be concluded that if wage differences fully compensate workers for the differences in the non-monetary characteristics (disamenities) among jobs there is no economic problem around the issue of job quality. The problem of the quality of working life is, consequently, a non-problem if (and this is a very important *if*) the required compensation for working in 'bad' (or not enough 'good') conditions is really fulfilled in the market for labour. And that will happen if these markets are sufficiently competitive (in theory, 'perfectly competitive'). In that situation, as firms compete among themselves to hire workers (at the same time that workers compete to be hired), the competition among them will lead each one to provide the *socially optimal level* of non-wage characteristics or 'amenities' in each workplace, with this socially required level defined in accordance with the preferences of the workers.[10] As workers in the *same* jobs and with the *same* qualifications will differ in their preferences for job characteristics, firms will differ in the working and employment conditions that they will offer. Workers will get different wages because employers will pay a compensating differential to those workers who *prefer and choose* working in workplaces with low level of amenities in exchange for such higher pay. When we compare jobs which are different in terms of their intrinsic 'pleasantness' but require equal qualifications (garbage collectors and hotel porters, for instance), the more unpleasant job will have to pay a higher wage to attract and retain workers.

As far as this theory is accurate and corresponds to the real functioning of labour markets, it is not the wage which is equated across jobs in a competitive labour market, but the wage *and* the bundle of amenities and disamenities of the job. Wage differentials equalize or compensate for the non-monetary differences among jobs. If that were the case, there would still be 'good' and 'bad' jobs in terms of specific characteristics: wages, intensity of work, physical working environment, etc., but not in terms of all characteristics simultaneously, because those with a lower level would have to be compensated by equally higher levels in the rest of the characteristics.[11] That is, to mainstream economics, the quality of jobs is a consequence of the preferences (and decisions) of workers, not imposed on them.

From a formal perspective, the argument presented above can be expressed as follows. Let us assume that a representative worker's behaviour can be described as a process of maximization of a utility function that depends on two arguments: his market or job activity (L) and his nonmarket activity (C):

$$U = U(L, C) \qquad [2.1]$$

In order to model the occupational choice of a specific worker (given his human capital) in the presence of differences in the quality of jobs,[12] it will be assumed for the moment that the worker can only do one type of occupation (and only one kind of nonmarket or consumption activity), but that the job can be done under different conditions. These job conditions are like the consumer goods that individuals acquire as inputs in their domestic production functions. Many or perhaps the majority of these job conditions will be qualitative; however, in the model they will be treated as quantitative variables. Consequently, *better* will be modelled as *more*.

Labour activity (L) can be understood as dependent of two variables: the quantity of working-time (t_L) and a vector of characteristics or attributes a job can have (a). In order to simplify the model, we will assume that there is only one attribute.

$$L = L(t_L, a) \qquad [2.2]$$

The consuming activity, the domestic production function or technology of consumption, depends on the consumption time (t_C) and the quantity of goods (c):

$$C = C(t_C, c) \qquad [2.3]$$

Therefore, the utility function can be rewritten as

$$U = U(L(t_L, a), C(t_C, c)) = U(t_L, a, t_C, c) \qquad [2.4]$$

For convenience, the existence of decreasing returns in the 'production functions' of the market and nonmarket activities is assumed, that is,

- $Ut_L = \partial U / \partial t_L \lessgtr 0$; $Ut_L t_L = \partial^2 U / \partial t_L^2 < 0$ (since labour can be directly an economic good or a bad, so the marginal utility of work can be positive or negative and it is decreasing)[13]
- $Ut_C = \partial U / \partial t_C > 0$; $Ut_C t_C = \partial^2 U / \partial t_C^2 < 0$ (the marginal utility of consumption time is positive and decreasing)
- $Ua = \partial U / \partial a > 0$; $Uaa = \partial^2 U / \partial a^2 < 0$ (the marginal utility of the quantity of the job amenity is positive and decreasing)
- $Uc = \partial U / \partial c > 0$; $Ucc = \partial^2 U / \partial c^2 < 0$ (the marginal utility of the consumption good is positive and decreasing)
- $Ut_L a = \partial^2 U / \partial t_L \partial a > 0$ (the marginal utility of work grows as the job attributes grows)
- $Ut_C c = \partial^2 U / \partial t_C \partial c > 0$ (the marginal utility of consumption activity grows as the quantity of consumption good used rises)
- $Ut_L t_C = \partial^2 U / \partial t_L \partial t_C = Ut_L c = \partial^2 U / \partial t_L \partial c = Ut_C t_L = \partial^2 U / \partial t_C \partial t_L = Ut_C a = \partial^2 U / \partial t_C \partial a = 0$ (the two activities are independent, that is, the marginal utility of work is not affected by a variation of the consumption time or the quantity of good consumed, and the marginal utility of the consuming activity does not depend on the working time and the level of job attributes)

For the worker, the job attribute or desirable characteristic a has an implicit price or shadow price, p_a, that represents the opportunity cost of having this desired attribute in terms of a lower monetary wage. Therefore, in a particular job in which the level of attribute a is a_0, its value $- p_a a_0$, represents the in-kind remuneration. In other words, it is as if the employer was also the seller of the 'good' a to his employee in a kind of inner labour market in each occupation.[14]

A rational worker will try to maximize the utility function (equation [2.4]) subject to the three restrictions: a time restriction, a total income restriction and a monetary income restriction.

The *time restriction* states that the available total quantity of time (T) is employed either working or in the nonmarket activity.

$$T = t_L + t_C \qquad\qquad [2.5]$$

$$\omega t_L = p_c c + p_a a \qquad\qquad [2.6]$$

The second restriction refers to the *total income restriction*. The worker uses his total wage (ω) or value of his marginal productivity to buy either the consumption good in the explicit market or the job-attribute in the inner and implicit labour market.

$$wt_L = p_C c \qquad [2.7]$$

The third restriction is the *monetary income restriction*, according to which the monetary wage (w) is employed to buy the consumption good.

The relationship between total hourly wage (ω), hourly monetary wage (w) and in-kind hourly wage per hour ($p_a a$) / t_L can be obtained from the previous equations as follows:

$$\omega = w + \frac{p_a a}{t_L} \qquad [2.8]$$

The quantity of working time, the level of the job-attribute and the consumption good that maximizes the utility function is the result of the maximization of the Lagrangian equation:

$$L(t_L, a, t_C, c; \lambda, \mu, \eta) \equiv U(t_L, a, t_C, c) + \lambda(T - t_L - t_C)$$

$$+ \mu(\omega t_L - wt_L - p_a a) + \eta(wt_L - p_C c) \qquad [2.9]$$

The set first-order conditions of this problem include the three restrictions and the following four equations:

$$\frac{\partial L}{\partial t_L}(t_L^*, a^*, t_C^*, c^*; \lambda^*, \mu^*, \eta^*)$$

$$= Ut_L(t_L^*, a^*, t_C^*, c^*) - \lambda^* + \mu^*(\omega - w^*) + \eta^* w^* = 0 \quad [2.10]$$

$$\frac{\partial L}{\partial t_C}(t_L^*, a^*, t_C^*, c^*; \lambda^*, \mu^*, \eta^*) = Ut_C(t_L^*, a^*, t_C^*, c^*) - \lambda^* = 0 \ [2.11]$$

$$\frac{\partial L}{\partial a}(t_L^*, a^*, t_C^*, c^*; \lambda^*, \mu^*, \eta^*) = Ua(a^*, c^*) - \mu^* p_a = 0 \qquad [2.12]$$

$$\frac{\partial L}{\partial c}(a^*, c^*; \lambda^*, \mu^*, \eta^*) = Uc(a^*, c^*) - \eta^* p_C = 0 \qquad [2.13]$$

The satisfaction of this set of equations along with the set of restrictions determines the optimum levels of working time (or time devoted to nonmarket activities), the consumption level and job amenities (and, indirectly, the monetary wage) – that is, (t_L^*, t_C^*, c^*, a^*, w^*) – that maximize individual utility given the marginal productivity of the worker (ω) and the price level of the consumption good (p_C) and the implicit price of job attributes (p_a). It must be stressed that the worker decides autonomously the level of his monetary wage (w^*) after choosing the level of job attributes (a^*) and the working time (t_L^*) according to

$$w* = \omega - \frac{a*}{t_L^*}p_a \qquad [2.14]$$

From the [2.12] and [2.13], one can easily obtain that μ is the marginal utility of in-kind income ($\mu = Ua / p_a$) and η is the marginal utility of monetary income ($\eta = Uc / p_C$). In equilibrium, it is obvious that $\mu = \eta$. By substituting in the first condition, one gets

$$Ut_L(t_L^*, a*, t_C^*, c*) - Ut_C(t_L, a*, t_C, c*)$$

$$+ \frac{Ua(t_L^*, a*, t_C^*, c*)}{p_a}(\omega* - w*) + \frac{Uc(t_L^*, a*, t_C^*, c*)}{p_C}w* = 0 \qquad [2.15]$$

or

$$\frac{Ua(t_L^*, a*, t_C^*, c*)}{p_a}(\omega* - w*) + \frac{Uc(t_L^*, a*, t_C^*, c*)}{p_C}w*$$

$$= Ut_L(t_L^*, a*, t_C^*, c*) - Ut_C(t_L^*, a*, t_C^*, c*) \qquad [2.16]$$

In other words, in equilibrium, the value in utility terms of the income obtained from using time in the working activity (monetary plus in-kind wages) must equal the difference between the marginal utility of consuming time and the marginal utility of working time (or, in other words, the direct marginal utility – or disutility – of working activity plus its indirect marginal utility – the utility of in-kind and monetary income – is equal to the marginal utility of the time in the consumption activity).

Now, by substituting [2.8] in [2.16], we have

$$\frac{Ua(t_L^*, a*, t_C^*, c*)}{p_a}\frac{p_a a*}{t_L^*} + \frac{Uc(t_L^*, a*, t_C^*, c*)}{p_C}w*$$

$$= Ut_L(t_L^*, a*, t_C^*, c*) - Ut_C(t_L^*, a*, t_C^*, c*) \qquad [2.17]$$

and

$$w* = \frac{p_C}{Uc(t_L^*, a*, t_C^*, c*)}\left[Ut_L(t_L^*, a*, t_C^*, c*) - Ut_C(t_L^*, a*, t_C^*, c*) \right.$$

$$\left. - \frac{Ua(t_L^*, a*, t_C^*, c*)}{p_a}\frac{p_a a*}{t_L^*} \right] \qquad [2.18]$$

This last expression describes the set of possible combinations of levels of job attribute (a) and monetary wage (w) corresponding to different levels of working time and utility. With all the maximization conditions, the utility level is $U*$, the working-time is t_L^* and the rest of the variables are in their optimum values (a^*, w^*, c^*) given the prices p_a, ω, p_C. We can ask about the other possible combinations of levels of job attribute and monetary wage that are compatible with the utility level U^*, and the quantity of working time t_L^*. This set of values of w^* and a satisfy the last equation and can be thought of as representing different jobs with the same working hours (t_L^*) among which the worker is indifferent, in the sense that his/her level of utility will be the same. In consequence, each one of these combinations of monetary wage and level of job attribute represent a job of the same *quality* to the worker.

In this respect, the quality (Q_L) of a job can be defined as the combination of wage and job attributes that yields the same utility to a worker given a fixed working time,[15] that is,

$$Q_L = Q(w, a; U, t_L) \qquad [2.19]$$

For each utility level and working-time level, there will be a curve that shows the different ways (bundles of monetary wage and level of job attributes) a job can involve, holding constant the job quality to the worker. Such curves can be labelled as isoquality-job curves. Equation [2.14] describes the map of these isoquality-job curves, each one corresponding to a utility level and a quantity of working time (Figure 2.11).

The slope of each isoquality-job curve is given by

$$\frac{\partial w}{\partial a} = \frac{p_C}{Uc}\left(- Ut_La - \frac{Ua}{t_L} - \frac{a}{t_L}Uaa \right) \qquad [2.20]$$

and it will be negative if

$$- aUaa - Ua < t_L Ut_La \qquad [2.21]$$

Graphically (Figure 2.10), in equilibrium, a worker with a marginal productivity ω who works t_L^* hours chooses the variety of job L which offers to him the maximum quality Q^*, that is, a monetary wage w^* and a level of job attribute a^*.

However, nothing guarantees that this type of job actually exists in the job market, so it will be usual to find that a worker cannot get the maximum job quality (Q^*) and, thus, he must conform with the most satisfying but existent quality (Q'), accepting a monetary wage w' and a level of job attribute a'. The difference between his desired level of utility, U^*, and his real level, U', will appear as his/her declared job dissatisfaction in the studies of happiness economics.

How would a worker compare the qualities of different jobs? For

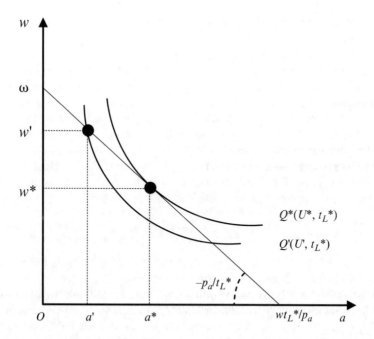

Source: Authors' elaboration.

Figure 2.10   *Combination of wage and amenities leading to the same level of utility*

example, the jobs L_1 and L_2 are two possible ways in which a job can be found in the labour market, each one offering a particular combination of monetary wage and job attributes. In job L_1, the worker gets a monetary wage w_1 and an a_1 level of job attribute, while the job L_2 yields w_2 and a_2. As the quality is the same, $Q(w_1, a_1; U^*, t_L^*) = Q(w_2, a_2; U^*, t_L^*)$, both types of the same job satisfy the equations

$$w_1 = \frac{p_C}{Uc^*}\left(Ut_C^* - Ut_L^* - \frac{Ua^*}{t_L^*}a_1\right)$$ [2.22]

$$w_2 = \frac{p_C}{Uc^*}\left(Ut_C^* - Ut_L^* - \frac{Ua^*}{t_L^*}a_2\right)$$ [2.23]

and, consequently,

$$w_1 - w_2 = \frac{p_C}{Uc^*}\frac{Ua^*}{t_L^*}(a_1 - a_2)$$ [2.24]

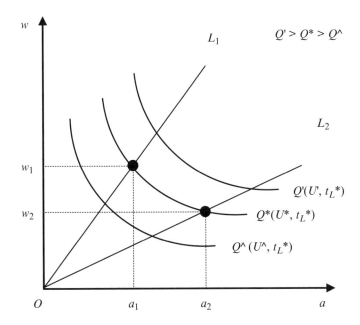

Source: Authors' elaboration.

Figure 2.11 *A graphical illustration of the theory of compensating differentials*

This expression implies that any differences between the monetary value of the utility levels corresponding to the different levels of job attributes in different quality types of the same job must be compensated by a difference in their monetary wages. If w_1 is greater than w_2, the job attributes of job L_1 are of a lesser value to the individual than the level of attributes of L_2 (see Figure 2.11).

A similar, though more complicated conclusion can be drawn when we consider a situation in which the worker can do different jobs because he/she is less specialized or because his/her human capital endowment allows such possibility. Let's assume, for simplicity, that the worker can do not one but two types of jobs. Jobs A, which combine working time $t_L{}^A$ and job attributes a, and jobs B which combine working time $t_L{}^B$ and job attributes b. The optimal behaviour of the individual worker is the result of the maximization of the Lagrangian:

$$L(t_L, a, t_C, c; \lambda, \mu, \eta) \equiv U(t_L^A, a, t_L^B, b, t_C, c) + \lambda(T - t_L^A - t_L^B - t_C)$$
$$+ \mu(\omega t_L - w^A t_L^A - w^B t_L^B - p_a a - p_b b) + \eta(w^A t_L^A + w^B t_L^B - p_c c)$$

$$[2.25]$$

Solving the problem in a similar way as above we obtain the following condition:

$$w^A - w^B = \frac{p_C}{Uc^*}\left(Ut_L^{B*} + \frac{Ua^*}{t_L^{B*}}b - Ut_L^{A*} - \frac{Ua^*}{t_L^{A*}} \right) \qquad [2.26]$$

That is, the individual worker distributes optimally his/her working time between the two labour activities when the difference in the monetary wage rates of the two jobs compensate the difference in monetary income or marginal utility of the jobs plus the difference in the value of the in-kind attributes. Therefore, people are paid more in a job to offset the discomfort arising from doing it and/or its low level of desired job attributes. If such compensation were a real feature of the labour markets, the question of the quality of jobs would be largely a descriptive, uncontroversial issue, as workers would choose the quality of their jobs. That is precisely the corollary of the hypothesis of the compensating differentials theory.

It is important to stress that the predicted outcome of the compensating wage differentials theory is not that employees working in 'bad' conditions will receive more than those working under 'good' conditions. The expectation is that, *holding worker's characteristics constant*, employees with similar qualifications working in 'bad' jobs will receive higher wages than those working in the same or similar jobs under more pleasant conditions.[16]

This prediction will be effective as long as the assumptions of the theory are satisfied. Three of these assumptions must be stressed: (a) labour markets must be competitive: there must be many firms offering the same type of job with different levels of amenities competing for the same kind of workers; (b) there must be a high level of worker mobility (so workers with different preferences for non-pecuniary aspects of jobs would go to those jobs with their preferred characteristics); and (c) workers must have complete information about the non-pecuniary aspects of their jobs (compensating wage differentials only holds for those job characteristics that workers are aware of). These are, obviously, very stringent conditions that undermine the empirical validity of the compensating differentials approach in many real-life labour markets.

Starting with the second assumption, the existence of a high level of workers' mobility implies the absence of unemployment (i.e., workers should be able to move to another job). This was noticed by another of the great classical economists, John Stuart Mill (1806–1873), who in the third edition of his *Principles of Political Economy with some of their Applications to Social Philosophy* (1848) added the following paragraph, which is worth quoting at length:

These inequalities of remuneration, which are supposed to compensate for the disagreeable circumstances of particular employments, would, under certain conditions, be natural consequences of perfectly free competition [. . .]. But it is altogether a false view of the state of facts, to present this as the relation which generally exists between agreeable and disagreeable employments. The really exhausting and the really repulsive labours, instead of being better paid than others, are almost invariably paid the worst of all, because performed by those who have no choice. It would be otherwise in a favourable state of the general labour market. If the labourers in the aggregate, instead of exceeding, fell short of the amount of employment, work which was generally disliked would not be undertaken, except for more than ordinary wages. But when the supply of labour so far exceeds the demand that to find employment at all is an uncertainty, and to be offered it on any terms a favour, the case is totally the reverse. Desirable labourers, those whom every one is anxious to have, can still exercise a choice. The undesirable must take what they can get. The more revolting the occupation, the more certain it is to receive the minimum of remuneration, because it devolves on the most helpless and degraded, on those who from squalid poverty, or from want of skill and education, are rejected from all other employments. Partly from this cause, and partly from the natural and artificial monopolies which will be spoken of presently, the inequalities of wages are generally in an opposite direction to the equitable principle of compensation erroneously represented by Adam Smith as the general law of the remuneration of labour. The hardships and the earnings, instead of being directly proportional, as in any just arrangements of society they would be, are generally in an inverse ratio to one another. (Mill [1848] 1965 Book II, Chapter XIV)

In this respect, as noted by Purse (2004), the comparison between the results of Viscusi (1979) and Robinson (1991) on the relation between hazardous work and job turnover are very revealing. While Viscusi, using labour turnover data from 1969 to 1976, a period of low unemployment, finds a positive relation between the two variables, Robinson observes a downward trend in labour turnover for hazardous jobs over the period 1977–87, a period of high and persistent unemployment. In the words of Purse 'in the light of this, the strongest claim that can be made for the theory is that, if compensating wage differentials occur at all, they do so under atypical circumstances [. . .] of tight labour markets' (Purse 2004, p. 610).

The third condition mentioned above is very stringent as well. Available studies on the awareness of workers to exposure of hazardous conditions, although not abundant, point to the low existence of awareness to environmental hazards among workers. For example, Behrens and Brackbill (1993) compare the degree of exposure of US workers to chemical and physical hazard according to a national exposure survey with the workers' perception of exposure, obtaining differences of 62 percentage points for hospital workers and exposure to chemical and 42 points for exposure to radiation. For workers in construction the difference for exposure to noise was 54 points, and 63 to vibration. A different research centred in the awareness of carcinogenic exposure among Greek employees produced similar results, with only 6.6 per cent of the men exposed aware of their occupational exposure (Chatzis *et al.* 2004). The existence of cognitive dissonance also in relation to the exposure to environmental hazards means that having the proper information is not sufficient as such information has to be processed accordingly, and not played down.

It could be argued that for other types of disamenities, working on weekends, for example, the negative impact is straight, so the required information would be available for all workers. In that case the most that we can say is that compensating wage differentials only would hold for some job characteristics (those that workers are aware of) but not for others.

The existence of compensating differentials in the labour markets has three other corollaries that are worth mentioning. First, compensating differentials provide the key to the valuation of the non-pecuniary aspects of the employment and work relationships. In fact, recent studies have used the estimates of wage compensation associated to a given risk to infer the statistical value of a worker's life (Viscusi and Aldy 2003). Second, in the presence of fully compensating differentials, public and administrative interventions limiting the disamenities of a given job (through the establishment of regulations, for example) will be considered economically non-desirable as they might constrain the possibilities for employers and employees to reach freely their most preferred positions. Third, according to the theory of compensating differentials the best way of improving the quality of jobs in real labour markets, as perceived by workers, is not directly by state regulation of the level of many of the non-pecuniary job characteristics, but indirectly, by policy aiming to make the labour markets more efficient and competitive and the workers better informed about the impact of the non-pecuniary characteristics of jobs on their welfare.

(B)   Reality check: the empirical evidence on compensating differentials.
As we have seen above, the assumptions underlying the theory of compensating differentials are very demanding, so just by acknowledging them we could infer that the prospects for the existence of compensating differentials are not very encouraging. Nevertheless, it can be argued, following the old methodological dictum of Milton Friedman (1953) that the test of a theory is not so much the reality of the assumptions behind such theory but its potential to explain reality. In this respect, many authors have studied whether working conditions in different jobs could explain differences in pay. Within this type of research, one of the areas that has attracted more attention is the relation between work-related fatalities

and wages, for two different reasons. First, if there are compensating differentials, the risk of death should be highly paid in the market, making easier the identification of the link between higher occupational death risk and higher wage. Second, death hazard is less prone to measurement error.

Most studies of what we can call the 'first wave' of empirical research on the existence of compensating differentials for occupational death risk and other disamenities (Thaler and Rosen 1976, Viscusi 1980, Dorsey and Walzer 1983, for the US, and Martin and Psacharopoulos 1982, for the UK) conclude that there is some nexus between work-related fatalities and wage, although the results are far from being univocal.[17] In fact, Brown (1980), after reviewing 11 papers of this first wave of empirical work, concludes that 'the overall pattern that emerges [. . .] is one of mixed results: some clear support for the theory but an uncomfortable number of exceptions' (Brown 1980, p. 118). The most common explanation for such lack of consistency is the omission of important variables reflecting differences in workers' abilities. In order to solve this problem, Brown presents his own estimates using longitudinal data richer in information about workers' abilities, concluding that the hypothesis of lack of support of the theory of compensating differential due to the omission of important dimensions of workers' quality is not supported by the data. Using the NBER-Thorndike-Hagen sample, Mathios (1989) reports the effects on earnings of variables such as convenient hours, convenient location, availability of free time, challenging and interesting work, that go in the expected directions in terms of compensating differentials.[18] However, other effects, such as status of the job and future financial rewards are inconsistent with equalizing differences. In a different paper, this author concludes that 'earnings might be an adequate proxy for compensation for those with low levels of education, whereas the opposite holds for highly educated individuals' (Mathios 1988, p. 456). In short, compensating differential might work for some characteristics of work, but not for others, and for some workers, but not for others. A similar result is reported by Duncan and Holmlund (1983): they found little wage response for positions demanding hard physical labour and inflexible hours of work constraints but strong positive effects of wages on dangerous and stressful working conditions.

While the defenders of the existence of compensating differentials consider that the lack of information on important characteristics of workers can be blamed for the absence of definitive conclusions, other authors, like Purse (2004), from a critical perspective, argue that the positive results obtained from the mainstream perspective abound in econometrical problems that make them largely useless. Among such problems, Purse highlights difficulties with the construction of the risk variable and the existence of omitted variables. An example of the first type of problem is the much-quoted paper of Thaler and Rosen (1976), where the risk variable is incorrectly specified, failing to separate the risk of death from occupational and non-occupational causes, meaning that they actually measure the risk of death of people in particular occupations. An example of the second problem is the omission of inter-industry wage differentials from the wage equations. Such differences might account for as much as 37 per cent of the wage difference in the US for a given occupation (Krueger and Summers 1988). In fact, according to Leigh (1995), when inter-industry differences are considered in analysis of compensating differentials, much of the correlation between death rates and higher wages disappears.[19]

The review of other papers on the issue buttresses the inconclusiveness of what we could call the 'compensating differential controversy'. This result, by itself, can be interpreted in terms of the lack of general existence of supportive evidence. An example of the most recent literature is the paper of Bonhomme and Jolivet (2009), who explore the existence of compensating differentials using European data (Austria, Denmark, Spain, Finland, France, Italy, the Netherlands and Portugal) from the European Community Household Panel for the years 1994–2001, considering five amenities (apart from the wage). The estimates of the authors reveal the existence of strong preferences for some job characteristics (especially job security) that does not translate into the existence of compensating wage differentials in cross-sectional data. Fernández and Nordman (2009), using quantile regressions and UK data conclude that 'jobs offering poor working conditions carry lower earnings, contrary to what the theory of compensating differentials might suggest' (Fernández and Nordman 2009, p. 203). Such penalty is mostly significant in the middle part of the distribution. A few other examples will help us to see how diverse is the casuistic related with the existence of compensating differentials. The study of Ose (2005) on working conditions, compensation and absenteeism in Norway concludes that workers may not be fully compensated when experiencing high levels of noise in the work area, or when the job involves a high degree of monotonous work, heavy or frequent lifting or poor work postures. In contrast, Lanfranchi *et al.* (2002) find a significant shift earnings premium for French male full-time blue collar workers, the wage rate for shift workers being 16 per cent higher than for day workers. This result is coherent with the data supplied by many Spanish collective agreements, where the night shift premium for specific sectors of economic activity can be as high as 25 per cent. Still, such premiums are not really the result of market mechanisms, but rather of institutional factors such as collective bargaining or labour regulation.

Last, two interesting studies of the use of condoms by female sex workers in Calcutta, India, and Ciudad Juarez in Mexico (Rao *et al.* 2003, De la Torre *et al.* 2010), show the existence of higher average prices (i.e. compensating differentials) for unprotected sex, with a wage premium of 31 per cent in Mexico and larger in the former case.[20] Interestingly, key predictors of a decrease in the price premium for unprotected sex included age, a bad financial situation, frequent alcohol consumption before or during sex, and frequent drug use before or during sex; in all cases, elements that can be interpreted as signalling fewer alternatives to the acceptance of the risk.[21]

Summing up, we can conclude that the compensating differentials are far from being a general phenomenon. Although researchers have been able to detect compensating differentials for some specific risks and groups of workers, in most cases what has been dominant is, paraphrasing one of the papers reviewed above, their pervasive absence. This result should not come as a surprise since, as we have seen above, labour markets seldom meet the assumptions behind the principle of the theory.

2.2.1.2. The radical alternative: exploitation and job quality

The theory of compensating wage differentials, dominant as it is in the economic academic world, has nevertheless found fierce opposition since the time it was enunciated, not only in non-economic academic domains like politics and sociology, but also in other strands of the economic thought. Without any doubt, the fiercest of all critiques has been the position held by Karl Marx and his followers. For Marx, workers will always be exploited under capitalism, whether the labour market is competitive or not (although they would be relatively more exploited where the demand side of labour markets is less competitive). No compensating wage differentials could be expected to hold in the same jobs and for the same workers except in short-run periods of economic expansion. In contrast, in the long run: (a) the concentration and centralization of capital tend to restrain the competition between firms in monopoly capitalism, and (b) the spells of unemployment will force workers to accept any job offered, independently of the wage and disamenities involved, to survive. Therefore there was only a floor or ultimate limit to the 'bad' conditions of jobs, the limit set by the necessary socio-physical reproduction of the labour force. Therefore, for Marxists, workers in capitalism would generally have 'bad' jobs with low wages (unless, obviously, the workers could gain enough economic and political force to fight for the betterment of these conditions). From this perspective, raising the low level of non-pecuniary aspects of jobs would be a task for trade unions and political parties. And, consequently, defining what is or must be a 'good' job will be less a technical question but a political one reflecting the power relations in a society.

2.2.1.3.   The behavioural approach: two points of view

There are two further (non-conflicting) economic explanations for the persistence of poor quality jobs – those with non-fully compensating wages *and* dangerous working conditions, excessive working days, contractual instability, lack of autonomy in the job, and so on. Paradoxically, these perspectives explain the existence of these 'bad quality' jobs as the *efficient* response of the labour markets to the *revealed* preferences of workers when they show a preoccupation for their relative position or income, or when they become trapped in pre-existing norms and traditions regulating the conditions of the workplace. We review these two further economic approaches in the following pages.

(a) Workers are obviously interested in the *absolute* levels of the wages they get in return for their work since such levels are the means to buy the goods they need to increase their levels of utility or welfare. But the fact that they are interested in their *absolute* levels of income does not mean that they are not also interested in their *relative* income level, i.e., how their wages compare with the wages earned by other workers within their reference groups. At least, we can think about three justifications for the relevance of the relative position as a determinant of people's subjective evaluation of their situation. First, the anecdotal evidence about the role played by moral 'weaknesses' such as envy or jealousy in human behaviour. But although this kind of emotion can be imputed to individuals as a human correlate of genetic traits that some Darwinists would defend, on its own it cannot provide a solid basis for a scientific theorization. Thus, economists have mostly relied on two other justifications. One is the existence of what are known as *positional goods* or goods with positional characteristics (Hirsch 1977). These types of goods are those whose consumption cannot be generalized because it is physically impossible or because their quality would decrease with the increase in their supply. In fact, in contrast to 'standard' goods, in order to be able to acquire goods with positional attributes, the important thing is not to have money but to have more money than the rest of the people who compete for the same goods. Relative income is also a very important consideration for people when the level of income is used to 'buy' a starting position for their offspring (by allowing them to pay for a better education, for instance) or is a signal or mark of success used to gain a better standpoint in any other kind of social or economic race.

There is wide and accumulating evidence coming from psychology, biology and economics showing that people are continuously comparing themselves with others, ranking relatively their performance, abilities, possessions, earnings, etc.[22] Such literature has shown that these inter-individual comparisons and positional competition sometimes affect the aggregate behaviour producing non-desired (non-efficient) collective outcomes. An obvious example of these unintended consequences of this kind of relative or positional competition is precisely in the 'markets' for amenities in labour markets. When this kind of comparative relation is pervasive among workers, one of the means open to each worker to outdo others is by accepting to work more hours, or in bad conditions. But when all the individual workers pursue independently this strategy, all receive more money but will all also work longer or in poor conditions without improving the relative standing of each one. So their individual level of welfare is lower.

If workers are interested in their relative standing in the income scale, there will be a larger than desired quantity of 'bad' jobs because *they*, the workers, will *voluntarily* choose a lower level of 'amenities' in their jobs (and correspondingly higher wages) than the one they would choose if they could coordinate their decisions. Under these circumstances, the exogenous or collective definition of some job quality standards affecting all workers in a type of job, constraining their self-interested willingness to trade disamenities for a better relative wage, will be important not as a means to protect workers from exploitation by employers, as the radical approach holds, but as a means to avoid a type of destructive competition amongst themselves and the possibility that workers end up 'exploiting' themselves.

An example – taken from Frank (2008) – may clarify the type of impact of positional preferences on the quality of jobs. Suppose that we have a 'group' of workers composed of two people, Smith and Jones, and that each one faces a choice between working in a 'good' job (for instance, a mine with safety measures) at a weekly salary of 500€ or a 'bad' job (an unsafe or dusty mine) at a weekly salary of 550€, the difference between salaries reflecting the costs of providing better working conditions. The consequence of working in the unsafe job is a defined reduction in life expectancy. Each worker chooses independently selecting the job that promises to deliver the highest welfare or utility. Such utility depends on three factors: (1) absolute income, (2) relative income, and (3) job conditions.

Suppose, additionally, that Smith and Jones have the same preferences in evaluating these factors, so their welfare depends additively on these three elements. To put the argument in its simplest terms, we can suppose that the two miners know perfectly the risks they run if they choose to work in the unsafe job, so they are perfectly informed about the jobs and can make rational decisions. We may also suppose that the labour market is perfectly competitive, so the theory of compensating wage differentials has full applicability in this example. Consequently, the weekly 50€ differential wage would reflect the costs per worker of installing the safety

Measuring more than money

Smith choice

		'Good' job (500€ a week)	'Bad' job (550€ a week)
	'Good' job (500€ a week)	2nd best for Jones (551€) / 2nd best for Smith (551€)	Worst for Jones (351€) / Best for Smith (750€)
Jones choice	'Bad' job (550€ a week)	Best for Jones (750€) / Worst for Smith (351€)	3rd best for Smith (550€) / 3rd best for Smith (550€)

Source: Adapted from Frank (2008, p. 502).

Figure 2.12   Pay-offs to different choices of good and bad jobs

devices (to filter the dust). Now, if we suppose that the two workers value the health provided by the safety devices (the clean air) at 51€ a week or more (for instance, 52€) then, if the only argument of their utility function is absolute income, they will choose working in the safe mine at 500€ per week, and the mine owners will be ready to make the necessary expenses in safety devices. So, Smith and Jones will get the 'good' jobs they want. But their choice will be completely different if, in their preferences, the relative level or income ranks high up, because when relative income matters, the attractiveness of each choice for each worker depends on the choice made by the other worker. Suppose now that the importance of the relative position in the preferences of both workers results in the four possible combinations of choices as outlined in Figure 2.12.[23]

Now, when relative income matters, the interdependence of preferences means that both Smith and Jones will freely *choose* to work in the 'bad' job when the other worker chooses to work in the 'good' one but also when the other chooses to work in the 'bad' job, so both workers would choose to work in bad jobs (that is their *dominant strategy*) and consequently, if each one chooses independently in a self-interested way, both get their third-best preference. This is clearly a collectively bad result attending to the obvious fact that both workers will be better if they choose to work in good jobs because, if that were their choice, both of them would get their second-best preference in their rankings of preferences. But this *socially rational* solution will not be attainable if the workers are *individually rational* and make their labour market choices following their private interests. Therefore, if Smith and Jones would work initially in 'good' jobs, each one making his choices rationally will have the incentive to refuse to follow suit, each one trading a higher wage for worse working conditions.

The kind of interaction between the workers' decisions represented in the figure is known in Game Theory as 'Prisoner's Dilemma', one example of the kinds of social interdependences where there is a contradiction between individual and social rationality. The problem we confront in these kinds of social interactions is that it does not pay to either worker, acting alone, to choose the alternative that would be better for both. In this situation it is easy to see why Smith and Jones might want to enter a binding agreement to work in the 'good' job, and it can also be seen why, if we ignore the presence and importance of relative income considerations, it might be concluded mistakenly that a regulation which imposes safety devices, or defines exogenously what conditions a job must have, makes each worker worse off. Since, before the regulation, both workers chose rationally and freely to work in the 'bad' jobs it would seem, from the perspective of the theory of compensating differentials, that additional safety devices would be of a lesser worth for them than 50€ per week, and so the regulation would harm the workers forcing them to purchase some amenities whose worth is less to them than its cost. From the opposite perspective, it could be concluded that the workers were being exploited because, as a group, they reach their third-best position in their preference rankings.

Both conclusions would be erroneous. Neither the safety devices cost less than 50€ per week per worker, nor are the workers being exploited by their employers. Simply, the kind of direct interaction amongst workers when relative considerations matter would lead the workers to freely agree with their firms a level of 'amenities' that would not be socially optimal, that is, would not reflect the preferences of the collectivity of workers.[24] This conclusion does not completely invalidate the compensating wage differential approach; it does, however, show its shortcomings. The same kind of argument could be used to explain the emergence of regulations and other social norms which put limits to the length of the working week or require employers to pay a wage premium whenever workers do overtime. Once again, these regulations cannot be understood by using the traditional model of compensating differentials because there is no justification for workers supporting a legislation that put limits to the workweek or discourages employers to pay for overtime work: the same can be said about other 'amenities' in the workplace. Once more, if workers care not only about the absolute income but also about relative income, it can be predicted – as Frank notes – that the quality of work life will be worse than it would be desirable. So the definition of the optimal level of 'amenities' in the workplace cannot be left only to the labour markets.

(b) Some useful conclusions can be reached from another strand of economic thought known as the Economics of Conformism (Jones 1984; Akerlof 1980). According to this approach, individual behaviour will be affected by group membership. As opposed to the isolated behaviour described above, behaviour is different inside a group as the individual takes into account the rewards and penalties of his behaviour in accordance or deviance with the internal norms of the group. If we consider groups of workers within a workplace from this perspective, we find that the collective action by workers in the past, leading to some specific set of norms and rules of action affecting various aspects of job quality (procedures, rhythms, intensity, etc.), might impose themselves over other norms more suitable to the present conditions. The pressure that any individual worker experiences to conform to the pre-existing pattern of how the work must be done seriously hampers his/her ability to freely negotiate new working conditions, a new bundle of compensating differential wages and amenities. This approach highlights the possibility that the groups of workers could find themselves locked in an inefficient or 'bad' level of working conditions as a result of past decisions and norms. The path dependence of the definition and level of job quality in each place and time means that this level could be inefficient, which again calls for a definition external to the individual worker. Here too, the capacity of a worker to participate in the establishment of those internal-group rules is in itself a dimension of quality in a job.[25]

2.2.1.4. Final remarks

Summing up, the mainstream economic approach to job quality defends the existence of compensating differentials in the labour market warranting, given a set of assumptions, that workers with the same skills will be offered different bundles of wage and disamenities leading to the same job quality. Workers then will choose whatever combination best suits their preferences. Two different approaches criticize the applicability of compensating differentials in the labour market. The first perspective casts doubts about the fulfilment in real labour markets of the assumptions that have to be met to allow for the full functioning of the principle of compensating differentials, namely, perfect information of workers of the value of the disamenities associated with a given job, perfect competition and full employment. The second perspective considers that workers take their relative income into account or they take decisions not in isolation but as members of groups, and as such the compensating wage differential approach must be qualified. According to these alternative theories, even in a world of perfectly competitive labour markets with workers enjoying full information about the non-pecuniary features of their jobs and in a full employment economy, the free bargaining between workers and employers will not completely reach an efficient spectrum of wage and non-wage characteristics reflecting the preferences of workers. Therefore, the observed wage differentials will not compensate adequately the non-pecuniary aspects of the jobs and, in that case, the question of job quality becomes relevant in the evaluation of the efficiency of labour markets. The existence of partial compensating differentials highlights, on the other hand, the importance of using both wage and non-pecuniary disamenities when measuring job quality. Any evaluation of job quality based on either wages or disamenities could lead to wrong conclusions if there is compensation between both aspects of work.

Finally, it is important to highlight that from the economic perspective, the issue of job quality cannot be reduced to a purely moral question. Without any justice considerations, it concerns the efficiency with which labour markets supply some special 'goods' (the amenities that define a 'good' job) to their 'users' (the workers). If, for whatever reasons (unemployment, non-competitive labour market, internal-group norms, positional competition), differential wages do not fully compensate the disamenities, from an economic point of view this will be the result of an efficiency problem, a signal of an incorrect assignment of resources, as with any other efficiency problem it can be found in any other market.

2.2.2 Other Approaches to Job Quality from the Social Sciences

2.2.2.1. Alienation and intrinsic quality of work

As we have seen, the traditional economic approach to job quality is based on the idea that work is, in itself, a disutility (which produces dissatisfaction and 'ill-being'). Work is a necessary evil, something in which human beings have to engage in order to gain access to resources for surviving or consuming, but which would be avoided otherwise. Of course, not all jobs are equally unpleasant: some are more unpleasant than others, and because in a capitalist economy the labour force is free, the remuneration of jobs will have to reflect the differential unpleasantness of jobs (to compensate for the relative disutility of each job compared to the other jobs available). Hence the theory of compensating differentials discussed above.

According to this traditional economic approach, as pay compensates for the unpleasantness of work, there is no need to care explicitly about job quality. Poor-quality jobs will receive more pay and vice versa, so under given circumstances the combination of unpleasantness and pay shall be more or less the same for all jobs (if we could calculate the ratio of *unpleasantness per unit of pay*, this ratio should be the same for all workers). From a mainstream economic point of view, only if there are external factors hindering the proper functioning of labour markets this compensating mechanism would not work and there would be some jobs not properly compensated (Green 2006, p. 9). Therefore, in order to improve job quality, we should only make sure that labour markets are free from external interventions.

It is somewhat paradoxical that this has been the standard view of quality of work in liberal economics since Adam Smith first proposed it in the Wealth of Nations. As Weber argued a long time ago (Weber [1905] 1930), the foundations of capitalism lay in the development of a Protestant Ethic which sanctified mundane work as proof of one's virtue and eventual salvation, an ethical system in which diligence and application in the performance of one's profession (vocation) is a moral good in itself. This implies a non-utilitarian view of work, in which the motivation for work is not primarily instrumental but intrinsic, because industriousness in mundane work activity is what elevates (saves) human beings from evil.[26]

The paradox becomes fully circular when Marx secularizes the Protestant work ethic to mount a powerful critique of capitalism as a productive system through his concept of alienation. If Protestantism considered productive work to be God's calling and proof of one's sanctity, Marx considers purposeful creative work as the essence of humanity, the key to realize our potential as human beings. Therefore, according to the young Marx of the *Manuscripts*, the separation of workers from the process and fruits of production which characterizes capitalism as a productive system, denies workers the realization of their potential, their very essence, as human beings (Marx, [1844] 1968). For Marx, work is not only a means to an end, as for classical economists, but also a (or even *the*) crucial element of realization and fulfilment of men and women. This concept implies a turn to the intrinsic qualities of work (very importantly, to the social conditions under which work takes place), moving beyond the exclusive focus on pay and compensation implied in an instrumental concept of work.

Karl Marx's concept of alienation is the starting point of the sociological tradition in the study of job quality, which emphasizes the intrinsic qualities of work as key determinants of the well-being of workers (without necessarily denying the importance of wages). We can identify two main strands in this tradition: one which has a more objective approach and focuses on autonomy and skills (Braverman [1974] 1998) and one more subjectivist focused on workers' feelings of powerlessness, meaninglessness and isolation (Blauner 1964).

2.2.2.1.1.   The objectivist approach: the debate on autonomy and skills   In the 1970s, Braverman directly took up the Marxist tradition to argue that the developments of industrial organization in the first half of the twentieth century (the Fordist/Taylorist system) had exacerbated the problem of alienation that Marx spoke about more than a century earlier: by separating conception and execution, accumulating all knowledge and authority in the hands of managers, such production system transformed workers into 'trained gorillas' (as Taylor himself famously put it). The autonomy, skills and pride of earlier craft workers were wiped out by this process of mechanization and rationalization of modern industry: the twentieth century was a period of degradation of work (Braverman [1974] 1998, pp. 316–25).

Around the same time that Braverman published his theses in *Labour and Monopoly Capital*, another sociologist (Daniel Bell) presented a symmetrically opposite view of the impact of modern technology on the quality of work, based on the central idea that the United States was no longer an industrial society (Bell 1973). After the Second World War, all developed capitalist economies experienced a fast-paced process of structural transformation that made them service, rather than industrial, economies. In this new economic structure, knowledge is the key factor of production, which according to Bell implies a very significant upskilling of the labour force rather than a de-skilling as argued by Braverman (as well as increased autonomy and flattened power structures; Bell 1973, p. 161). This debate over whether structural change in the economy leads to deskilling or upskilling continues in a lively fashion today, with some new empirical evidence pointing to a skill polarization (which suggests that both Braverman and Bell could have been simultaneously right; see Autor *et al.* 2006).

The deskilling debate has very important implications for the analysis of job quality. On the one hand, and most importantly for our purposes, it emphasizes the importance of two objective characteristics of work organization (skills and autonomy) for the intrinsic quality of work; on the other, it puts these two characteristics in the wider context of technological progress, the division of labour and managerial practices.

2.2.2.1.2.   The subjectivist approach: alienation and job satisfaction   Karl Marx's concept of alienation also had an obvious subjective component, even if somewhat elusive. Several sociologists and social psychologists have tried to operationalize the concept and measure it empirically in real-life situations – which in practice moved the concept into the area of job satisfaction. The classic study of this second strand was 'Alienation and Freedom' by Blauner (1964), who researched four types of work organizations associated with different production technologies: craft (printing), machine-tending (textile), assembly-line (automobile) and process technology (chemicals). Although the four types of technology studied by Blauner were obviously contemporary, he considered that they represented four typical stages in the evolution of productive technology, implying that the historical trend in the degree of alienation at work would follow an inverted u-curve (alienation, as he measured it, was low in craft production, higher in machine-tending and highest in assembly-line, decreasing again in process technology).

To carry out his study, Blauner operationalized Marx's concept of alienation along four dimensions: powerlessness, meaninglessness, social isolation and self-estrangement. To evaluate each of those dimensions, Blauner studied the subjective feelings of the workers themselves, using several pre-existing surveys on job satisfaction and attitudes to job redesign. In fact, Blauner's (and his followers) approach to alienation has been criticized for being more about job satisfaction than alienation in the original Marxian sense (Edgell 2006, p. 36). Part of this criticism derives from the elusive and purely philosophical nature of Marx's concept of alienation, which makes any attempt at empirical application very open to criticism. However, it is true that alienation in the traditional Marxian sense referred to an *objective* state of separation between the worker and the means and fruits of production: by focusing on the perceptions of workers themselves rather than in their objective situation, Blauner's approach would be insensitive to mechanisms as important to the original Marxian concept as false conscience (what happens if workers are happy about their situation even if they are totally alienated from the means and fruits of production?). It is in this sense that it can be said that the operationalization of alienation by Blauner, in the end, does not differ much from job satisfaction studies. On the other hand, the approach by Blauner and followers has the advantage of anchoring job satisfaction on the structural and technological conditions of work, something which is often lacking in the psychological tradition of job satisfaction studies.

The four dimensions of subjective alienation at work identified by Blauner have been applied to different countries and work environments (see, for instance, Kohn 1976; Shepard 1977; Hull *et al.* 1982; Vallas 1988). They constitute, therefore, a relatively tested set of dimensions to measure the impact of the structural and technological characteristics of work on the feeling of realization and psychological well-being of workers.

2.2.2.2. Segmentation and the importance of employment conditions
In its origin (which lies somewhere between institutional economics and Marxist sociological analysis of power relations in the workplace),

segmentation theory was a reaction to the neoclassical economic view of the labour market. Its basic argument is that instead of a single labour market functioning according to competitive rules of supply and demand, there are different segments which function with different rules: 'The competitive form is only one mode of labour market organization, coexisting along other modes of organization' (Peck 1996, p. 47).

This theory was first proposed by Doeringer and Piore (1970), who, rather than segmentation, spoke about *dualism*. The labour market, they observed, is segmented into a primary and a secondary sector. The primary sector contains the good jobs, with high wages, secure employment and good prospects of career advancement: this sector corresponds to large companies which use technologically advanced production processes. The secondary sector contains the bad jobs, with low wages and poor working conditions, usually in smaller firms in less technologically advanced activities.

The explanation given by Doeringer and Piore to this dualistic pattern is primarily technological: the most technologically advanced sectors of the economy require a stable supply of highly skilled labour, so it is in their interest to create internal labour markets (i.e. non-competitive, protected) to attract and retain the highly specialized workers they need. The secondary sector, on the other hand, is not only technologically backward and requires less specific skills, but also has to provide the flexibility that the primary sector lacks. Even primary sector companies rely on the secondary sector when they need flexibility, by hiring temporary workers (secondary workers within primary sector companies) or by directly subcontracting work to the secondary sector.

The radical school of segmentation theories (Gordon *et al.* 1982) agreed with Doeringer and Piore with respect to the fundamentally dual nature of contemporary labour markets, but disagreed in the causal mechanisms behind such pattern. According to these Marxist theorists, the technological developments of monopoly capital lead to an increasing homogeneity rather than segmentation, but this homogeneity and the levels of discontent associated with deskilling and work degradation (following Braverman) implies a challenge to the capitalist order. Segmentation is, therefore, a conscious strategy of management to undermining working class solidarity and mobilization by exploiting and further developing the internal divisions of the working class.

Later segmentation theories (for a review, see Peck 1996, pp. 56–79) are less univocal in their explanation and in their analysis: rather than a single causal mechanism (be it technology or workplace politics), they consider segmentation a result of a multiplicity of factors, including social reproduction, discrimination, industrial relations systems and state regulation;

and rather than dualism, they emphasize the multiple segmentation of contemporary labour markets. These theories provide a sound theoretical framework for understanding the increasingly fragmented labour markets brought about by the flexibilization policies of the 1980s and 1990s across OECD economies (see for instance Heery and Salmon 2000).

Segmentation theories emphasize the link between the conditions and characteristics of work within firms and the conditions and characteristics of employment in the labour market, and therefore provide a basis for an integrated approach to job quality (referring both to work and employment conditions). In particular, the segmentation approach highlights the importance of the conditions of the employment relation itself for job quality: most importantly, contractual status and stability of employment, opportunities for skill development and career progression.

2.2.2.3. The effect of work on health: the health and safety literature

The field of health and safety studies has its origins in two different traditions: on the one hand, occupational medicine, which even before the Industrial Revolution had systematically studied diseases associated with specific occupations (going back to Ramazzini's classical study of the health conditions of 50 occupations of seventeenth-century Italy). On the other hand, health and safety studies can be traced back to nineteenth-century studies and pamphlets denunciating the appalling conditions of work and life of the proletariat in the early years of the Industrial Revolution, carried out by social reformers and revolutionaries such as Owen and Engels. But it is with the development of the Welfare State and modern labour regulation in the first half of the twentieth century that this field was consolidated and institutionalized – not only in terms of research, but also in terms of regulation and state intervention, arguably more than most other areas of work and employment.

The traditional approach of health and safety considered the workplace as a harbinger of illnesses and accidents: an environment which exposed workers to a number of physical and psychological agents that made them sick or generated risk of accidents (which leads to an intervention strategy focused on minimizing exposure to such hazards; see Navarro 1982). Such an approach seems linked to the traditional economic approach of work as a disutility in itself, even though the perspective is obviously different. More recent approaches tend to take a more integrated, organizational approach, and assign a central role to the social determinants of health and safety problems, including motivation, decision latitude and equity (Wilkinson 2001).

Most health and safety studies are strongly empirical in character, and consist of the evaluation of the impact of certain conditions of work on the health of workers. The range of conditions and outcomes studied has evolved following the changing nature of work in the twentieth century. Up to the 1970s, most health and safety literature focused on the types of risks and hazards typically found in industrial organizations, mostly those of a physical nature. In those earlier studies, the social aspects of work organization were often neglected, focusing rather on the degree of pressure and load that the production system required of workers (Wilkinson 2001, p. 10). After the 1980s, with the decline in manufacturing and the increasing dominance of office and service work, the social environment received increasing attention, and the focus moved towards psychosocial risks and the various types and determinants of stress.

2.2.2.4. Work does not take place in a vacuum: the increasing importance of work–life balance

In some ways, work–life balance (WLB) has always been a concern for those studying both quality of work and quality of life (the notion that there must be a balance between work and non-working life is a crucial element in any system of work values, and has been always present in discussions of work and leisure, the role of work in human life, etc.), but WLB has only come to the forefront of social research in the last 25 years. The increasing centrality of this issue is probably related to the massive incorporation of women into the labour force after the 1970s (Gallie 2007, p. 5). It is not that before the 1970s work–life balance was unproblematic, but it remained relatively hidden behind a division of economic roles by gender that assigned women the reproductive tasks at home and men the productive tasks in the labour market. The struggle of women for equality in the access to economic resources (paid work) demonstrates that this *pre-1970s work–life balance arrangement* was far from sustainable (or equally acceptable to both parts), because of the power imbalances between genders it brought about. It is when (married) women join the labour force in massive numbers that the (at least, potential) conflict between the demands of working and non-working life becomes visible, and work–life balance becomes a salient social issue.

Despite the abundant literature on WLB in recent years (not only in academic journals, but also in the popular media), there is no clear and widely agreed definition of what WLB actually is. After an extensive review of this literature, in which they identify six different conceptualizations, Kalliath and Brough propose the following general definition: 'work–life balance is the individual perception that work and non-work activities are compatible and promote growth in accordance with an individual's current life priorities' (Kalliath and Brough 2008, p. 326; for an alternative definition, see Guest 2002).

We can divide the literature on WLB into three categories: (1) studies of the objective levels of demands of work and non-work activities, and their impact on the well-being of the workers; (2) studies of the norms and values around work and non-working life, and their relation to workers' expectations and preferences; and (3) studies of the subjective evaluation of workers of their situation regarding WLB (most importantly, their satisfaction with it), and its determinants. It is important to emphasize that, as mentioned earlier, most work–life balance research is either focused on gender or at least very concerned with it, as in advanced Western societies gender is the social cleavage that most directly affects the level of demands of work and non-working life on individuals, as well as the norms and values around work and family life.

It seems quite clear that any job quality indicator must include information on this increasingly important area of research and social concern – especially if the indicator has to be gender mainstreamed. But what approach fits best? Of course, the sub-indicators on work–life balance should refer to the demands of work rather than to the demands of non-working life on the individual worker – after all, the idea is to make a quality of work, not a quality of life, indicator. But there would be two potential approaches: one would consist of measuring the demands of work on workers themselves (assuming that, *ceteris paribus*, more demands imply more difficulties to reconcile work and non-work commitments), the other on measuring the satisfaction of each worker with his/her work–life balance at present (ignoring the actual level of work demands). The dilemma of choosing an objective or a subjective approach here is analogous to the discussion of whether using objective or subjective measures of job quality (see section 2.3.1), so we will not repeat the same arguments.

Taking into account work–life balance from an objective approach would imply covering in some detail the level of work demands to the individual worker. In practical terms, this means collecting information about two main aspects of work: (1) working time, with respect to the specific areas of duration of work, scheduling, flexibility (to be able to adapt working hours to other commitments), regularity (necessary to structure non-working life) and the existence of clear boundaries between work and non-working time (an area of increasing concern: technical advances such as the Blackberry may be blurring the boundaries, which has obvious implications for work–life balance); (2) the intensity of the work effort may also have implications for work–life balance, beyond its impact on working time (exhaustion and stress can lead to disruptions of life outside work).

2.3. CONCLUSIONS: DIMENSIONS OF QUALITY OF WORK DERIVED FROM SOCIAL RESEARCH

In this chapter we have made a brief overview of three broadly different approaches for operationalizing job quality. A first perspective focuses on workers' satisfaction, considering that the level of job satisfaction of workers is directly related to job quality. This approach allows the researcher to skip the difficult process of selecting the attributes important in terms of job quality and measuring them. The second approach is also subjective in nature, making workers select themselves the attributes defining job quality using surveys, but differs from the first strategy because, once selected the relevant dimensions, objective data is used to measure the quality of jobs. The third approach draws on contemporary social science literature to identify the main elements of job quality.

From our point of view, the purely subjective approach is, as explained in this section, the least satisfactory, so we would favour a mix of the second and third methodological strategies. In fact, these three approaches, and in particular the last two, are only partially exclusive: when workers are asked about the importance of different attributes in defining what is a good job they are usually confronted with a predefined list of alternatives, and such a list is not randomly chosen from all the possible characteristics of jobs. On the contrary, researchers usually draw from the available literature on dimensions of job quality to construct such a list. Given the limitations associated with the approach based on job satisfaction, and the interrelations between the other two approaches, it seems reasonable to conclude that the best practice for developing a sound model of job quality would draw from the latter approach.

After the review and discussion of the different approaches to job quality undertaken in this chapter it should be clear that job quality is a multidimensional concept, that there are several different attributes of jobs that have to be taken into account in order to evaluate the impact of work and employment on the well-being of workers. This discussion should serve as a good starting point for the design of a model of job quality, or more specifically, for the selection of the dimensions to consider in such a multidimensional model. Table 2.4 summarizes the main elements proposed by each of the social sciences traditions covered in this chapter.

Table 2.4 *Dimensions of job quality suggested by the different traditions*

The orthodox economic approach: compensating differentials	The radical economic approach: exploitation	Behavioural economic approaches	The traditional sociological approach: alienation and intrinsic quality of work	The institutional approach: segmentation and employment quality	Occupational medicine and health and safety literature: risks and impact of work on health	Work–life balance studies
Labour compensation: (1) Wages	*Power relations:* (2) Industrial democracy as a compensating power	(3) Participation	*Objective strand:* (4) skills; (5) autonomy *Subjective strand:* (6) powerlessness; (7) meaninglessness; (8) social isolation; (9) self-estrangement	(10) Contractual status and stability of employment; (11) Opportunities for skills development and career progression	*Conditions:* (12) Physical risks; (13) Psychosocial risks; *Outcomes:* (14) Perceived impact of work on health; (15) Absenteeism	*Working time:* (16) Duration (17) Scheduling (18) Flexibility (19) Regularity (20) Clear boundaries *Intensity:* (21) Pace of work and workload (22) Stress and exhaustion

Source: Authors' elaboration.

NOTES

1. These scores are based on the country averages of the answers given to the following question: 'How satisfied are you in your (main) job?'. The possible answers range from completely unsatisfied (0) to completely satisfied (6). We have rescaled this variable to the more standard 0–10 scale to facilitate the interpretation of results.
2. The level of satisfaction in the 1997 wave of the ISSP for the countries in both samples was also very high, in fact higher than in 2005 (7.43 *versus* 7.11).
3. The presence of this kind of cultural mediation has been used to explain some surprising results such as the low levels of satisfaction reported in many high developed and stable Asiatic countries. In this case, the weight of Confucian and Buddhist conceptions has been wielded as an important element to explain such low results. Following a similar reasoning, the relatively high level of happiness reported in many Latin American and Caribbean countries, given their lower levels of economic development and their social and political unrest, has been explained by the mediation of a specific Latino culture that allows its people to master the art of living.
4. An important further point to emphasize here is that job satisfaction is not suitable either as one of the dimensions within a composite index of job quality (which is done in some of the indices discussed later). Because job satisfaction depends on the overall evaluation that the worker makes of his/her job, including it as an element within a composite index would mean including *input* and *output* together in the same index, and therefore, counting twice the impact of the variables considered.
5. This difference, though, is mostly the result of the different answers given in Eastern European countries.
6. In the words of the Memorial Nobel Amartya Sen:

    > The need to take a transformation – to be exact, a strictly concave – of the income variable relates to the fact that the valued object ultimately is not income itself, but the things we are able to do with the help of income, and it also gives recognition to the further fact that there is likely to be some diminishing returns in that conversion (Sen 2000, p. 100).

7. For simplicity and the radically different institutional environments, we intentionally exclude from the analysis low- and middle-income countries and OECD countries other than European ones.
8. In fact, if this were true, there would be no shared concept of what is a good job, because each individual worker would only refer to his or her own experience: the attributes of a good job for a society would coincide to the attributes of existing jobs.
9. When we limit the analysis to high income countries or European Union states the results hold as well.
10. The kinds of 'amenities' considered must be interpreted in a wide sense including health and safety, social benefits, location, employment security, unemployment risk, etc., as it is explained more thoroughly later on.
11. Note that it is perfectly possible that one, or some, *particular* individuals might prefer being garbage collectors than hotel porters even if the wage were the same or lower. This means no problem for the compensating wage differential approach given that it is the *equilibrium* wage in the occupation and the compensating wage differentials among occupations that are determined by the general or market demand and supply for each occupation.
12. It exists generally an inverse relationship between the specialization in some sort of human capital and the number of possible occupations open to the individuals. While the jack-of-all-trades type of workers can do a wide variety of manual tasks, the number of occupations open to a nuclear engineer or an astrophysicist is much more limited.
13. Strictly speaking, the activity A is an economic good for the worker if $\partial U / \partial A > 0$, and

an economic bad if $\delta U/\delta A <0$, but as $Ut_L = (\partial U/\partial A)(\partial A/\partial t_L)$ and $\delta A/\delta t_L>0$, this condition is the same as in the text.

14. It is clear that they are job attributes that cannot be thought of as merchandises sold by the employers because they are provided by the group of workers. For instance, a good social ambient is a desirable job attribute that workers do not have to pay for.

15. For expositive convenience, in the model presented in these pages working time will be considered as an independent argument of the utility function and not as one of the many attributes of our variable amenities. This last alternative is preferred in the index of job quality developed in Chapter 6.

16. The common observation that the most unpleasant and dangerous jobs are *always* occupied by the lowest-paid workers does not necessarily invalidate the compensating wage differential theory. These sorts of jobs are occupied by the low-income workers, but this is *also* a prediction of the compensating wage theory because people with high earning incomes (because they have more human capital or experience, for example) will demand jobs with higher levels of amenities since these amenities are 'normal goods' in economic language, that is, goods for which its demand grows with income.

17. See Rosen (1986) for a complete review of the evidence.

18. In 1955, Robert L. Thorndike and Elizabeth Hagan collected information on earnings, schooling, and occupation for a sample of 9700 men drawn from a population of 75 000 white males accepted as candidates for Aviation Cadet status in the Army Air Force in the last half of 1943. Candidates were given 17 specific tests that measured five basic types of ability: general intelligence, numerical ability, visual perception, psychomotor control, and mechanical ability. In 1969 and in 1971, the National Bureau of Economic Research mailed questionnaires to the members of the Thorndike-Hagan 1955 sample.

19. For a mainstream response to this criticism, see section 1.2.6 of Viscusi and Aldy (2003).

20. Other interesting papers on the issue focusing on Mexico are Bucardo *et al.* (2004) and Gertler *et al.* (2005).

21. An unrelated, but still interesting question in the contradiction between female sex workers demanding higher payment to compensate the higher risk of HIV from unprotected sex and supposedly rational clients willing to pay more for exactly the same thing (a higher health risk).

22. From an economic analysis point of view see Veblen (1899), Hirsch (1977), Frank (1985), Lane (2000) and Veenhoven (1991), among others. Examples from other perspectives as different as biology, psychology or sociology are Buunk and Gibbons (1997), de Botton (2004), Marmot (2004) and Wilkinson and Pickett (2010).

23. That will be so if Smith's welfare function is, for example, $W = X + R + S$, where X is Smith's monthly wage, R is Smith's satisfaction from the relative position measured in money, so thus $R = 200$, if Smith's wage exceeds Jones's, $R = 0€$ if their wages are the same and $R= -200€$ if Smith's wage is less than Jones'; and $S = 51€$ if Smith has a 'good' job and $S = 0$ if his job is 'bad'. Jones' welfare function is symmetrically defined. In consequence, when both of them choose the 'good'-job option, both have a welfare measured in monetary terms as $W = 500 + 0 + 51 = 551€$; when both choose the 'bad'-job option, they get a welfare whose monetary value is $W = 550 + 0 = 550€$; and when their choices differ, the one who chooses the 'good'-job option gets $W = 500 - 200 + 51 = 351€$, and the one who chooses the 'bad'-job option gets $W = 550 + 200 = 750€$. Obviously, a worker would choose to work in the 'bad' job if he hopes to increase his earnings both in absolute and relative terms, but this is only possible if the other one chooses to work in the 'good' job, because when both of them choose the 'bad' option the relative advantage disappears, and this is the sure result because the forward movement in the income scale to a worker if he chooses the 'bad' job means a backward movement in relative terms for the other, and rather than falling behind, the other worker will feel pressed to choose the same 'bad' option, and in the end, both of them remain equal in positional terms but working in 'bad' conditions.

24. It seems dubious that workers would risk their lives to improve their relative standing. But, as Frank notes:

    Clearly most people desire to avoid illness and injury. Yet they also want their children to keep up with (or exceed) community standards with respect to education and other important advantages. People are also strongly motivated to emulate the consumption habits of their neighbours. Taking a riskier job will often mean being able to come up with a down payment for a house in a better school district, or not having to drive the oldest car on the block (Frank 2004, p. 687).

    As Frank points out, the workers who clean up radiation spills in the nuclear industry provide a striking example of the willingness to trade risk for extra pay.
25. This argument is developed, among others, in Solow (1992).
26. It could be argued that the Protestant Work Ethic also implies an instrumental concept of work, only that the ultimate objective is eternal rather than mundane retribution. But it is not so much the Protestant Ethic in itself that matters, but its worldly derivation, the Spirit of Capitalism.

3. Measurement problems and data sources

3.1. PRELIMINARY REMARKS: PROBLEMS AND OPTIONS

After reviewing the different theoretical approaches to job quality in the previous chapter, this one focuses on the methodological problems and options to be taken into consideration in the process of constructing an indicator (or system of indicators) of job quality. In the first section, we review several conceptual and technical problems that have to be confronted in the process of designing an indicator of job quality, and the different alternative solutions. Section 3.2 discusses how job quality interacts with other institutions like the Welfare State or family structure, collectively affecting workers' well-being. The existence of such interrelations implies that the same job attribute can have very different implications across countries in terms of workers well-being, depending on the types of social provisions or family backing existing in each country. Finally, section 3.3 presents a summary of the main sources of information currently available for the measurement of the main dimensions of job quality identified in Chapter 2.

3.1.1. Results versus Procedures

Although most measures of job quality focus on outcomes (the actual levels of employment security, autonomy and so on), it is possible also to develop measures based on evaluating the existence of procedures and mechanisms that facilitate or ensure that the conditions of work are adequate. For instance, a procedural indicator of job quality could be whether there are channels of participation open for workers to determine their own working conditions, or whether there are safety standards in place, or whether there is adequate information on health and safety issues.

For the purposes of measuring job quality, it is preferable to measure results rather than procedures, but the latter approach is often a second best solution justified by the lack of reliable information about the output. In some cases, it can be argued that procedures themselves can be an important (and positive) attribute of a job. For example, the existence of channels of participation in the process of decision-making at the firm level can be interpreted in terms of better job quality irrespective of its impact on other specific dimensions of job quality, as it gives workers a voice and more capacity to control their work situation. In our view, if participation is to form part of a job quality index, it should be justified from a results rather than a procedure perspective: that is, as a desirable job attribute in itself.

3.1.2. Static or Dynamic

During the last two decades, labour market transitions have received increasing attention from labour economists. The relevance of dynamics as a key ingredient of job quality is based on the fact that the implications and consequences of a certain employment status – for instance, temporary work – might vary if such a state persists over time – for example, becoming a sort of trap of non-stable employment. However, as our interest is focused on quality of work, the focus should be on the jobs, not on the people hired to perform them. If a worker moves from a low-quality to a high-quality job, but both jobs were already in the economy, nothing changes from the point of view of the quality of the existing jobs. Based on this reasoning, an index of job quality does not require considering any dynamic dimension as such.

There are two precautions to be taken regarding this issue. First, it can be argued that the implications of working in a 'bad' job are different if individuals work in those jobs for life, or if those types of jobs are just a temporary stage in their career. In that case, it might be interesting to include the degree of transition as a separate indicator, complementing the information on job quality in a given country. Second, from a subjective perspective, having a job with good prospects of advancement, even if the present quality of the job is not so good, can be considered an important asset of the job. Nevertheless, the researcher can capture this dimension through some question about the opportunities of advancement in the current job position.

3.1.3. Constructed at Individual or Aggregate Level?

Job quality refers to the impact of the attributes of existing jobs on the well-being of workers. Therefore, in one way or another, all measures of job quality will necessarily be based on information collected at the level of individual workers.[1]

However, job quality is a multidimensional concept, and therefore, any holistic account of job quality requires making some form of aggregation of the information on the different job attributes collected at the individual level.[2] Depending on what will be the use of the job quality index (or system of indicators, see section 3.1.5), it is possible to do the aggregation of the measures of the different dimensions at a higher level than the individual. In fact, if our only aim is to compare overall job quality across countries, regions or sectors, there is no difference between doing the aggregation at the higher level (based on averages or other summary functions) and doing it at the individual level and then comparing the country averages. Constructing the indicator at the aggregate level has the added (and important) advantage of allowing more flexibility for drawing information from different sources (different surveys or registers, for instance). In a job quality indicator constructed at the individual level, this is a practical impossibility: such an indicator requires having measures of the different attributes for the same individual, which is only possible in practice by drawing from a single source.[3]

For these reasons (namely, that it is sufficient for comparative purposes and more flexible in terms of data sources), most of the indicators on job quality reviewed here are constructed at the country rather than individual level (see Chapter 4). As mentioned, this is perfectly legitimate if the main (or only) aim is comparative. But whenever our aims are a bit wider, this approach has very important disadvantages, which have to be acknowledged.

First, indicators constructed at the aggregate level do not allow the study of the distribution of the particular measure *within* the populations of interest. Characterizing the whole distribution of any variable with a single number necessarily implies losing an enormous amount of information, and can hide important differences in the distribution of the variable across different subpopulations (the same overall result can be the outcome of completely different distributions). This is particularly damaging for issues such as job quality, which is very likely to vary more *within* than *between* countries (for most of the EU, this is certainly the case, though maybe not for all countries: for some examples, see Parent-Thirion *et al.* 2007). It is also particularly damaging because often the policy focus is not so much on the overall level of job quality but on whether there may be some disadvantaged or discriminated groups which systematically get the worst jobs.

There is a way to partially account for the distribution even within an indicator constructed at the aggregate level: by including (aggregate) distributional measures within the indicator. For instance, the pay dimension can be calculated by aggregating two sub-indicators: one measuring the average pay level and the other the level of inequality (measured, for instance, with the Gini index). This way, the outcome of this dimension will be sensitive not only to the average pay levels, but also to their distribution (for instance, a country with a very high average wage but a large proportion of people in poverty will receive a lower score than another country with a similar median wage but a more equal distribution). Since most of the dimensions of job quality vary considerably within countries, it is certainly advisable that any job quality indicator constructed at the country level includes such distributional measures. However, this only reduces this problem and it does not eliminate it. As recently argued by Tony Atkinson (2006), it is still much better to construct the indicators at the individual level whenever it is possible. Even if measures sensitive to the distribution are added to the indicator, it will be fundamentally inflexible for doing distributional analysis. The distributional characteristics of the job attributes of interest will have to be known in advance in order to design the distributional measures to be included in the indicator, and once the indicator is constructed, this distributional element will be completely fixed – there will be no way to explore further the distribution of job quality for other groups or in other ways. This inflexibility can be quite important for an EU job quality indicator, because the distributional aspects of job quality do vary across countries (in some countries, gender might be the key determinant of wage inequality, whereas in others it might be ethnicity) and over time (for instance, a surge of immigration such as the one experienced by Spain in recent years has completely changed the distribution of good and bad jobs across the population). In sum, if a job quality indicator is constructed at the aggregate level, it is better to make it sensitive to the distribution of the variables covered, but it will still not be really adequate for distributional analysis. Only an indicator constructed at the individual level is fit for such purpose.

Another common strategy to make the measure sensitive to the distribution of job quality for specific subgroups of the population (such as gender), followed in several indicators reviewed in Chapter 4, is to include a separate indicator reflecting the gender gap in a given variable (usually wages). In our opinion a better way to address this issue is to build separate indicators of job quality (considering all variables) by gender, and then calculate the overall gender gap. This option allows considering *all* dimensions of job quality from the gender (or ethnicity, age, etc.) perspective, offering a full picture of the gender distribution of job quality. As shown by Smith *et al.* (2008, p. 586), very often gender (along with occupation status, sector and other job characteristics) 'have more influence on an individual's job quality than the country [. . .] in which they are situated'. Furthermore, such a method is more correct from a methodological point of view since it does not require the introduction in the index of variables which are not directly related to job quality (i.e., belonging to a particular subgroup).

A second general disadvantage of constructing the indicator at the aggregate level is that it does not permit the study of interactions (intersections and compensations) between the different dimensions forming the index or system of indicators. Again, as job quality *happens* at the individual level, it is only at the individual level that these interactions can be studied, so by constructing the indicator at the aggregate level we are necessarily losing very important information. An example can clarify this. Let us suppose an indicator of job quality with two dimensions, long hours (more than 48 a week) and low pay (earnings below 60 per cent of the median). Suppose that, in a specific country, there is 40 per cent of the working population that work long hours and 40 per cent that receive low wages. If the aggregation of information is done at the level of the whole population (probably, because we do not have data at the individual level for both dimensions), there is no way of knowing whether the 40 per cent of people working long hours *is the same* as the 40 per cent receiving low wages, which is obviously of great importance. If the two attributes tend to affect the same people (if the two variables *intersect*), the job quality of the people affected will certainly be much worse than if the two bad attributes affect different people (if there is no intersection), but an indicator constructed at the national level is blind to this. Only an indicator constructed at the individual level can take into account not only the aggregate incidence of each individual attribute, but the intersection between them.

Another example of the importance of the interaction between the different dimensions at the individual level is the existence of compensation mechanisms as implied, for instance, by the theory of compensating differentials discussed in the previous chapter. According to this theory, bad working conditions are compensated by higher wages, other things being equal. An indicator constructed at the aggregate level can measure the overall level of wages and the overall incidence of bad working conditions, and it can somehow aggregate the information of the two domains: but it cannot reflect whether there is a trade-off between the two dimensions (because again, such compensation takes place at the individual level, and can therefore only be measured at that level).

Summing up, we can say that an indicator or system of indicators constructed at the aggregate (country) level can be sufficient if the only aim is to compare the overall levels of job quality between different countries (or alternatively, the evolution of overall job quality within each country). This approach has the important advantage of allowing the use of different sources of information for the individual dimensions and indicators. Nevertheless, to construct the indicator at the aggregate level narrows considerably its potential for the analysis of job quality from a wider perspective. It does not allow studying the distribution of job quality, the concentration of 'good' or 'bad' jobs on specific groups of workers, the intersection between the different dimensions of job quality or the existence of compensation mechanisms between them. Only an indicator constructed at the individual level can fulfil those broader objectives.

3.1.4. One Size Fits All?

At a very high level of generality, it can be more or less agreed that job quality refers to the characteristics of work and employment that affect the well-being of the worker. But when we try to operationalize this very broad definition in order to be able to apply it to different countries, enormous difficulties arise, because there are structural and cultural differences that make those 'characteristics that affect the well-being of the worker' likely to differ across countries. In terms of structural differences, probably the main issue is the big diversity that exists in the design of social systems across countries. Employment is embedded within an institutional and economic context: the characteristics of employment interact with the features of social systems in ways that can make similar employment characteristics have very different implications for the well-being of the worker in different countries. A couple of examples can illustrate this. Employment security appears systematically in most indicators of job quality, but social systems which are very generous with the unemployed in terms of income replacement and duration of benefits will certainly make employment security *per se* a much less important element of the quality of employment for the individuals concerned (the advantages for the worker of the Danish flexicurity model, mentioned above, do not lie in an increased level of employment security, which is in fact considerably lower due to the lower firing costs faced by Danish firms compared to other EU countries, but in the fact that it makes employment insecurity much less negative for the worker). The different levels of social protection and social services available to the worker can also distort the impact of pay on the well-being of the worker: if labour income has to cover health and pension costs, its impact will be much larger than if most of these social risks are *decommodified* and provided as part of the social security system (or rather, the covering of those risks by the employer may be an important element of pay in some countries, as happens with health insurance and pensions for some workers in the US).

Cultural differences across countries are equally problematic, because they imply systematic differences in how people evaluate their own situation, and therefore in how their working environment will affect their (subjective) well-being. For instance, a culture that emphasizes conformity can make the impact of low autonomy at work much less detrimental for the well-being of the worker than a cultural context that emphasizes autonomy and personal achievement. These cultural variations lead also to considerable technical difficulties for measuring the different dimensions of job quality across countries in a truly comparable way (it makes it difficult to be sure that we are comparing the same thing rather than different understandings of the same concept).

In fact, what we have to confront is the familiar problems of comparative research. 'In cross-national survey work, the differences in culture and social structure mean that for many types of questions the frame of reference of the respondent will be unknown and may vary systematically from society to society' (Verba 2007, p. 248). Any international comparison of issues such as job quality must try to take into account that not only the issues being measured vary across countries, but also the contexts that interact with them: the measures and the analysis have to be embedded in the structural and cultural contexts, as is the reality itself that we try to measure.

In terms of the construction of measures and indicators, international social research has dealt with this contextualization problem mainly through the principle of functional equivalence, which implies allowing to some degree a different (but equivalent) operationalization of the concepts being studied in the different contexts. These different operationalizations can be based on the criteria of experts or on the criteria of the people concerned themselves (in this case, the workers). For comparisons of large groups of countries such as the EU, and for concepts as normatively charged as job quality, the latter option seems particularly appealing. At a minimum, there must be a common definition of the overall issue being studied, even if at a very high level of generality: in our case, the earlier definition of job quality as the characteristics of work and employment affecting the well-being of the worker can be a sufficient starting point. This definition can be the basis of a simple question to workers about how their jobs affect their well-being: this is more or less the approach implicit in the international comparison of broad indicators of job satisfaction – the assumption being that the worker himself/herself is best positioned to evaluate how his/her job affects his/her well-being. The main problem of such an approach is that workers tend to adapt their expectations to their actual conditions if they cannot change the conditions, so that it is difficult to know whether job satisfaction measures job quality or simply the adaptability of workers (as discussed in the previous chapter). Less radical alternatives would, for instance, allow workers to define the main elements of job quality and then ask them how they rate themselves according to those elements, or to ask them about the elements considered most important on average within each country.[4] Even more homogeneity can be achieved by providing the workers with a predefined list of dimensions of job quality and ask them to rate them, using their ratings to nationally weigh the different sub-indicators within an overall composite index of job quality. At the minimum, internationally defined lists of elements can be weighted according to the correlations between them in the different countries (for instance, by using factor analysis).

The logic behind these different methods is the same: because the realities being studied are embedded in structural and cultural contexts, the ways of operationalizing them into indicators have to vary across countries, ensuring functional equivalence through context-sensitive variability of measurement. These methods try to make meaningful comparisons of similar concepts across different countries. The idea of functional equivalence is not alien to EU employment policies. For instance, in the context of the discussion on flexicurity, the European Commission (2007) has itself argued that there may be different paths to achieve a similar policy result:

> The implementation of the common principles of flexicurity in the Member States requires the establishment of carefully planned and negotiated combinations and sequences of policies and measures. *Since Member States vary considerably in their socio-economic, cultural and institutional background, the specific combinations and sequences will also vary.* [emphasis added]

One could think of a similar approach to employment quality. Whereas it is a policy goal to monitor and develop the quality of employment, it could be argued that because of the different structural and cultural contexts of employment, what is a good job should be nationally defined rather than settled at an EU level. Then, it could be discussed whether those national definitions should be based on experts' opinions, political agreements or the workers' own views (as discussed earlier). However, what would be the policy implications of such a national-specific definition and operationalization of job quality? One can easily see the intrinsic interest of such a monitoring tool (for understanding the development of working life in each country in terms of the well-being of the workers), but it is important to acknowledge that such an approach is likely to be very problematic for policy making and policy monitoring purposes.

The more sensitive to the national specificities the construction of the indicator is, the more compromised the comparability of its results becomes. In the extreme case of totally different definitions and measurements, we would be in fact comparing totally different issues, even if they are based on a common underlying concept. Such an indicator would certainly be useful for policy making within each individual country, and probably also very informative for broad comparisons of overall levels of job quality (and its evolution) across Europe, but what possible use would it have for policy making or policy monitoring at an international level? How would the differences be evaluated, resulting as they would from totally different definitions (and measures) of what constitutes a good and a bad job?

Any international comparison has to deal with the problem of how to compare different realities in ways which are sensitive to national specificities (so that the national results capture the national realities) yet reasonably harmonized (so that the actual comparison can be made and the reasons behind the differences can be understood). The correct balance between the degree of harmonization and the degree of national sensitivity depends, as always, on the objectives behind the comparison. If the comparison has a policy purpose behind it (for instance, for EU policy making), harmonization can be more important than national sensitivity, to give more political force to the comparison (and to make the drawing of policy conclusions a bit easier). If the comparison has a scientific purpose, there can be much more flexibility with respect to the strict comparability of methods and indicators, as long as they remain functional equivalents and are founded on a clear internationally agreed concept and model of job quality. In our own proposal of a job quality index for the EU (see Chapters 5 and 6), we will opt for a fully harmonized approach, based on a specific EU-level survey (the European Working Conditions Survey (EWCS)), because our intention is to propose an index that could be used for policy purposes.

3.1.5. Composite Index or a System of Indicators?

The policy purpose of comparing job quality across countries can be fulfilled by a system of indicators (that is, a coherent and interrelated set of measures of the different attributes of jobs that have an impact on the well-being of workers) or by a composite index (a single aggregate measure synthesizing the information of all the different attributes of job quality). Both ways of measuring and comparing job quality are perfectly valid, and – as it will be shown later – in practice the differences between them are not as large as it may seem, but they have different implications for the interpretation of results which have to be taken into account.

In both cases, the goal is the same: to simplify a complex and multidimensional reality in order to understand it better. In both cases, we have to depart from a clear idea of the subject or phenomenon of our interest (in this case job quality) and why do we want to measure it (in this case, in order to compare the quality of the jobs available in the different countries and to monitor their evolution). Also in both cases, it is necessary to develop a theoretical model that sets out clearly what is the structure of the phenomenon we are trying to measure, specifying its dimensions and sub-dimensions (if it is multidimensional), and how do they relate to each other. Then, a set of observable variables that measure adequately each of the dimensions or sub-dimensions must be identified, checked against the structure of the model, and if necessary aggregated into higher-level dimensions.[5] All the steps up to this point are the same no matter whether we construct a composite index or a system of indicators. It is only in this final step that there is a difference: a system of indicators would stop there, once we have scores for the dimensions of the model, whereas a composite index would go one step further and aggregate the dimensions to a single number. Obviously, the dimensions will be still there: in most cases, both the overall index and its components are presented when the analysis of job quality is done with composite indices, so that in practice the composite index *includes* (it is based upon) a system of indicators.

Nevertheless, even though a composite index can be understood as nothing more than a system of indicators aggregated in a single number, this final aggregation has very important implications for the overall interpretation of the results, especially in political terms. Precisely because the composite index aggregates all of the information within a single measure, it implies a single, univocal and unidirectional understanding of what job quality is (no matter how many components it is based upon), which will unambiguously position the different countries (or whatever social group we are interested in studying) within a unidimensional axis going from bad to good (a ranking). In contrast, a system of indicators only implies defining a set of dimensions of job quality and providing measures for them: of course, this also implies normative choices, and within each dimension there will be better and worse performers; but the more dimensions there are, the more ambiguous (and therefore, the less politically sensitive) the overall evaluation of each country will be.

Therefore, a system of indicators will not – in principle – impose a univocal interpretation of the results. The system of indicators is, in this sense, closer to the reality of job quality itself, which is widely acknowledged to be multidimensional. The comparisons based on systems of indicators will necessarily be richer than those based on composite indices. On the other hand, a system of indicators will lead to ambiguous results, from which it can be difficult to draw useful political conclusions. For instance, if the aim is to compare countries, unless country A is better in all dimensions than country B, it will not be possible to say that country A provides better jobs to its citizens – even if in all dimensions but one it is better than B. The same can happen when studying the evolution of job quality within a single country: if a country has improved in some dimensions but becomes worse in others, what conclusion should we draw?

The advantages and disadvantages of the composite index mirror those of the system of indicators. A composite index implies a harsh simplification of a reality which is by nature complex and multidimensional. If not well constructed, it can easily lead to mercilessly wrong conclusions, which could have a very bad impact on the credibility and the usefulness of the whole effort of index building. Even though, as we have said, composite indices tend to be reported together with the detailed systems of indicators on which they are based, the numeric results, rankings, etc., deriving from the index are so attractive that they tend to draw all of the attention. On the other hand, for the reasons already mentioned, composite indices can be very useful for policy evaluation and design, and they can certainly have a bigger impact (and more political force) than a system of indicators because of its apparent lack of ambiguity.

What has to be emphasized, in any case, is that if a composite index is to be used for policy purposes, it has to be constructed not only with the highest scientific standards, but with a clear and univocal definition of what is desirable and what is not with respect to the conditions of work and employment.

Technically, the aggregation of different pieces of information within composite indices involves a two-step process: first, the different elements (variables, indicators or dimensions) have to be standardized,[6] so that their scales become equivalent and they can be summed together; second, each of the standardized elements must receive a weight (a multiplication factor proportional to the importance that we want to assign to each element).[7] Once the components of the index have been standardized and weighted, they can be summed together.[8]

The determination of the weights to apply to each of the elements that form a composite index is one of the trickiest parts of the whole process, but there is no escape from it: any aggregation of different pieces of information will require a choice of how much influence we want to assign to each of the individual elements in the overall measure. Not applying any weight is the same as applying an equal weight to all of the elements, which is as much of a choice (and as debatable) as applying unequal weights, proportional to the importance we believe each of the individual elements have for the phenomenon of interest.

There are two main ways to decide which weights to assign to the different elements of a composite index: a data-driven way and a theory/policy-driven way. The former approach implies analysing the structure of correlations between the different variables measuring the dimensions and letting the statistical procedure assign the weights in proportion with how they correlate with each other. This method implies assuming that all the variables included in the analysis are measures of the same latent (unobservable) phenomenon: the structure of correlations between them can be used to infer the latent variable from the observed variables. The main problem with this method is that it is a black-box, the logic linking the elements and the composite index being mathematical (and often difficult to grasp) rather than human or theory-based. The resulting composite index can be the best possible summary of the individual elements included in the analysis, but not necessarily a good and meaningful measure of job quality. For this reason, especially for indices constructed for policy purposes, it is much better to base the weights of the index on a sound theoretical/policy model of the concept to be measured, providing a transparent justification for the choices made in this matter.

The issue of weighting seems solely problematic in composite indices, as the main result in this case is a weighted aggregation of different pieces of information (the dimensions of job quality). But it is an error to think that by using systems of indicators we avoid the problem of weighting. On the one hand, the different indicators that compose the system are often themselves the result of a process of aggregation of individual variables very similar to the process of producing a composite index. On the other hand, a system of indicators is a set of different pieces of information put together: if we have a system of indicators with five dimensions all given the same importance in the presentation of results, is that not very similar to producing a composite index with equal weights for each of the five dimensions? And after all, it is impossible to avoid that the users of the system of indicators will produce *in their own mind* an overall impression of the level of job quality in the different countries after looking at the different dimensions of the system of indicators (aggregating themselves the sub-dimensions mentally and drawing their own conclusions).

3.1.6. Periodicity

Job quality indices constructed for policy purposes not only aim at comparing countries, but also at monitoring the evolution of job quality (within and between countries) over time. This implies updating periodically the indicators. But how often should they be updated?

There are three main considerations to be taken into account in the determination of the periodicity of job quality indicators: first, to adapt this periodicity to the needs of the users; second, to adapt the periodicity of the indicators to the pace of change of job quality itself; and third, the more prosaic concern with the availability of periodically updated data.

Regarding the first point, when the indicators have been constructed with policy purposes, it seems logical to try to fix a periodicity that fits those purposes. In particular, the information provided by the indicators can be intended to feed specific political processes, such as collective bargaining periods or revisions of employment policies. A yearly periodicity is often fixed because it is frequent enough as to be able to fit most policy cycles, and to feed the increasing impatience of public opinion with respect to statistical information.

But in fact, the periodicity that fits the policy purposes of the indicators might not be best suited to the pace of change of the phenomenon being studied. Empirical evidence suggests that most of the elements of job quality change relatively slowly, in the medium and long term rather than in the short term. For instance, after four waves and 15 years of the EWCS, the European Foundation could find only relatively marginal changes in most areas of job quality (Eurofound 2006). The pace of change of job quality, in particular, contrasts strongly with the pace of change of job *quantity*: the latter can change dramatically in a very short period (as this is being written, we are witnessing such a process with the effects of the economic crisis on employment levels across Europe), whereas the former will rarely experience a sudden change in any direction, except maybe in cases of radical policy shifts.

To complicate things even further, the different elements of job quality can also have different rates of change. We can group the dimensions of job quality under two headings: employment (which refers to the conditions of the employment relation) and work (which refers to the conditions within which the activity of work itself takes place). In general, the conditions of employment tend to change more quickly than the conditions of work, because they are more sensitive to the situation of the labour market (especially, to the general level of unemployment) and can be abruptly affected by changes in labour regulation. The conditions of work, on the other hand, mainly depend on the technological and organizational characteristics of the production processes, which change relatively slowly and incrementally, so that only in the long term can their effects be felt clearly and unambiguously. Therefore, it may be reasonable to update the indicator of job quality in a modular way, yearly for the areas of employment which change more quickly (although even in this case a yearly cycle might be too frequent) and every four or five years for the conditions of work that tend to change at a slower pace.

In fact, this leads us to the final consideration to be taken into account when deciding a periodicity for the updating of job quality indicators: the availability of data. As we will see in detail in section 3.3, the two main existing sources on job quality in Europe are the European Labour Force Survey (ELFS) and the EWCS. The ELFS is updated every three months (as it is the main source for estimating employment numbers, which have a fast pace of change as already mentioned) and covers most of the job quality dimensions of employment. The EWCS is updated every five years and covers all the dimensions of work quality (in fact, it covers employment quality as well). Considering our earlier discussions about the different pace of change of the components of employment and work of job quality, the periodicities of these two main sources do not seem unfortunate, as they would permit an update of the elements of employment yearly (or even quarterly, although that would probably be unnecessarily frequent) and the elements of work every five years. The only problem of such an approach is that it would not permit a link at the individual level between both elements of job quality (the dimensions of employment and work would come from different sources). A single source with two modules (one updated yearly and the other every five years) would be the best solution.

3.2. THE IMPORTANCE OF THE CONTEXT: INSTITUTIONS AND JOB QUALITY

Jobs do not exist in a vacuum, but in a social context conformed by public and private institutions like the Welfare State and the family. Therefore, the impact of a given job characteristic on workers' well-being will depend on the interplay of such characteristics with the existing welfare arrangements and the supporting role played by the family. For example, a given working schedule might conflict or not with the employee's work–life balance depending on the existence of a sufficient and affordable supply of nursery places and kindergartens to which the worker can trust the caring of the dependent members of the family while at work. If there is a wide programme of public kindergartens, or a helping retired grandma or grandpa willing to watch over the younger ones while their parents are working, the lack of family-friendly provisions at work might not interfere with the work–life balance of workers. This is especially important from a gender perspective, as it is normally women who face more pressure to balance work and family commitments. Something similar can be said about wages. A low wage might have different implications if there is public housing or a system of income tax credit complementing directly or indirectly take-home pay.

As the existence of such interconnections between job characteristics, social policy and family supporting roles (to which we could add the employment level itself)[9] have clear and important implications in terms of workers' well-being, it is convenient to debate whether the indicator of job quality should account for the complementary role played by such aspects or not.

From one point of view, it could be argued that if the important thing is the impact of a given job attribute on the workers' well-being, the existence of a specific public provision compensating for a negative job attribute (for example, an earned income tax credit complementing wage of low-paid workers) should be directly part of the indicator. Otherwise we could – wrongly – conclude that a segment of workers are facing an insufficient income while that is not the case thanks to the existence of an income supplement provided by the public sector through the system of tax credits.

A particularly relevant case related to this problem is the existence of employer-provided social benefits as a dimension of employment quality. In the United States, an important proportion of jobs have employer-provided health insurance, while in Europe only a minority of employees enjoy such type of complementary social benefits. Should we conclude then the quality of European jobs is worse in this respect? Obviously that is not the case, as in most, if not all European countries, workers have access to a public universal health system. The principle of homogeneity or comparability would then support the introduction in the indicator of those areas of public intervention (as health or pensions, for example) with a direct impact on worker well-being; otherwise, the results in terms of job quality could be biased against those countries with bigger Welfare States.

From a different perspective it can be argued, though, that to include in the system of job quality indicators a dimension of state-provided social benefits to workers would undermine one of the most important criteria defended so far in the construction of an indicator of job quality: to limit the job quality dimensions considered to those characteristics directly related to the job. If the unit of reference is the job, then whatever happens outside the job realm should not be taken into consideration in the measurement of job quality. But it is important to acknowledge that, if the institutional context affects the impact of the different job characteristics on the well-being of workers, they will have to be taken into account before drawing any implications from the crude comparisons of the scores of the indicator. The interrelations between job quality and social institutions must always be explicitly considered when doing international comparisons of job quality, especially when (as in the previous example of social benefits in the US and EU) there are important differences in the social systems of the countries involved in the comparison.[10]

To appreciate the complexity of the issue we are dealing with, we have to acknowledge the fact that many public interventions affecting job quality, in fact all regulations of working conditions (from redundancy payments to paid vacation and health and safety standards), with compulsory compliance by the firms, are direct determinants of key dimensions of job quality. Thus, we are isolating private job characteristics (whether product of unilateral decision taken by the firm, negotiated with workers, or imposed by the public administration) from other public (or private) interventions outside the realm of the work-employment relation.

A possible solution to this problem is to construct a kind of *satellite account*[11] to include those elements of social policy with a direct impact on workers' well-being, interacting with job characteristics. Such an approach would obey the criteria of concentrating on the job realm when measuring job quality, but at the same time would force the user of the indicator to consider the way in which public intervention through social policy softens the negative impact of disamenities (and complements the amenities) of job quality on workers' well-being. This type of account should include those elements of social policy affecting job quality, for example:

- *Unemployment provisions and active labour market policy.* The existence of unemployment provisions and active labour policies, like training, might mitigate the negative impact of job insecurity. In fact, the acclaimed flexicurity model is an example of how such public-policy compensation for privately generated work disamenities can work in practice.
- *Public health insurance and public pensions.* The existence of public pensions and public health system will make at least partially redundant the existence of employer-provided health insurance and pensions. For example, according to Eurostat in 2006, public health expenditure was 8.7 per cent of GDP in France and the Netherlands, compared to 3.8 per cent in Poland or Estonia.
- *Public provisions to facilitate work–life balance.* Such public provisions would include child care, early education services and long-term care services. For example, in 2005 in Denmark over 60 per cent of children up to two years of age are in childcare and early education services, in Spain, 20 per cent, and in Germany, Italy, Greece, Hungary, Poland or the Czech Republic less than 10 per cent (Eurofound 2009).
- *Tax credits or direct income transfers specifically those favouring low-wage workers.*

The idea of satellite accounts to complement a comparative job quality index seems like the best alternative to deal with the problem of embeddedness of job quality within the different institutional and social environments. Nevertheless, it requires an enormous extra effort, as in practice it means constructing ancillary indices drawing on different sources. For these reasons, and to focus our efforts on job quality as such, in our own proposal of a job quality index for the EU (Chapters 5 and 6) we will not attempt the construction of such satellite accounts, which is left for further research.

3.3. EXISTING SOURCES FOR THE STUDY OF JOB QUALITY IN EUROPE

In this section, we briefly present the main characteristics of the existing pan-European data sources which include information relevant for the study of job quality (see Table 3.1), and which therefore could be used for developing job quality indicators at the EU level. The data sources covered here are all European in scope, periodically updated and statistically representative of the European working population. There are five European sources fitting these restrictive parameters: the ELFS, the EWCS, the European Survey on Income and Living Conditions (EU-SILC), the European Structure of Earnings Survey (ESES) and the International Social Survey Program (ISSP).

The ELFS is an excellent source for the study of employment quality: it has a large sample, it is updated four times a year and permits long consistent time series. But its coverage of quality of work issues (especially, intrinsic value of work, health and safety) is either lacking or extremely limited, so it cannot provide the basis of a holistic account of job quality at the EU level.

The EWCS is, by far, the survey that covers the widest range of areas of work and employment quality. In Chapters 5 and 6 of this book, we will present our own proposal of a job quality index for the European Union which is fully based in the 2005 edition of this survey. Therefore, in section 3.3.1 we will discuss its characteristics in more detail.

The EU-SILC is the EU reference source for comparative statistics on income, poverty and social exclusion. Job quality is secondary to the objectives of the survey, and, hence, the number of areas of interest covered by it is rather limited. In contrast, it has the advantage of being longitudinal and including a good measure of income.

The ESES is even more limited and does not cover the whole working population, but has the best comparable measure of wages available, so that it can be useful to compile information on labour earnings for very specific groups of workers. It also includes detailed information on the hours worked and some basic information on employment and contractual status (including sector, occupation and type of contract).

Table 3.1 Main characteristics of the existing sources for the study of job quality in Europe

		European Labour Force Survey	European Working Conditions Survey	European Union Statistics on Income and Living Conditions	European Structure of Earnings Survey	International Social Survey Program
Logistics	Funding organization	National governments and Eurostat.	Eurofound.	National governments and Eurostat.	National governments and Eurostat.	Each country, no central funds.
	Design organization	Eurostat and National Statistics Offices.	Eurofound (with a team of international experts).	Eurostat and National Statistics Offices.	Eurostat and National Statistics Offices.	Strong coordination in sampling and questionnaire design.
	International coordination	Eurostat.	Eurofound and main contractor.	Eurostat.	Eurostat.	ISSP general assembly.
	Data collection	National Statistics Offices.	National contractor.	National Statistics Offices.	National Statistics Offices.	National partner.
Methodology	Sample design	Rotating random sample.	Random sample.	Rotating random sample.	Random sample.	Random sample.
	Reference population	All persons in private households.	All employed people in private households.	All persons in private households.	All employees working at firms (excepting most of public sector and the primary sector).	All persons in private households.
	Degree of harmonization	Low (mainly general recommendations).	High (the same questionnaire).	Low (mainly general recommendations).	Low (mainly general recommendations).	Very low (broad variability in timing).

Table 3.1 (continued)

	European Labour Force Survey	European Working Conditions Survey	European Union Statistics on Income and Living Conditions	European Structure of Earnings Survey	International Social Survey Program
Sample size per country	Variable, but in many cases very large.	Roughly 1000 cases per country (600 in some of them)	Variable, but in many cases quite large.	Variable, but in many cases very large.	Minimum at 1000 cases. Normally, 1500–2000.
Periodicity	Quarterly.	Every four or five years.	Yearly.	Every four years.	Yearly, but different modules.
Degree of harmonization	Low	High	Low	High	Medium
Questionnaire Stability of questions	High in the concepts, lower in implementation.	Medium	High	Medium (changes in the sampled population)	Modules are repeated every four years.
Areas covered	In general, employment conditions.	All areas of working and employment conditions.	Earnings, working time, type of contract.	Earnings, working time, type of contract.	Autonomy, skills, meaning, social environment, psychosocial risks, working time.

Source: Authors' elaboration.

Finally, the ISSP does not only cover most European countries, but also many countries outside Europe, and although its main goal is not to collect information on work and employment, three yearly waves of this survey (1989, 1997 and 2005) were specifically aimed at the measurement of 'work orientations', and are quite rich in information on intrinsic aspects of job quality. Although the ISSP has a limited sample size, a very sparse periodicity, and its methodology has a relatively low degree of harmonization, its coverage of some of the intrinsic aspects of job quality is good, and the fact that it goes beyond Europe means that it can be used for comparing job quality in Europe with other regions of the world.

3.3.1. The European Working Conditions Survey (EWCS)

The EWCS is without any doubt the most important statistical source on working conditions in Europe. In fact, even with respect to employment issues, the coverage of the EWCS is unsurpassed by any other existing European survey. This is because, among all the surveys discussed here, the EWCS is the only one whose explicit aim is to collect information about the conditions of work and employment of Europeans (whereas the ELFS, for instance, is focused towards measuring employment and unemployment levels, rather than employment conditions as such).

The EWCS is funded, designed and coordinated by the European Foundation for the Improvement of Living and Working Conditions, an EU agency based in Dublin whose mandate is to gather knowledge that can contribute to the planning and design of policies to improve the conditions of life and work of Europeans. The questionnaire is designed by a group of experts and policy makers in the area of work and employment, together with the Foundation research staff. The Foundation also prepares the principles for the sampling and fieldwork methodology, which are then part of the technical conditions of a tender. The successful tenderer, a large EU-wide fieldwork company (Gallup in the 2005 EWCS), then finalizes the design together with the Foundation and carries out the fieldwork under the supervision of the Foundation staff (see Fernández-Macías and Petrakos 2006).

One of the key advantages of the EWCS with respect to other surveys (especially, with respect to Eurostat's ones) is the fact that the whole endeavour is funded, designed and coordinated centrally, by dedicated Foundation staff and the fieldwork contractor. This ensures a level of comparability which is much higher than the ELFS, at least in principle: not only the concepts, definitions and classifications are the same across Europe, but even the questions and specific items are the same. Of course, there is some flexibility for national adaptations – the translation process itself implies an adaptation of the questionnaire to national specificities (Hurley 2006). Another very important advantage of the EWCS with respect to the other surveys included in Table 3.1 is the high degree of transparency and documentation of the whole research process (Fernández-Macías and Petrakos 2006).

The sample of the EWCS is representative of all persons in employment in private households of all EU Member States (and some European non-Member States, such as Switzerland or Turkey, see Parent-Thirion *et al.* 2007). The fieldwork procedures also follow strictly the same principles across Europe: in all countries, the sample is stratified by region and settlement size, and the interviews are clustered by geographic proximity. The actual selection of households is done by the random walk method, and within the selected household one employed individual is randomly selected.

The sample size of the survey was established with the main aim of making adequate estimations at the national and EU levels, keeping the budget within reasonable limits. The European Foundation provides all the funding for the survey from beginning to end (which is also exceptional: in most other surveys, the funding comes partly from the coordinating centre and partly from the national parties). The size of the sample for the latest EWCS was 1000 cases per country (except in six smaller countries, where the sample size was kept at 600 cases). This, in fact, is the main problem of the EWCS. This sample size allows for the production of good estimates of the overall incidence at the national level of the phenomena captured in the survey, but if we want to go deeper and break down the results within countries by gender, sectors of activity, occupational level or whatever other variables, the number of cases used for specific estimations very quickly becomes too small and therefore the estimation is unreliable.

The other problematic characteristic of EWCS for monitoring job quality in the EU with composite indicators is its periodicity. It is only carried out every five years, whereas most indicators of job quality aim at being updated at least every year. Whether the EWCS should be done more often or, on the contrary, the indicators of job quality should be updated less frequently is, in fact, debatable. As can be seen in a Eurofound report on the trends in working conditions from 1991 to 2005 (using the four waves carried out so far; see Eurofound 2006), the pace of change of these issues has been empirically quite low for the last 15 years in Europe (especially in *work* issues, not so much in employment – type of contract, working time, etc.). This suggests that a survey cycle of five years may be enough. Of course, the reasons for preferring a yearly cycle are not scientific but *political* (in a wide sense): it coincides better with policy cycles, it is better for ensuring public attention for the indicator and for engaging with public discourse.

To summarize, we can say that the EWCS is without any doubt the best existing source for the study of job quality in Europe. Its coverage of issues is more than adequate, the items are very well designed and strictly comparable across countries, while the level of documentation and transparency of the whole process is exceptional. On the downside, the size of the sample is quite limited for carrying out detailed analysis of working conditions for specific groups within countries, and the periodicity might be a bit sparse for the objectives of monitoring job quality with a composite index.

NOTES

1. The only potential alternative would be to try to measure the attributes of the jobs themselves, understanding jobs as positions within productive organizations which correspond to coherent sets of tasks and responsibilities (for an example of such an approach, see Fernández-Macías and Hurley 2008). However, in fact, even in this case, information is collected at the level of individual workers (or jobholders) rather than at the job itself. Simply put: without jobholders, there are no jobs.
2. By aggregation here we only mean putting together different pieces of information within a coherent and structured model of job quality (even if the pieces are not mathematically added as in a composite index but just put together as in a system of indicators; for a detailed discussion, see Chapters 4 and 5).
3. In this case, possibly surveys, since administrative registers do not usually contain very detailed information on worker's characteristics.
4. This methodology is proposed by Jencks *et al.* (1988).
5. For instance, if our model posits that five variables are measures of the same dimension of job quality, normally they should be highly correlated statistically, which can be tested empirically once we have identified the measurement variables (for instance, using Cronbach's Alpha coefficient).
6. By standardization we simply mean transforming the different dimensions so that their scales are equivalent and can be aggregated. The most frequent standardization is converting to zeta units (subtracting the average and dividing by the standard deviation), but this is neither the only nor the best method in all situations (because it transforms the differences into relativities, it can obscure differences in the distribution which can be quite important, so in some cases it is better to use other standardization methods, as described in OECD, 2008).
7. For a detailed discussion of the technical issues involved in generating composite indices, see OECD (2008).
8. There are different ways of doing this final aggregation. The most popular method is the arithmetic average, but there are many alternatives, such as other additive measures based on thresholds, the geometric mean, rules based on multi-criteria decision analysis and social choice theory or non-compensatory multi-criteria approaches (OECD 2008). We will argue in Chapter 5 that a geometric aggregation presents very interesting statistical properties (for instance, allowing for only partial compensation among dimensions or a decreasing contribution of each dimension to overall job quality) that make it a desirable option for the construction of a job quality index.
9. It can be argued that the negative implications of the lack of employment security are different in a context of rising labour demand and in a context of rising unemployment.
10. In fact this question is a specific example of the general problem discussed in section 3.1.4 dealing with whether it is possible to have a single set of indicators for countries

very diverse in terms of economic and social development and with different public-private mix.

11. According to the *OECD Glossary of Statistics*, 'Satellite accounts provide a framework linked to the central accounts and which enables attention to be focussed on a certain field or aspect of economic and social life in the context of national accounts; common examples are satellite accounts for the environment, or tourism, or unpaid household work'.

4. Mapping the terrain: review of existent indicators of job quality

4.1. REVIEW OF EXISTING INDICATORS

In this chapter, we review over twenty proposals of job quality indices or systems of indicators. These measures are grouped according to two different criteria: first, according to their scope (national or international); and second, according to the origin of the proposal (policy or academic institutions). In most cases, they are still relatively new proposals, with tentative concepts and methodologies and probably still open to change. The lack of a widely accepted indicator of job quality (compared to other areas, such as development and the Human Development Index) is in itself proof of the immaturity of this area of policy and research. Our survey of existing proposals starts with international institutional indicators, then proceeds with national institutional indicators and finishes with the individual (mostly academic) international and national proposals. Section 4.2 summarizes the main characteristics, overlaps and differences, strengths and shortcomings of the indicators surveyed.

4.1.1. The Laeken Indicators of Job Quality

In spite of the minor role played by the EU with respect to social and employment policy, European authorities have been expressing concern about job quality issues for more than a decade. In 2000, the Lisbon and Nice European Councils strongly supported the creation of a system of indicators to monitor poverty and social exclusion in the member countries, recognizing as well the need of indicators for assessing job quality.[1] The first step towards a practical application of the EU interest in job quality was taken in 2001, as a result of the Stockholm European Council, where Member States decided that the Commission and Council would jointly develop a set of indicators of job quality to be presented at the following European Council in Laeken (Belgium) on December 2001.

The output of this process of European reflection on job quality was the definition of two broad dimensions, named 'Characteristics of the Job Itself' and 'The Work and Wider Labour Market Context'. While the former comprises indicators of 'Intrinsic job quality' and 'Lifelong learning and career development', the latter includes the remaining areas covered by Laeken measures: 'Gender equality', 'Health and safety at work', 'Flexibility and security', 'Inclusion and access to the labour market', 'Work organization and work–life balance', 'Social dialogue and workers' involvement', 'Diversity and non-discrimination' and 'Overall economic performance and productivity'. The European authorities defined several specific indicators for evaluating each dimension, except in the case of social dialogue, where no agreement was reached. These indicators are presented in Table 4.1. All the indicators were to be measured using the main data sources available at European level at that time, that is, the European Community Household Panel, the European Labour Force Survey and other variables included in the Eurostat database. They represent a system of indicators, with no aggregation between the different dimensions being proposed (hence, the EU avoids any judgement of their relative importance).

Although the Laeken indicators constitute the biggest effort so far towards the measurement of job quality made by the European institutions, they have several important weaknesses, which we discuss below.

First, there are several variables – even entire dimensions – that do not measure anything related to job quality (certainly not directly), but other issues such as overall labour market or economic performance. Some examples of this problem are those variables measuring access to the labour market (dimension 6), overall economic performance and productivity (dimension 10) and all those other variables that measure the *quantity* of jobs (that is, employment or unemployment rates) or transitions from employment, unemployment or inactivity situations.

Second, both output and conditions variables are simultaneously included among the Laeken measures. In particular, the inclusion of job satisfaction as a key determinant of the first dimension is problematic. Even if we disregard the difficulties for interpreting the results of this variable (see Chapter 2), job satisfaction can be considered an overall evaluation of job quality made by the workers themselves, and therefore it should not be included together with other objective elements of job quality. The other elements of job quality should be determinants of job satisfaction: by including these determinants and their results (job satisfaction itself) one would be simply including redundant information.

A third problem is the inclusion of gender or age gaps, or, in general, the consideration of variables referring to specific subgroups of the population. The differences in job quality for specific subgroups are of course of great importance, but the way to reflect them is to compute the variables of job quality for each of the subgroups and compare the overall results

Table 4.1   The Laeken indicators of job quality

Dimensions		Indicator
I. Charac-teristics of the job itself	1) Intrinsic job quality	Transitions between non-employment and employment and, within employment, by pay level
		Transitions between non-employment and employment and, with employment, by type of contract
		Satisfaction with type of work in present job
	2) Lifelong learning and career development	Percentage of the working population age in education and training by gender, age group, employment status and education level
		Percentage of the labour force using computers in work, with or without specific training
II. The Work and Wider Labour Market Context	3) Gender equality	Ratio of women's gross hourly earnings to men's for paid employees at work
		Employment rate gap between men and women
		Gender segregation in occupations
		Gender segregation in sectors
	4) Health and safety at work	The evolution of the incidence rate (accidents)
	5) Flexibility and security	No. of employees working part-time and with fixed-term contracts as a percentage of the total number of employees
	6) Inclusion and access to the labour market	Transitions between employment, unemployment and inactivity
		Transitions between non-employment and employment or training
		Total employment rate, and by age group and education level
		Total long-term unemployment rate, and by gender
		Percentage of early school leavers
		Youth unemployment ration
	7) Work organization and the work–life balance	Difference in employment rates for individuals aged 20 to 50 in households having or not a child aged between 0 and 6 years
		Children cared for (other than the family) as a proportion of all children in the same group

Table 4.1 (continued)

Dimensions	Indicator
	Employees who left their job over the last year for family duties and intend to go to work but are currently unavailable for work
8) Social dialogue and workers' involvement	No agreement
9) Diversity and non-discrimination	Employment rate gap for workers aged between 55 to 64 years old
	Employment and unemployment rate gaps for ethnic minorities and immigrants
10) Overall economic performance and productivity	Growth in labour productivity (both per hour worked and per person employed)
	Total output (both per hour worked and per person employed)
	Percentage of the population having achieved at least upper secondary education by gender, age group and employment status

Source: Authors' elaboration from European Commission (2001).

between them. The existence of a gap in a specific dimension (or dimensions) of job quality is surely very important for evaluating the wider implications of the quality of existing jobs, but is not part of job quality itself.

And, finally, there is a striking absence in the extensive list of issues covered by the Laeken indicators: wages. Even though in most of the models and theoretical discussions of job quality wages play a prominent role, not a single indicator on wage levels is included. Only labour productivity, which is indirectly related to wages, is included.[2]

There are other minor problems to be mentioned. For example, the indicator on part-time employment does not take account whether part-time is voluntary or involuntary. The fact that the indicators are aggregated does not allow for a detailed analysis of job quality by subgroups (as mentioned earlier, the system of indicator includes some distributional information by covering some gaps). The absence of any variables measuring social dialogue and workers' involvement (because of a lack of agreement on the measures, despite the inclusion of this dimension) is also an important weakness of the Laeken indicators.

The actual policy impact of the Laeken indicators seems quite mixed, even within European institutions. It is quite striking that the 2008–2010 Employment Guidelines (European Council 2008), although repeatedly referring to desirable job attributes beyond remuneration, makes no explicit reference to the Laeken indicators established in 2001. The so-called 'EU Structural Statistical Indicators' and 'Euro Indicators' (produced by Eurostat) include some labour market variables, such as labour cost or tax wedge on wages, which were not part of the Laeken measures. In fact, the recently refurbished Eurostat database does not contain a specific section devoted to the Laeken indicators of job quality.

The 2008 *Employment in Europe* report (European Commission 2008) proposed alternatives to solve some of the problems referred to above. Particularly, it discussed the weaknesses of some indicators related to the socio-economic context, the absence of any wage measures, the lack of measures of more qualitative aspects of training and indicators of work intensity. The variables proposed to be incorporated to the Laeken indicators are outlined below:

- Perception of being well paid for the work done.
- Wages.
- In-work at risk of poverty.
- Prospects for career advancement in the job.
- Painful/tiring positions and work.
- Tasks' repetitiveness.
- Health at risk because of work.
- Working to tight deadlines.
- Working at very high speed.
- Consulted about changes in social organization.
- Long working days.
- Working at night.

In addition, some variables were reformulated or their scope was broadened. For example, the report suggested including involuntary part-time and fixed-time employees, proportion of people in education and more types of gender and age gaps. Though these proposals imply a clear improvement over the original Laeken indicators, some of the original shortcomings remain. For example, some of the new variables go beyond the scope of work itself, such as the proportion of people in education. The indicators remain measured only at the aggregate level, and to deal with distributional aspects, some indicators are measured as gaps, without a separate calculation of employment quality for each of the subgroups.

The 2008 *Employment in Europe* report developed an aggregate indicator

Table 4.2   Variables used for constructing a synthetic index of job quality by the European Commission (2008)

Variable	Direction of the impact on job quality
One year transitions from employment to unemployment	+
Long-term unemployment rate	–
Involuntary part-time	–
Share of employment with fixed-term contracts	–
Older workers (55–64) employment gap	–
Gender employment gap	–
Gender pay gap	–
Gender occupational segregation	–
Participation in education and training	+
Upper secondary education attainment	+
Non-standard hours	–
In-work accidents rate	–

Source: Authors' elaboration from European Commission (2008).

to rank the countries on the basis of an index and monitoring the evolution of job quality over time, according to the following principles. First, variables to be included were standardized in order to make them comparable. Second, synthetic indicators were calculated by adding or subtracting the standardized variables according to their likely impact on job quality, respectively, positive or negative. Only variables that have an unambiguous impact on job quality were included (see Table 4.2). Finally, those values were summated in order to obtain the synthetic index.

The absence of some key dimensions of job quality (wages, intensity, and so on) means that this index has serious limitations compared to some of the other indices discussed below. Furthermore, from the 12 variables considered, only half might be regarded as being clearly related to job quality. Of the other half, two are related to job *quantity* and its implications, one to education, and four to distributional issues in terms of gender and age: all obviously very important issues on their own, but with little relevance for the measurement of the quality of existing jobs. The results for 2004 are presented in Figure 4.1. Probably because of the mentioned shortcomings, it is easy to see some evident inconsistencies. Although, as in most of the other indicators reviewed here, Nordic countries rank quite highly, countries like the Czech Republic, Hungary or even Latvia have a better score than France, Spain and Italy, which is inconsistent with

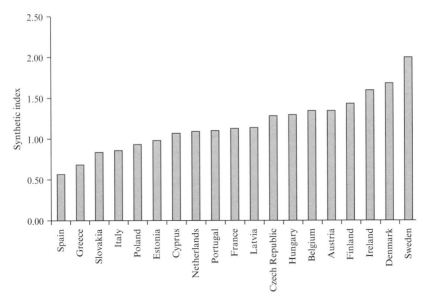

Note: Data from the Netherlands correspond to 1998, the last year available.

Source: Authors' analysis from European Commission (2008, annex 2).

Figure 4.1   Synthetic index of job quality for European Union countries in 2004

previous research (as can be easily checked by comparing these results with all the other indicators reviewed in this chapter).

4.1.2.   The European Job Quality Index

In order to contribute to the monitoring and evaluation of the progress of the different Member States towards the European Employment Strategy goal of 'more and better jobs', the European Trade Union Institute (ETUI) developed in 2008 the *European Job Quality Index*. ETUI is the research arm of the European Trade Union Congress (ETUC), the most important representative body of workers at the EU level, and therefore itself a major player (as a social partner) in the EU policy area of work and employment.

Although so far it has only been published once, the European Job Quality Index (EJQI) will be updated yearly, with results for the EU as a whole as well as for each Member State (broken down by gender). This index is completely focused on job quality from the perspective of workers:

therefore, all the variables refer to information measured at the level of individual workers, with only two exceptions (the degree of training for the overall population of working age and the extent of union representation at workplace level). Nevertheless, only job quality at the national level is computed (and reported), based on averages and percentages of different variables. This means that it is impossible to break down this index in order to do detailed analysis for specific subgroups of workers, by sector or type of contract, for instance: only the national scores can be compared. Nevertheless, there is a remarkable exception to this rule: the ETUI publishes the index broken down by gender.

Because the EJQI is an index computed only at the national level, it has more flexibility to draw from different data sources, which widens the scope of information that can be covered. The EJQI uses five different sources: the European Labour Force Survey (ELFS), the European Working Conditions Surveys (EWCS), the Annual Macro-Economic Database of the EU (AMECO), the European Survey on Income and Living Conditions (EU-SILC) and the Database on Institutional Characteristics of Trade Unions, Wage Setting, State Intervention and Social Pacts (ICTWSS). Not all these databases are updated every year, which means that some dimensions of the EJQI cannot be updated annually either, but in longer cycles depending on the database upon which the measures are built. The EWCS database, in particular, is only updated every five years. We could not find any specific mention as to whether the ICTWSS is updated annually or not. The implication of this dependence on the updating procedure of different specific sources is that the year-on-year changes in the index, except for the years coinciding with an update in the EWCS, will be the result of changes only in the dimensions based on the ELFS, AMECO or EU-SILC.

The EJQI contains six dimensions, based on 16 indicators which in turn are drawn from many more individual variables taken from the different sources mentioned earlier. They are outlined below:

1. *Wages.* Entirely based on the AMECO database, and therefore updated yearly. It includes two indicators: nominal compensation per employee in Power Purchasing Parity and in-work poverty (percentage of workers living in households whose disposable income is below 60 per cent of the national median).
2. *Non-standard forms of employment.* This information comes from the ELFS, and therefore it can be updated yearly. It includes two indicators: percentage of temporary employees (and what share of them was involuntary) and percentage of part-time employees (and what proportion of them is involuntary).

3. *Working time and work–life balance.* The measurement of this dimension is based on ELFS, EU-SILC and EWCS, and therefore only partially updated every year. It includes: share of employees working more than 48 hours a week (ELFS), share of workers on shift-work and unsocial hours schedules (evening, nights and weekends, also based on ELFS), share of voluntary part-time workers (EU-SILC) and share of workers who are satisfied with their work–life balance (based on EWCS, and therefore updated only every five years).
4. *Working conditions and job security.* By far, this is the dimension based on more individual items, all of them computed from the EWCS. Therefore, it is only updated every five years. It includes the following indicators: work intensity, work autonomy, physical work factors, and perceived job security.
5. *Skills and career development.* The analysis of this dimension is based on the ELFS and the EWCS, and, hence, only partially updated every year. It comprises two indicators: the share of population (25–64) participating in education and training (from the ELFS) and perceived career prospects from current job (from the EWCS). The inclusion of the first indicator is surprising, because it seems unclear why the share of population between 25 and 64 participating in training or education should be an element of job quality. The justification for this inclusion is that 'the extent of skills development at the workplace will vary depending on the extent and formalization of initial education' (Leschke *et al.* 2008, p. 12), which is certainly true, but it is difficult to see how this variable solves the problem. In any case, this is the only indicator included in this proposal that might be regarded as unrelated to job quality.
6. *Collective interest representation.* This dimension is based on the ICTWSS database and the EWCS. It is not clear in the documentation of the EJQI whether the ICTWSS database is updated yearly. This dimension is clearly related to job quality, although as argued in a previous section, it refers to procedures rather than results; that is, the existence of collective interest representation at the workplace allows workers to defend their interests better, and therefore should improve job quality, but it is not necessarily an indicator of job quality in itself (unless we understand that the existence of voice mechanisms is good in itself, for its expressive or socializing functions, but this does not seem to be the idea behind this dimension of the EJQI). This dimension comprises three indicators: collective bargaining coverage, trade union density (drawn from the ICTWSS) and whether the worker has been consulted about changes in work organization (EWCS).

Overall, the EJQI is one of the indices that covers a wider range of the areas of job quality identified in the specialized literature (see Table 2.4), although it leaves out deployment of skills at work, subjective feelings of meaningfulness, social environment issues and exposure to psychosocial risks. Except for the case of participation in education and training, all the variables used are clearly and unambiguously related to job quality, and the documentation of the index provides some justification for every inclusion (even if the justification is more policy-oriented than theoretical, according to the aims of the index).

The measure is additive: that is, the construction of the index is based on adding the normalized scores of the indicators to the dimensions, and, then, adding the scores of the dimensions to the overall index. As argued in the documentation of the index, this way it is possible to determine 'to what extent countries cumulate "good" or "bad" job quality characteristics or, in contrast, offset good or bad elements along one dimension with opposite characteristics in another' (Leschke, *et al.* 2008, p. 14). However, this procedure does not take into account that a more balanced structure of job attributes can be preferable than another where the scores of the different components present more extreme values, even when both cases yield the same EJQI.

The indicators are normalized by re-scaling each value to the proportion they represent with respect to the difference between the maximum and minimum values for the base year (which is set to 2000 for EU15 and 2007 for EU27). This system of normalization, a widely used method for comparing country performance (for example, in the construction of the Human Development Index), has the advantage of putting each value in relation to the best and worst cases.

With respect to the weighting of the indicators for the construction of the overall index, the EJQI uses unequal weighting for the (normalized) indicators within each dimension, but equal weighting for the dimensions that add up to the overall index. Therefore, each of the six dimensions is equally important for the overall result of the index, which implies an unavoidable discretionary decision by the researcher, but has the advantage of making the analysis and comparisons of the relative importance of each dimension more intuitive. The individual dimensions, on the contrary, are computed adding the lower level indicators after applying unequal weighting factors. For instance, the dimension 'wages' is composed by two indicators: nominal compensation per employee in PPS (which weights 70 per cent in the overall result for the dimension) and in-work poverty (which means 30 per cent). Again, this weighting system is arbitrary, but not more arbitrary than just adding the indicators (which in fact implies assigning equal weights). In all cases the weights are documented and seem rather reasonable. In the main methodological paper of the EJQI (Leschke *et al.* 2008), the authors include an annex with a sensitivity analysis of the weights (checking how much do the country rankings change when the weights are slightly shifted), which proves that the results are quite stable even after moderate adjustments in the weights.

In sum, the EJQI is a well-balanced and extensively documented index. It covers most (though not all) of the important areas of job quality appearing in the Social Sciences literature, and it is transparent and honest in its methodological choices, all of which are well documented and available for consultation. On the downside, its main problem is that it is an aggregate index that is only computed for whole countries (even if separately for women and men), which means that it is not possible to do detailed analysis of the *distribution* of job quality within each member state. In addition, the use of an arithmetic method of aggregation means that it does not take into account that improvements in some dimensions might have a larger impact on job quality the lower is their initial value and the larger are the scores in other dimensions. A specific, and relatively easy to address problem is the consideration of in-work poverty rate instead of the low-wage work rate (under 60 per cent of median wage); the former indicator is affected by elements external to job quality (family structure, existence of social transfers, etc.).

The results (Figure 4.2) obtained by the application of the index by ETUI researchers for 2007 (the only year for which the index has been calculated so far) places Northern European countries at the top of the list (an outcome that is remarkably consistent across all the different proposals), and Eastern and Southern European Member States at the bottom (also a quite consistent pattern). As the authors themselves acknowledge (Leschke and Watt 2008, p. 25), the two countries whose scores seem somewhat surprising are the UK (which appears very high, at the very top of the list, especially for females) and Germany (which appears relatively low, below the EU27 average). For the UK, as they argue, this result is in fact quite consistent with other job quality indices (including our own, as we shall see in Chapter 6).[3] As for Germany, the authors of the EJQI show that its scores are rather low in terms of non-standard employment, working conditions and job security, even if its scores are higher than average on wages. The fact that the index is easily decomposable facilitates enormously the analysis of the possible reasons behind the different country scores.

4.1.3. Employers' Reflections on Job Quality

It is not only trade unions who have expressed their concern for job quality but also European employers (UNICE 2001), grouped in the employers'

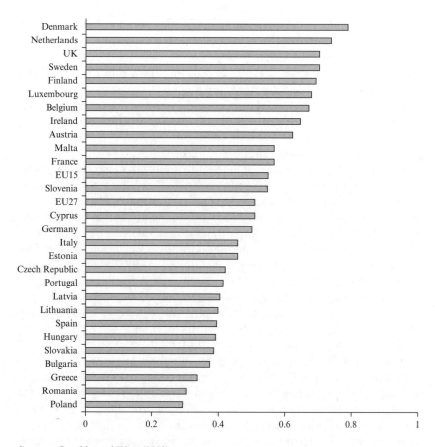

Source: Leschke and Watt (2008).

Figure 4.2 *European Job Quality Index for European Union countries in 2006*

confederation Business Europe (formerly named Union of Industrials and Employers' Confederations of Europe, UNICE). Rather than proposing its own job quality index, as ETUI, European employers recommend focusing on the following items:

– Number of fatal and serious accidents at work.
– Rates of occupational diseases.
– Total number of days lost due to sickness.
– Labour productivity.
– Proportion of working population with low, medium and high

levels of education (if possible with breakdown by gender and/or age groups).
- Proportion of population with basic, medium and high levels of ICT literacy (if possible with breakdown by gender and/or age groups).
- Average time taken to find the first or a new job (with breakdown by gender and/or age group).
- Employment rate and unemployment rate by gender, age group and educational level.
- Proportion of working age population creating their own enterprise (with breakdown by gender, age groups and educational level).

Though it is of course positive that employers contribute to the debate on measuring job quality, the indicators proposed by UNICE do not seem very appropriate for this objective, as only the first three show clear measures of job quality (at least, from the perspective of this book). Most of the indicators proposed by UNICE, in fact, do not appear in any of the other models or systems of indicators on job quality discussed in this chapter. The rest of the measures make reference to human capital formation, some measures of overall labour market and economic performance.

4.1.4. The European Working Conditions Survey

The European Working Conditions Survey (EWCS) is not really an index of job quality, but it can be considered a system of indicators of job quality (that is, a vector, or an index without the computation of a final single number summarizing an overall score). In fact, the five-yearly reports based on each new wave of the survey and published by the European Foundation constitute a very rich source of information for the analysis and evaluation of the evolution and distribution of job quality across the different EU Member States. And in any case, it is such an important source for the study of quality of work in the EU (used in many of the individual job quality indices), that it is well worth covering it here. In this section, we briefly describe the EWCS as a vector of indicators of quality of work, discussing the questionnaire and main results of the last published report (Parent-Thirion *et al.* 2007). The technical characteristics of the EWCS as a survey, which were covered in the previous chapter, are not summarized here.

The survey is carried out by the European Foundation for the Improvement of Living and Working Conditions (Eurofound), a tripartite EU agency whose mandate is to contribute to the planning and design of better living and working conditions in Europe. Eurofound never makes explicit evaluation of national policies or performance, but tries to increase the knowledge on living and working conditions in ways that help design better policies. It is probably because of this reason that so far it has not attempted to create any composite measure of job quality (which would require taking a specific political view on the issue and making direct policy evaluation and performance). In recent years, Eurofound has monitored developments of job quality across Europe through two main instruments: the European Working Conditions Survey and the European Working Conditions Observatory. In both cases, the point of departure has been a broad understanding of job quality and the main goal to try and monitor as many areas as possible on this issue, without attempting to evaluate explicitly the results. Many others (including several indices discussed here) have used this information as inputs for their own proposals.

The EWCS has been carried out every five years since 1991, and there have been four waves so far. It covers a wide (and expanding) range of issues related to work and employment, most of them relevant for purposes of job quality. Originally, the approach was closer to the Health and Safety tradition (see Chapter 3), but it quickly expanded to cover all the major areas of job quality of the Social Sciences literature. There are 63 questions and 118 individual items (many questions include several items). A core of key questions has been maintained since the 1991 edition of the survey, although most of the important variables for job quality were included in 1995 rather than 1991.

The questionnaire is developed and partially updated every five years by an "Expert Questionnaire Development Group", composed of representatives of national institutes carrying out surveys of working conditions, members of the tripartite Governing Board of the Foundation (employer associations, trade unions and governments), the European Commission and other EU bodies (Eurostat, the European Agency for Safety and Health at Work), international organizations (OECD, ILO), as well as leading European experts in the field of working conditions and survey methodology (see Parent-Thirion *et al.* 2007, p. 93). The questionnaire loosely follows the model of job quality published by Eurofound in 2002, which is depicted by Figure 4.3.

Unfortunately, the paper where this model is presented includes no justification or discussion of its structure and components (Eurofound 2002). The model includes four main dimensions that more or less correspond with four of the traditions in the Social Sciences literature identified in the previous chapter. The area that seems to be missing is the one related to the intrinsic rewards from work (autonomy, meaningfulness and social environment). However, in fact, this area is very well covered in the EWCS

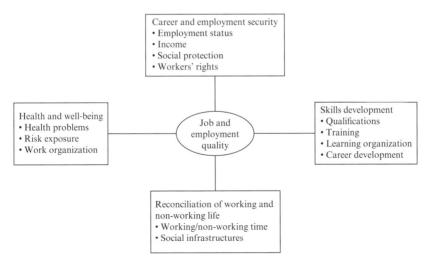

Source: Eurofound (2002, p. 6).

Figure 4.3   Eurofound's model of job quality

questionnaire, which clearly shows that the design of the questionnaire did not restrict itself to the model shown in Figure 4.3. Regarding the indicators included within each dimension in Figure 4.3, the list seems to be only indicative and not exhaustive. The position of some indicators seems a bit odd: for instance, work organization appears as an element of health and well-being, and income appears within career and employment security. The model is clearly underdeveloped and somewhat discretional, but this did not have a negative impact on the development of the questionnaire, which is extremely rich and detailed, and covers all the major areas of job quality identified in the literature.

4.1.5.   ILO Decent Work Indices

Jointly with social protection, job quality has been the primary focus of the International Labour Organization (ILO) since its origin. This concern was recently translated into the concept of *decent work* and a subsequent campaign in 1999 demanding the creation of 'good' jobs. The ILO original definition makes reference, in general terms, to *basic security for all*, and more specifically, is centred on four concrete areas: employment, social security, workers' rights and social dialogue. This broad concept represents more an expression of social or political goals for desirable working conditions than an operational concept.[4] However, based on the spirit of

Table 4.3　Indicators proposed by Ghai to calculate the index of decent work

Dimensions	Indicators
(1) Employment	Labour force participation
	Unemployment rate
	Gini index of income or consumption
(2) Social security	Public expenditure on social protection (% of GDP)
(3) Workers' rights	Female labour force participation
	Simple average of the share of female administrative and managerial workers and the share of female professional and technical workers
	Ratio of female to male unemployment rates
(4) Social dialogue	Union density

Source:　Authors' construction from Ghai (2003).

the definition, the staff of ILO has developed several indices and systems of indicators of decent work, which are presented below. In the following pages, we review four of these proposals.

4.1.5.1.　Ghai's decent work index (DWI-1)

The operationalization of the concept of Decent Work by Dharam Ghai (2003), advisor at the International Institute of Labour Studies at the ILO, focuses on developed countries, using as the main source of information the ILO cross-country databases on labour market and social protection. Table 4.3 presents the variables included by the author in order to account for the above-mentioned dimensions.

The computation of the index involves a simple procedure based on averaging the rankings of the countries on different dimensions (see the outline depicted in Figure 4.4). First, regarding employment, the author calculates the relative ranking of countries in terms of labour force participation, unemployment rate and income distribution (measured by the Gini index). Then, these three rankings are averaged obtaining a sort of mean ranking. Based on this average ranking, countries are ordered again, yielding an overall quality of employment ranking. The same procedure is applied to all the areas shown in Figure 4.4.

There are several problems in Ghai's selection of indicators. Firstly, many of them are not really indicators of job quality, but indicators of job quantity (unemployment rate or labour participation) or the social protection system (as the whole dimension of social rights). As argued previously, the inclusion of gaps between genders or ages as indicators of

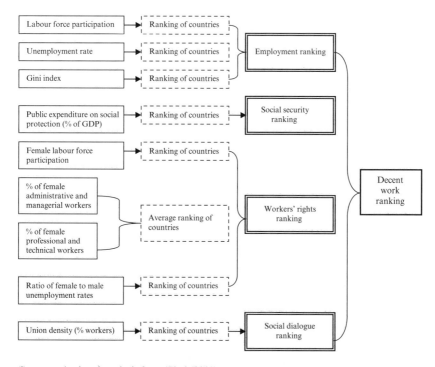

Source: Authors' analysis from Ghai (2003).

Figure 4.4   Ghai's Index of Decent Work

job quality is not free of problems either: one thing is the quality of existing jobs and another one is whether there is differential access to the good or bad jobs for different groups (which, we have argued, should be analysed by comparing the index results by subgroups, rather than making an index including gap variables). Secondly the aggregate nature of this index makes it impossible to do any kind of disaggregation. Similarly, social dialogue is approximated by using the proportion of workers affiliated to a trade union, an indicator far from perfect (as the author himself recognizes), as a non-negligible percentage of non-unionized workers are usually affected by collective agreements negotiated by main unions. However this shortcoming is common to other indicators trying to measure workers' voice. Lastly, the aggregation of dimensions is quite discretional, a common feature with other measures, casting more doubts about the robustness and convenience of this indicator. The author applies the index to 22 OECD countries: as usual, the results put the Nordic countries at the top and Mediterranean countries (Spain and Greece) at the bottom of the job quality ranking.

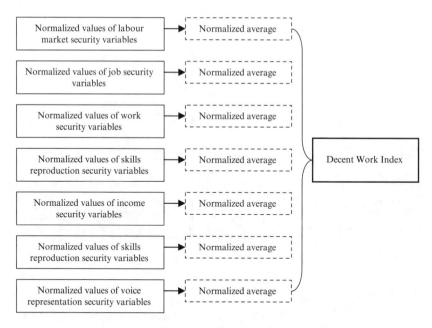

Source: Authors' analysis from Bonnet, Figueiredo and Standing (2003).

Figure 4.5   Bonnet, Figueiredo and Standing's index of decent work

4.1.5.2.   Bonnet, Figueiredo and Standing's decent work index (DWI-2)

A second operationalization of the concept of decent work is proposed by
Bonnet, Figueiredo and Standing (2003). Their starting point is the broad
definition of decent work as *basic security for all*, which they translate
into seven different dimensions of security: labour market, employment,
job, work, skills reproduction, income and voice representation. Though
they give some hints to adapt their proposal to lower levels of analysis,
their indicator is only defined at the macro level, that is, it is constructed
from data measured at the country level taken from ILO databases on
labour market indicators and social protection. The construction of the
index is based on the re-scaling procedures followed to compute the well-
known Human Development Index by the United Nations Development
Program (subtracting the minimum value and dividing the result between
the range), which yields a normalized index for each variable considered.
Then, these normalized values are averaged, obtaining an indicator of
security in each dimension. Finally, normalization provides a final index
of decent work ranging from 0 (minimum job quality) to 1 (maximum).
This procedure is summarized by Figure 4.5.

The specific indicators included by the authors in the analysis are presented in Table 4.4. As can be seen, the list is very exhaustive, including 67 static and objective variables aiming to capture many different dimensions of decent work. The final output is an aggregate index, which, in contrast to Ghai's proposal, has not only an ordinal but also a cardinal value. The DWI-2 is clearly a multipurpose indicator, as the indicators used in the construction of the index cover many areas not strictly related to job quality, from unemployment rate to life expectancy. As in the DWI-1, several distributional indicators are included and the authors also consider some variables involving specific characteristics of workers (for example, some ratios between male and female scores), instead of computing the quality of jobs for such separate demographic groups using a common index.

The index is applied by the authors to almost 100 countries. The results obtained by the authors place Nordic countries in a leading position. In general, none of the results obtained seems surprising or unexpected.

In sum, the DWI-2 makes a formidable effort to make the concept of decent work operative. The main strengths of this measure are the amount of information collected, their eminently objective nature and their aim of comprehensiveness. However, the DWI-2 also presents evident shortcomings. In the first place, its theoretical foundations are somewhat underdeveloped, and the method for aggregating its very long list of basic indicators, somewhat ad hoc. Secondly, although dispersion indicators are included in the analysis, it is not possible to compute the DWI-2 at individual level. Thirdly, it could be argued that a number of variables included in the index have nothing to do with job quality strictly speaking, for example, variables like literacy rates or the Gini index for the whole country. Fourthly and finally, the index can only be computed at country level and some indicators refer to gender or age gaps, which, as mentioned, is methodologically inappropriate.

4.1.5.3. Anker *et al.'s* decent work indicators (DWI-3)

Richard Anker, Igor Chernyshev, Philippe Egger, Farhad Mehran and Joseph Ritter (Anker *et al.* 2003), all of them at the ILO, propose a set of indicators based on aggregate data referring to 11 dimensions: employment opportunities, unacceptable work, adequate earnings and productive work, decent hours, stability and security of work, balancing work and family life, fair treatment in employment, safe work, social protection, social dialogue and workplace relations, and socio-economic context. A broad range of variables is suggested for each dimension (see Table 4.5). Anker *et al.* do not define a closed set of variables for the construction of their index, limiting themselves to point out which dimensions should be

Table 4.4   *Indicators proposed by Bonnet, Figueiredo and Standing to calculate the index of decent work*

Dimensions of security	Type of indicator	Indicators
(1) Labour market	Input indicators	Ratification of Employment Policy Convention, 1964 (No. 122)
		Government (or constitution) commitment to full employment
	Process indicators	Existence of a public employment service
		Public consumption (% of GDP)
		Average annual growth rate (%)
	Outcome indicators (divided by ½ if the country is known by its high level of unpaid work or low-paid leave)	Unemployment rate (%)
		Employment change during the last decade (%)
		Ratio of male to female unemployment rates
		Employment rate (% of working-age population)
		Ratio of male to female unemployment rates
		Wage employment share of people in income-earning activities (%, total and by sex)
(2) Employment	Input indicators	Ratification of Termination Employment Convention, 1982 (No. 158)
		Strictness of employment protection legislation
	Process indicators	Proportion of workers' coverage by collective bargaining agreements
		Existence of independent labour tribunals
	Outcome indicators (divided by ½ if the country is known by its high level of unpaid work or low-paid leave)	Proportion of employees in regular wage employment
		Proportion of employees in the public sector
(3) Job	Input indicators	Existence of a law prohibiting employment discrimination against women
		Existence of a law providing for maternity leave
		Existence of law banning discrimination among people with disabilities
	Process indicators	Overall literacy rate (%)
		Ratio of female to male literacy rates
		Ratio of the percentage of women completing post-secondary education to the percentage of population completing that level of education
		Duration of maternity leave
		Level of maternity benefits (% of average earnings)

Table 4.4 (continued)

Dimensions of security	Type of indicator	Indicators
	Outcome indicators	Share of professional occupations (% of employed)
		Ratio of the percentage of professional women in total female employment to the percentage of professional men in total male employment
		Transferability of parental leave between mothers and fathers
(4) Work	Input indicators	Ratification of seven specific ILO conventions
		Existence of national laws providing for occupational safety and health, protection of disabled workers, maternity leave and paid leave
	Process indicators	Expenditure on workers' compensation and labour management (% of GDP)
		Existence of tripartite or bipartite boards or committees for occupation safety and health
		Level of statutory disability or invalidity benefits provided to workers injured in work-related accidents (% of average earnings)
	Outcome indicators (divided by ½ if the country is known by its high level of unpaid work or low-paid leave)	Annual number of injuries by employed people
		Average annual pay leave (vacation days) adjusted for the share of workers in formal wage employment
		Share of the economically active population with guaranteed compensation for sick leave and occupational injury
		Working time (average hours per week)
(5) Skills reproduc-tion	Input indicators	Ratification of four specific ILO conventions
		Statutory number of years of compulsory schooling
	Process indicators	Public expenditure on education (% of GDP) corrected by the percentage of the population under 15 years old
		Expenditure on education per capita
	Outcome indicators (divided by ½ if the country is known by its high level of unpaid work or low-paid leave)	Literacy rate (% of people between 25 and 64 years old, total and by sex)
		Median number of years of schooling (with reference to population aged 25–64)
		Percentage of people aged 25–64 having completed tertiary-level education

Table 4.4   (continued)

Dimensions of security	Type of indicator	Indicators
(6) Income	Input indicators	Ratification of three ILO conventions on social security and minimum wages
		Existence of a minimum wage law
		Existence of unemployment benefits
		Existence of a state pension
	Process indicators	Public expenditure on social security (% of GDP)
		Coverage of all social security schemes (% of population covered by any programme)
	Outcome indicators	National poverty rate
		GDP per capita in PPP
		Gini coefficient of income
		Life expectancy at birth
		Unemployed receiving unemployment benefits (%)
		Wage share (% of GDP)
		Index of old-age income security generated from the ILO Social Security Database
		External debt (% GDP)
(7) Voice representation	Input indicators	Ratification of three ILO conventions on unionization and collective bargaining
		Absence of legal restrictions on unionization
	Process indicators	Existence of a national tripartite board or council dealing with labour and social policies
		Promotion of workers' interests by non-governmental organizations are allowed
		Proportion of workers covered by collective agreements
	Outcome indicators	Union density
		Change in unionization during the 1990s
		Proportion of wage and salaried workers in total employment
		Civil Liberties Index developed by the Freedom House
		Change in the Civil Liberties index during the 1990s

Source: Authors' construction from Bonnet, Figueiredo and Standing (2003).

considered and possible indicators for each one (37 in total). Since some of the areas (for instance, social protection) are unrelated to jobs defined in a strict sense, the DWI-3 can be categorized as multipurpose. It is worth mentioning that some variables are introduced with the aim of capturing the dispersion of attributes while others make reference to some specific

Table 4.5   *Indicators proposed by Anker* et al. *to calculate the index of decent work*

Dimensions	Suggested indicators
(1) Employment opportunities	Labour force participation rate
	Employment–population ratio
	Unemployment rate
	Youth unemployment rate
	Share of wage employment in non-agricultural employment
(2) Skills development	Children not in school by employment status
	Children in wage employment or self-employment
(3) Career and employment security	Share of workers with earnings below ½ of median hourly wage or absolute minimum, whichever is greater
	Average earnings in selected occupations
	Employees with recent job training
(4) Decent hours	Excessive hours of work (compared to the usual standards)
	Time-related underemployment rate
(5) Stability and security of work	Tenure less than one year
	Temporary work
(6) Balancing work and family life	Employment rate for women with children under compulsory school age
(7) Fair treatment in employment	Occupational segregation by sex
	Female share of employment in managerial and administrative occupations
(8) Safe work	Fatal injury rate (per 100 000 employees)
	Labour inspectors per 100 000 employees and per 100 000 covered employees
	Occupational injury insurance coverage
(9) Social protection	Public social security expenditure (% of GDP)
	Public expenditure on needs-based cash income support (% of GDP)
	Beneficiaries of cash income support (% of poor)
	Share of population over 65 benefiting from a pension
	Share of economically active population contributing to a pension fund
	Average monthly pension
(10) Social dialogue and workplace relations	Union density rate
	Collective bargaining coverage rate
	Strikes and lockouts (per 100 000 employees)
(11) Socio-economic context	Output per employed person (PPP level)
	Growth of output per employed person
	Inflation
	Education of adult population (several sub-indicators)
	Composition of employment by economic sector
	Informal economy employment
	Income inequality
	Absolute poverty

Source: Authors' elaboration from Anker *et al.* (2003).

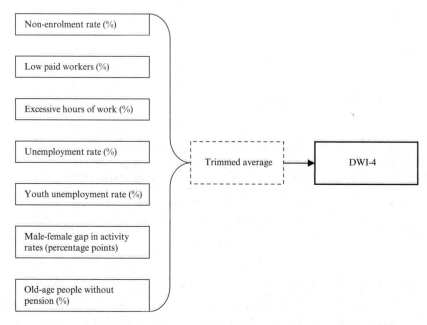

Source: Authors' analysis from Bescond, Châtaignier and Mehran (2003).

Figure 4.6   Bescond, Châtaignier and Mehran's Decent Work Index

groups of workers. There is not much more to say about the DWI-3, as it represents only a proposal to be developed rather than an index as such.

4.1.5.4.   Bescond, Châtaignier and Mehran Decent Work Index (DWI-4)
The last approach to the concept and measurement of decent work by the ILO is the one proposed by David Bescond, Anne Châtaignier and Farhad Mehran (2003). The computation of this index is quite straight-forward. Its main ingredients are child non-enrolment rate, proportion of low-paid workers (with earnings lower than 50 per cent of the median), proportion of workers with excessive working hours (more than 48 hours a week), unemployment rate, youth unemployment rate, male-female gap in labour force participation rates and the percentage of old-age people without pension. Therefore, the index can be derived from aggregate data. Bescond, Châtaignier and Mehran compute the DWI-4 as the average value of these indicators, excluding the two extreme values (that is, they calculate a trimmed average). This procedure is outlined in Figure 4.6 and yields a measure such that the lower is the DWI-4, the higher job quality. The nature of the index is clearly multipurpose, as some dimensions that

are not strictly related to jobs are also included, such as pension coverage or unemployment. On the other hand, all variables considered here are objective, static and linked to results. While no variable makes reference to distribution, the index includes several dimensions on gaps by gender or age, which, as argued earlier, can be considered as a shortcoming of the index (the measurement of job quality should not be affected by the characteristic of jobholders).

The index is computed for a wide range of developing, transition and developed economies, with Scandinavian countries positioned (once again) at the top of the ranking. The ILO databases on labour market issues and social security are the main source of data. However, some of the results are striking when we make cross-country comparisons. For example, Spain ranks below Yemen, Tanzania and Mexico, and Russia is ranked higher than Germany or Japan. Although probably the result responds to the existence of high unemployment levels among young people in some developed countries, these somewhat odd outcomes suggest the presence of serious problems in this DWI-4.

To conclude this review of decent work indicators, it is safe to say that probably the major shortcomings identified in these indicators derive partly from the fact that decent work is not entirely the same as job quality as understood here. While the perspective adopted in this report stresses the convenience of differentiating job quality from job quantity, the concept of decent work incorporates measures of both, as well as other dimensions as workers' rights or social protection. If decent work is not the same as job quality, it is obvious that the former should not necessarily be a good measure of the latter.

4.1.6. Good Jobs Index (GJI)

The GJI is a spin-off of a five-country study (covering Egypt, El Salvador, India, Russia, and South Africa) produced by the Global Policy Network in 2005 for the Ford Foundation (Avirgan *et al.* 2005).[5] The aim of the study was to research in depth the characteristics of informal work in these countries. The GJI was developed by Edgar Lara in the second phase of the research that looked at factors and policies contributing to the generation of good jobs.[6] Together with some of the proposals of the ILO, the GJI is one of the few proposals aimed at a worldwide application.

In the spirit of the concept of decent work developed by the ILO, the GJI, still in a testing stage, includes five different areas: equal opportunities for women, a living wage, job security (understood in terms of probability of employment), access to social security and respect for core labour law. Therefore, the GJI is a multipurpose index that includes a specific

Table 4.6   Indicators proposed to calculate the Good Job Index

GJI Subindices	Indicators needed to calculate the index
(1) Equal Opportunities Index	Number of employed and unemployed men and women Working age population Average salary for men and women
(2) Salary Index	Average wage Minimum wage Real wage Cost of minimum basket Index of consumer prices
(3) Employment Index	Output per employed person (PPP level) Growth of output per employed person Inflation Education of adult population (several sub-indicators)
(4) Social Security Index	Percentage of workers covered by social security
(5) Index of Respect to Labour Rights	Rate of unionization Rate of collective negotiation (workers who are protected by collective contracts (working population) Number of ratified ILO agreements

Source: Global Policy Network website.

dimension of employment. Table 4.6 reproduces the indicators proposed to measure each of the dimensions of the index.

These indicators are merely indicative, as according to one of the creators of the index, 'we found that what is important is for each country or region to choose the appropriate and available indicators and use those consistently' (Avirgan 2009). For example, the index developed for El Salvador, among other country-specific changes, introduces a fourth indicator in the construction of the dimension of equality of opportunities related to the gender gap in social security coverage. In fact the specific indicators used can differ from country to country depending on the specific information available and the characteristics of the country (in different countries the same dimension can be better captured by a different indicator). These make country-to-country comparisons difficult, a problem of which the sponsors of the index are fully aware.

As can be seen, the index includes indicators of procedures (the dimension of respect for labour rights) and indicators of distribution (in the dimension of equal opportunities, but also in the salary dimension). For example, one of the indicators used in the elaboration of the GJI in

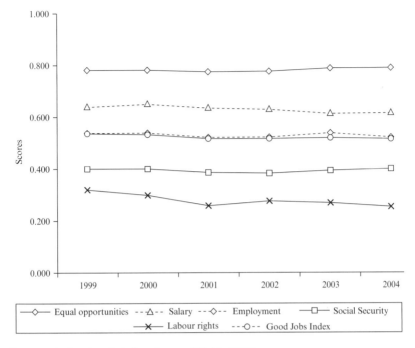

Source: Authors' analysis from Lara and Rubio (2006).

Figure 4.7 Good Jobs Index of El Salvador (1999–2004)

El Salvador, in the equal opportunities dimension, is the percentage of workers with wages over the poverty line.

The overall GJI is the simple average of the five dimensions; in order to generate the values of the different dimensions, the indicators used in each dimension are re-scaled using a procedure identical to the one described for the EJQI and the DWI-2.

The GJI was created as a tool to better understand the evolution of the labour market, on a regional or worldwide scale, in order to better understand the impact of the economic policies focused on job growth and employment stability as well as social security and respect of workers' rights. The GJI has proven its practicability, even in countries with lower economic and statistical development, in an interesting report on the evolution of job quality in El Salvador (1999–2004) (Avirgan *et al.* 2005). As it is shown in Figure 4.7, the combined analysis of the evolution of the GJI and the evolution of its five different dimensions provides a valuable information about the changes produced in the Salvadorian labour market in a decade of growth: stagnant job quality with improvements in the dimension of equal opportunities and drawbacks in the dimension of respects for labour laws.

4.1.7. Quality of Employment Indicators (QEI)

The QEI were proposed by Richard Brisbois, a Senior Researcher at the Canadian Policy Research Networks.[7] The QEI represent a good example of a theoretically-based system of indicators of job quality. It was developed in order to fill the informational gap in terms of job quality existing in Canada and computed from statistical sources provided by third parties (for example Statistics Canada).

Drawing from the model of the European Foundation for the Improvement of Living and Working Conditions, the QEI proposes five dimensions of job quality: health and well-being, skills development, career and employment security, reconciliation of working and non-working life and satisfaction with working conditions. These dimensions are measured with 11 variables, among which one can find both objective and subjective indicators (for instance, overall work satisfaction). The calculation is based on aggregated data, and hence it is not possible to determine the job quality enjoyed by specific groups of workers. The specific variables selected to measure job quality in each dimension are presented in Table 4.7. As can be seen, they make reference to both results and procedures but they do not include any measure of dispersion.

The author of the index, drawing on specific surveys on living conditions, computed the QEI for 11 OECD countries, making this information available at www.jobquality.ca. Most of the indicators are derived from the EWCS and the Ekos Rethinking North American Integration Survey (ERNAIS). Unfortunately, this information has not been updated recently. Some selected results of Brisbois' analysis are presented in Figure 4.8. He focuses on a group of developed countries with, according to general perception, quite different labour markets (Canada, USA, Sweden, Spain and Germany). As can be seen, the indicators are not – in general – redundant. We can see that a country like Sweden presents overall good scores, but it is far from leading on all the dimensions considered.

4.1.8. Indicators of Job Quality (IJQ)

The Indicators of Job Quality (IJQ) are produced by Andrew Jackson and Pradeep Kumar (Jackson and Kumar 1998), two Canadian economists linked to the major trade union in that country, the Canadian Labour Congress. Their proposal comprises a set of indicators referring to seven

Table 4.7   Dimensions and variables comprised by the QEI

Dimensions	Indicators
(1) Health and well-being	Work continuously at rapid rate
	Workers' health or safety is at risk
(2) Skills development	Skills match
	Received training
	Work with computers
(3) Career and employment security	Incidence of involuntary part-time employment
	Incidence of temporary employment
(4) Reconciliation of working and non-working life	Annual hours worked
	Incidence of long hours worked
	Work–life balance (*'how well do your work hours allow you to balance work and family or social commitments'*?)
(5) Satisfaction with working conditions	Overall self-reported satisfaction with working conditions

Source: Authors' elaboration from Brisbois (2003).

dimensions: pay, benefits, satisfaction with hours of work, work schedules, job security, physical well-being at work, and the human/social/work environment. In total 27 variables cover different objective and subjective areas in order to measure job quality (Table 4.8). It should be mentioned that a certain number of indicators cannot be illustrated with data because of partial or total lack of information for Canada (for example, work autonomy, paid vacation or reported satisfaction with work hours). The concept of job quality in IJQ is worker-oriented, and it comprises mainly static variables, related to both procedures and results. The set of indices are computed from aggregated data and include a wage polarization measure and the percentage of non-low-paid workers, so distribution is also taken into account into the IJQ. All the sub-indices are computed for men and women separately. The data comes from two Canadian surveys: the General Social Survey (GSS) and the Survey of Work Arrangements (SWA) and, to our knowledge, the IJQ is not published with any particular periodicity.

Although the IJQ is a system of indicators, each dimension is aggregated into an index obtained by simply averaging the scores of the variables considered in each category. The purpose of the IJQ is basically to assess the evolution of job quality in Canada over time, so the authors express the values for all variables with respect to a base year, when all variables take the value 100. An outline of this process is shown by Figure 4.9. There are

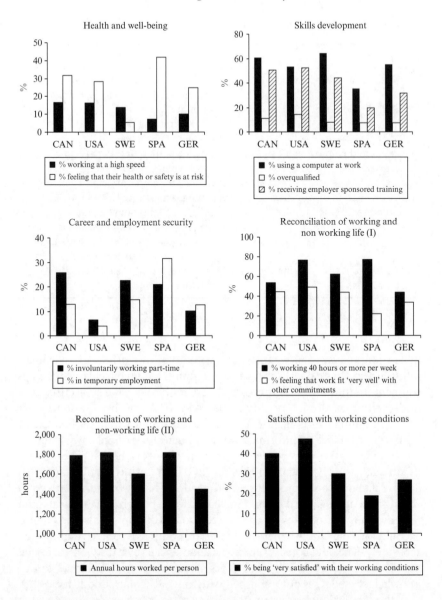

Source: Authors' analysis from www.jobquality.ca.

Figure 4.8   QEI for selected OECD countries around 2000

Table 4.8   Dimensions and indicators considered in the IJQ

Dimensions	Indicators
(1) Pay	Real median weekly earnings
	Not low paid
	Polarization (Ratio of average earnings of the
	10th decile to average earnings of the 1st decile)
(2) Social benefits	Pension plan coverage
	Other benefits
(3) Satisfaction with	Reported satisfaction
hours of work	Voluntary part-time as % part-time
	'Standard' work week
(4) Work schedules	Shift schedules
	Unsocial hours
	Flexitime
	Paid vacation
(5) Job security	Permanent lay-off rate
	Temporary lay-off rate
	Probability of new job lasting more than six months
	Permanent versus temporary jobs
	Stress from threat of lay-off
(6) Physical well-being	Incidence of occupational injuries
	Exposure to/damage from workplace health hazards
(7) Human/social/work	Union density
environment	Grievance procedure
	Access to training
	Promotion in jobs
	Work satisfaction
	Work autonomy/participation
	Demands of work
	Social support
	Harassment/discrimination

Source: Authors' elaboration from Jackson and Kumar (1998).

many dimensions for which information is scant, but the authors illustrate the application of the index using Canadian data. Figure 4.10 reproduces the evolution of male job quality during the period 1981–1993 and suggests a reduction in most dimensions of job quality among men during the period analysed.

As the index is designed for Canada and only applied to this country, not many points can be made from a comparative perspective. Several shortcomings of IJQ should be mentioned, especially three: first, the aggregate

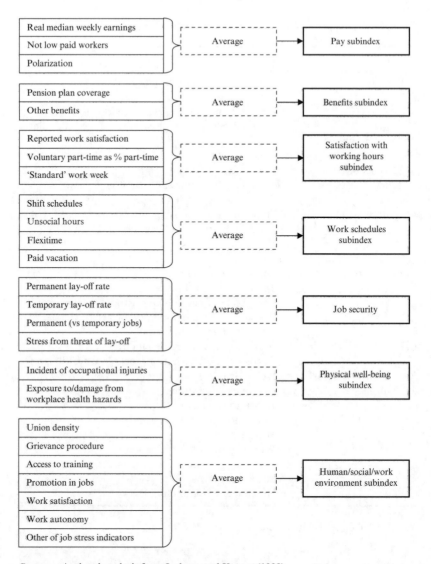

Source: Authors' analysis from Jackson and Kumar (1998).

Figure 4.9 Indicators of Job Quality

character of the indicators (it is not possible to calculate job quality for subgroups beyond the gender disaggregated index included in the publications); second, no variable related to work intensity is considered; last, the inclusion of job satisfaction as one of the sub-indices has several problems

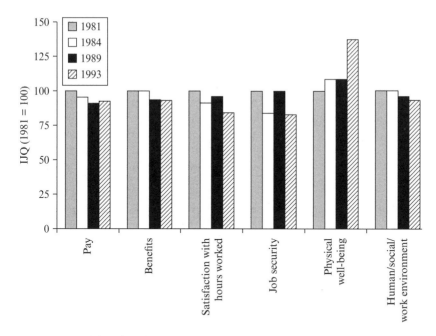

Source: Authors' analysis from Jackson and Kumar (1998).

Figure 4.10 Job quality in Canada according to the IJQ

discussed in Chapter 2 (including job satisfaction and its determinants involves an unnecessary double counting, and introduces elements which are alien to the actual quality of jobs, such as expectations or adaptability).

4.1.9. Subjective Quality of Working Life Index

The Subjective Quality of Working Life Index (SQWLI) is a product of a joint project, funded by the Czech Ministry of Labour and Social Affairs, of the Czech Occupational Safety Research Institute, the Institute of Sociology of Czech Academy of Sciences and the University of Economics in Prague (Vinopal 2009). Its aim is to propose a suitable instrument for measuring the quality of working life in population surveys. Particularly, the authors try to cover the maximum number of dimensions of job quality from a subjective point of view and weigh each attribute according to the relevance given to it by each worker. Therefore, the SQWLI is a totally subjective indicator. Six dimensions – all of them centred on the job, strictly speaking – are considered in the indicator: remuneration, self-realization, relationships, time, conditions and security. The provisional

Measuring more than money

Table 4.9.   Dimensions and indicators of SQWLI

Dimensions	Indicators
(1) Remuneration	Salary
	Remuneration fairness
	Non-financial benefits
(2) Social-realization	Self-activity
	On-the-job training
	Interestingness
(3) Relationships	With co-workers
	With higher-ups
	Bullying
(4) Time	Working time flexibility
	Time demands
	Harmonization
(5) Conditions	Equipment
	Tidiness
	Safety
(6) Security	Type of contract
	Post stability
	Chances of employment

Source: Authors' construction from Vinopal (2009).

final version of the SQWLI, really a pilot project, includes 18 variables aiming to characterize the six dimensions (Table 4.9).

The aggregation procedure is relatively simple. The researchers obtain two types of information from an ad hoc survey carried out in the Czech Republic: first, the importance given by each worker to each variable included in the index (from 1, *definitely unimportant attribute*, to 6, *definitely important job characteristic*); second, the individual worker's satisfaction with each of the attributes (using a similar scale from −3, *very dissatisfied*, to 3, *very satisfied with an attribute*). Each dimension of satisfaction is weighted by the relevance given to each area of job quality and then each dimension is normalized to 1 (Figure 4.11).[8] The index is clearly worker-oriented, both offering a menu of indicators for several dimensions and allowing the reader to have an overall perspective through the aggregate SQWLI. The variables used have a static nature and make reference to both procedures and results. In contrast with most indices, this one can be computed at the individual level.

As the SQWLI is an indicator in its first stages of development, the authors have only applied it to different groups of workers in the Czech

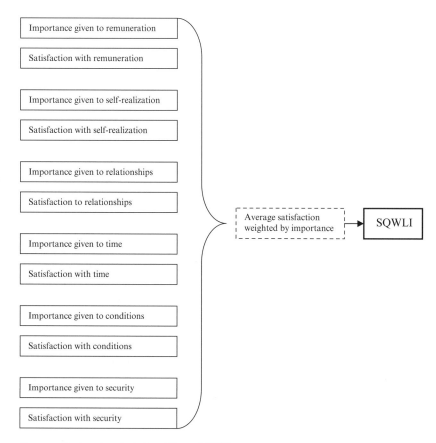

Source: Authors' analysis from Vinopal (2009).

Figure 4.11   Construction of the SQWLI

Republic and cross-country comparisons are not possible. The SQWLI is a valuable effort to measure subjective job quality, with all the advantages and disadvantages of indicators based on self-reported satisfaction. The dimensions considered by this indicator are all clearly pertinent for job quality (contrary to many other indicators reviewed elsewhere which incorporate some unrelated issues).

4.1.10.   DGB Good Work Index

This indicator is a proposal of the major umbrella organization of trade unions in Germany, the Confederation of German Trade Unions

(Deutscher Gewerkschaftsbund, DGB). The main goal of the DGB Good Work index (DGBI) is the measurement of quality of work from the employees' point of view. It has been calculated yearly since 2007 based on the information obtained by an ad hoc survey of German employees. Each wave contains roughly 6000 interviews. Some remarks on methodology and technical issues can be found in Mussmann (2009).

The DGBI comprises three broad dimensions: resources, load and stress, and job security and income. The resources dimension includes ten sub-dimensions: skill, training and personnel development, creativity, promotion opportunities, possibilities of influencing/shaping work, flow of information/communication, management quality, corporate culture, cooperation/social climate, meaningful work and working time. The second dimension (load and stress) is captured by three items: work intensity, emotional requirements/demands and physical requirements/demands. Finally, job quality linked to job security and income is ana-lysed using job security and future prospects and income. In turn, each sub-dimension is measured using a set of questions referred to different indicators of quality of work (each sub-dimension includes between one and three questions). The particular variables on which the DGBI is based are presented in Table 4.10.

The structure of all variables is similar, and quite simple: workers are asked about how often a condition occurs in the workplace (never, seldom, often, or always) and then the follow-up question is whether and to what extent the condition (e.g. working in noisy surroundings) is felt to be a burden by the person concerned. Similarly, in what are known in the survey as work-related resources (e.g. influence over job design), the first question is about their degree of availability (between to a great extent and not at all) and after that the interviewees are asked whether a lack of resources (e.g. little or no possibility of influence) is perceived as a burden. Then, on the basis of the responses, each individual is given a score between 0 and 100.

The process of aggregation, though not excessively sophisticated, is transparent: first, responses are averaged by sub-dimensions, obtaining an (average) score for each one. Then, all sub-dimensions within one of the three broad categories are averaged again. This yields three partial indices that are once again averaged in order to obtain the DGBI. This process of aggregation is sketched by Figure 4.12.

The DGBI is definitely worker-oriented. Though no indicator of overall job satisfaction is included, the nature of most variables is eminently sub-jective, though the degree of subjectivity varies greatly. Some questions are clearly factual (for instance, the occurrence of noise in the workplace) while others are purely evaluative. The DGBI comprises both procedure

Table 4.10   Dimensions and variables considered in the DGBI

Dimensions	Sub-dimensions		Variables
Resources	(1)	Skill training and personnel development	Opportunities to acquire skills Work environment conductive to learning
	(2)	Creativity	Opportunities to contribute ideas
	(3)	Promotion opportunities	Prospects of in-house promotion
	(4)	Possibilities of influencing/ shaping work	Freedom to plan schedule one's own work A say in the volume of work A say in how working hours are spent
	(5)	Flow of information/ communication	Access to all essential information Clear requirements
	(6)	Management quality	Appreciation/recognition shown by supervisors Work well planned by superiors Value placed on further training/HR development
	(7)	Corporate culture	Encouragement to cooperate Competent/appropriate management
	(8)	Cooperation/social climate	Help/support from the colleagues
	(9)	Meaningful work	Work valuable to society
	(10)	Working time	Freedom take overtime off when it suits Working hours reliably planned Personal needs considered in planning
Load and stress	(11)	Work intensity	Unwanted interruptions Rushed work/time pressure Job quality suffers from intense pace
	(12)	Emotional requirements/ demands	Need to hide feelings Condescending/undignified treatment
	(13)	Physical requirements/ demands	Heavy physical labour Physically monotonous labour Noise, loud environment
Job security and income	(14)	Job security and future prospects	Fears for occupation future
	(15)	Income	Income and performance well matched Enough income Enough pension from employment

Source: Authors' elaboration from Mussmann (2009).

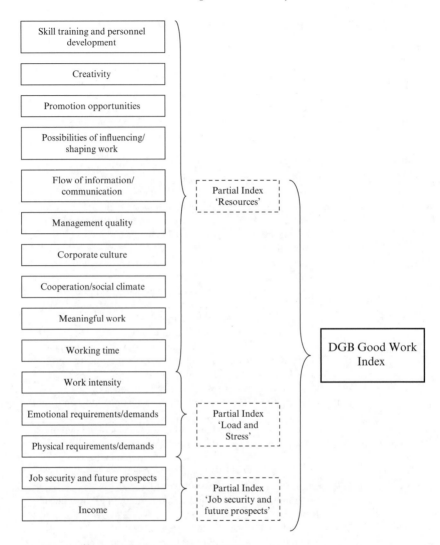

Source: Authors' analysis from Mussmann (2009).

Figure 4.12 Aggregation procedure of the DGB Good Work Index

and results variables and yields both an aggregate index and a system of indicators. In addition, one can look at any of the 31 variables included and determine the level of job quality in a particular area. All variables are measured using a similar scale, facilitating the interpretation of results. Another important strength of the index – an advantage shared by few of the indicators analysed here in this chapter – is the possibility of computing it at worker level, which allows the authors to differentiate the scores by gender, activity, occupation, unionization status and nationality, among others.

On the side of the disadvantages, apart from the potential problems of using subjective indicators for all the items (for example, a sub-dimension like wage is measured using qualitative questions), one can mention the particular set of weights adopted by the authors of the indicator: they select 31 variables which are grouped by theoretical criteria but, when aggregating, all sub-dimensions have equal influence on the final result of the index. For example, it is debatable why emotional requirements are as important as working time or earnings, and not more or less. This feature may be practical and transparent, but it is theoretically hard to justify and, thus, is open to criticism. A final difficulty has to do with the measurement of each variable. Particularly, workers' responses to each question are assigned values of 0, 16, 34, 50, 67, 83 and 100 according to the degree of agreement or disagreement with both the presence and the influence of each item considered. In other words, the questions – and, hence, the answers – are categorical and are transformed into a continuous variable according to the procedure explained above. An illustration of the application of the DGBI can be found in Figure 4.13, which shows the 2008 results for Germany.

The DGBI represents a well-delimited and worker-oriented index. It makes reference to most of the dimensions discussed in Chapters 2 and 3 and it can be calculated on an individual worker basis. Apart from the issue associated to the absence of any discussion on the way in which each dimension might substitute or complement the others – a common failure of all the measures reviewed here, the main (minor) shortcomings of the index are related to the subjectivity of the variables, the (unsolved) problem of the aggregation procedure and, finally, the need of a very specific survey to account for all the dimensions.

4.1.11. The Austrian Work Climate Index

The Work Climate Index (WCI) is an Austrian composite index of job quality commissioned by the Austrian Chamber of Labour of Upper Austria (Arbeiterkammer Oberösterreich), an organization representing Labour interests at the state level, and developed by the Institute for Empirical Social Research (IFES) and the Institute for Social Research and Analysis (SORA). It was conceived and first developed in 1995/1997 and has been continuously updated thereafter, every six months. The index has gained considerable public attention in Austria, where the quarterly press conferences with the new results often reach national news.

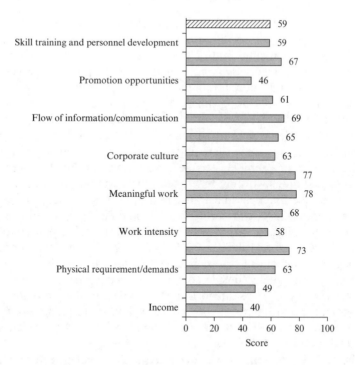

Source: Authors' analysis from Mussmann (2009).

Figure 4.13 Work quality according to the DGBI in Germany in 2008

The stated goal of the WCI is to track the changes in work satisfaction among Austrian employees; in the words of its authors, it means an attempt to register 'the consequences economic change has on the subjective experience and the perception of employed persons' (Höfinger and Michenthaler 1998, p. 1). However, despite this alleged goal, the WCI includes 'objective' dimensions (collected through workers' answers to a survey) such as the impact of work on health or absenteeism, and, hence, it can be considered an index of job quality, even if it has a strongly subjective orientation.

The index has four components, with 16 sub-dimensions and 25 basic indicators. The four higher-level dimensions are society, company, job and expectations. Although the index is strictly based on workers' responses to a dedicated survey module, those responses are not entirely restricted to work and employment, but include the perceptions of aspects related to the overall society and the company where he or she works. The dimension 'society' includes indicators of perception of the economic situation, the respondent's satisfaction with his/her social position and employee rights. The dimension 'company' includes indicators of the perception of the economic future of the respondent's company and satisfaction with the company's image, leadership and social security benefits. The dimension 'job', obviously the one most directly linked to the concept of job quality of this study, includes several indicators on job satisfaction (in general, with income, social relations, working hours and work–life balance), as well as the reported levels of stress, time pressure, loneliness and isolation, poor health conditions, accident risks and others. The fourth one, expectations, includes indicators on satisfaction with career opportunities, opportunities for further education and job market outlook.

The Austrian WCI uses as data source a dedicated module within an omnibus quarterly survey. This has many advantages: the variables used in the index were constructed *ex profeso* for this purpose, rather than being 'recycled' from pre-existing surveys (constructed with different aims), as is the case in most other indices; there is higher consistency in the data, since all the information comes from a single source; and because the index is constructed with individual data, it can be broken down as much as statistical concerns allow (the Austrian WCI has been used for regional breakdowns, for specific sectors or occupations, even for specific companies; for a few examples see Michenthaler 2006). All indicators are standardized and added with equal weights within each dimension (or sub-component), which are finally weighted unequally to the overall index (each dimension receives 20 per cent except for 'job' which receives 40 per cent). As in most other indices, there is no clear justification of the weighting used.

It is difficult to do an overall evaluation of the WCI, because its aims are slightly different to those of the other indices (it is less concerned with job quality as such than with job satisfaction) and its scope is national rather than European (for instance, there is not much documentation in English). Our impression is that the justification of the structure and components of the index is somewhat weak, without a solid theoretical foundation. An apparent problem of the WCI, shared with some other measures reviewed here, is the fact that it mixes variables that are very sensitive to the short-term economic situation (especially those within the dimensions 'society' and 'expectations') with variables that change very slowly and only in the long term (especially those in the 'job' dimension), which means that the former dominate almost completely the evolution of the index, as the authors themselves recognize (Preinfalk *et al.* 2006). This is problematic because it makes the WCI more an index of economic sentiment than an index of job quality or job satisfaction. Figure 4.14, taken from Michenthaler (2006), shows the changes in the index from 1997 to 2006.[9]

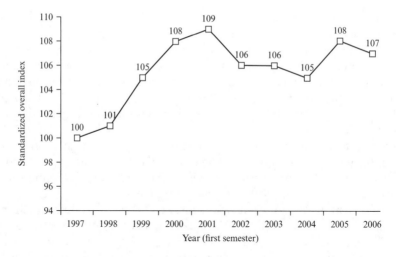

Source: Adapted from Michenthaler (2006, p. 11).

Figure 4.14   The Austrian Work Climate Index (1997–2006)

4.1.12.   Indicator of Quality of the Labour Market

The Indicator of Quality of the Labour Market (IQL) has been produced by the CIREM and the Spanish trade union UGT and published in the Socioeconomic Yearbook of the UGT of Catalonia since 2000.[10] The IQL is a synthetic indicator aiming to compare the quality of the labour market in Catalonia with other Spanish and (twelve) European regions. According to their proponents, the guiding principles of the IQL are simplicity, rigour and equilibrium between the goal of offering a complete view of the labour market and the danger of being over-exhaustive. With those aims the researchers were conscious of the need to restrict the number of indicators used in the construction of the IQT; therefore, they used only indicators that had proven their capacity in providing valuable information about the labour market and selected indicators with the double aim of allowing both comparisons of a country or region over time and comparisons across regions. It is computed from data from the National Statistics Institute (NSI) and the Ministry of Labour and Immigration (MLI).

   The IQL is composed by eight different dimensions plus a transversal dimension of equality between men and women, and 34 indicators. Table 4.11 reproduces the dimensions and indicator considered in the IQL national and regional versions.

Table 4.11   Dimensions and indicators considered in the IQL (for the European comparison)

Dimension	Indicators
(1) Access to labour	Employment rate (15–64 years old) (%)
	Full-time equivalent employment rate (15–64 years old) (%)
	Unemployment rate (15–64 years old) (%)
	Potential activity rate (%) (inactive persons that would like to work)
(2) Wage and income	Annual wage (PPP) (,000)
	GDP per capita (PPP) (,000)
	Rate of change of real hourly wage
	Agreed wage increase (deflated by the CPI)
	% for employees with wage under the 60% of median wage
	Wage dispersion index (Q3/Q1)
(3) Job security	Temporal employment rate
	Annual turnover rate
	Quarterly turnover rate
(4) Health and safety at work	Fatal accidents at work per 100 000 workers
	Serious accidents at work per 100 000 workers
	Standardized index of accidents at work per 100 000 workers
(5) Work–life balance	Weekly working hours
	Non-split working day
	Unsocial hours
	Overtime
	Time spent commuting to work
	Involuntary part-time work
	Impact of mother/fatherhood on employment
(6) Labour insertion of groups with problems	Youth unemployment rate
	Long term unemployment rate
	Immigrants unemployment rate
	Unemployment rate of handicapped population
(7) Work satisfaction	% of workers not satisfied with their job
	Match between education and work
	Access to training
	% of workers underemployed in terms of skills
	Unskilled labour
(8) Social Protection	Minimum wage PPA
	'generosity' of unemployment benefits in the initial phase of unemployment
	'generosity' of unemployment benefits in the long run
	% of unemployed receiving unemployment benefits
	Unemployed workers receiving training
	Risk of poverty rate

Source: Caprile and Potrony (2006)

The first thing to highlight in our review of the IQL is the fact that its scope is not at all confined to job quality: in fact, the aim of this indicator is rather to measure the quality of labour markets (even if the term market is missing from the IQL acronym). Obviously, the quality of jobs of a given labour market is an important element of the quality of such labour market, but there are other elements not linked to job quality but important when measuring the quality of the labour market. For example, the access to employment (dimension 1) is not really an element of job quality, but an indicator of the functioning of the labour market. The same can be said in relation to dimension 6, dealing with the problems of specific groups such as young workers, immigrants or handicapped in the labour market. Another example is the dimension of social protection, which actually refers mostly to people who are out of work. Altogether around two thirds of the variables considered in the IQL are directly related with job quality, while the other third are related with the labour market, the economy (GDP per capita), social protection external to the employment relationship or other areas clearly unrelated with a worker-centred concept of job quality (commuting time).

The IQL is an aggregate index that permits the comparison of countries or regions for the values obtained in the different dimensions considered as well as the aggregate value of quality of the labour market. The method used in the construction of the aggregate index is the following: (1) each indicator is standardized by the following procedure: $(IIc - IIa)/\sigma$, where IIc is index I of country c, IIa is the average value of index I of the countries/regions of the sample and σ is the standard deviation of the index. This process of standardization permits the interpretation of a value over 0 in terms of a higher value than the average, making it possible at the same time to aggregate variables with different units of measurement; (2) the value of each dimension (the simple arithmetic average of its sub-components) is transformed into a single index of quality of the labour market, the IQL, by means of a weighted average with the following weighting factors: 25 per cent for the first dimension (access to labour market), 15 per cent for dimensions 2–4 (wage, security and health and safety), 10 per cent for dimensions 5–7 (work–life balance, labour insertion of specific groups and satisfaction), and 5 per cent for social protection. Unfortunately no rationale is offered for this specific weighting scheme. To address the gender aspect of job quality, the standardized values of women and men are presented separately. Figure 4.15 reproduces the ranking and value of the IQL of Spanish Regions in 2007.

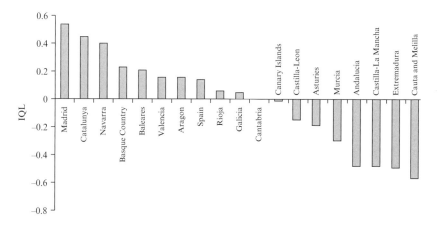

Source: Authors' analysis from Toharia *et al.* (2008).

Figure 4.15 Ranking of Spanish Regions according to the IQL in 2007

4.1.13. Quality of Work in Flanders (QWF)

This set of indicators of job quality is produced by the Flanders Social and Economic Council. The construction of these indicators was the central piece of a research project carried out in the Flemish part of Belgium. The study comprised the period 2004–2007 and it is organized around an ad hoc survey carried out among Flemish employees and self-employed workers. It is a system of indicators, not providing any aggregate index. It includes two broad groups of variables: risk indicators and workability indicators. Risk indicators include reported worker's workload, emotional load, skill variety, autonomy, social support and physical working conditions. The workability dimension comprises stress at work, well-being at work, learning opportunities and work–family balance (see Figure 4.16). All variables are evaluated by asking workers how problematic they find certain features (for example, emotional load). The available responses are 'not problematic', 'problematic' and 'acutely problematic'.

Though, in principle, all variables can be considered objective, the particular method of collecting the information make the QWF indicators quite close to subjective measures of job quality. Aggregation is achieved by simply counting the number of dimensions where a worker reports a problematic situation. An important limitation of the index is the exclusion of any variables related to remuneration, something which could be particularly problematic if compensating wage differentials (at least partially) exist. Aggregation is not sophisticated and has no obvious

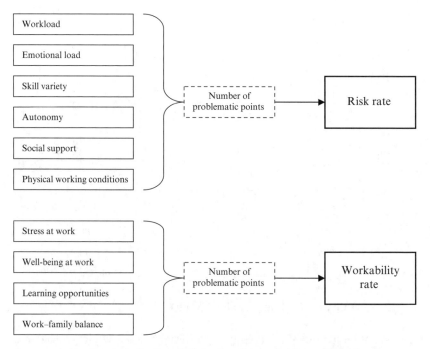

Source: Authors' analysis from Flanders Social and Economic Council (2009).

Figure 4.16 Construction procedure of the Quality of Work in Flanders

theoretical foundation, but at least it is transparent. The index is only applied to Flanders, allowing the researcher and the general public to assess the evolution of some key variables of well-being at work (see an example in Figure 4.17).

4.1.14. Tangian's Composite Indicator of Working Conditions

In several academic papers, Andranik Tangian (researcher in the Hans Böckler Foundation in Germany) presents a composite indicator of working conditions based entirely on the European Working Conditions Survey (Tangian 2005 and 2007). As such, Tangian's proposal can be interpreted as a personal application of the data of the survey to the construction of an index of job quality. The aim of Tangian's composite indicator is explicitly to contribute to EU policy monitoring and evaluation: the papers are an attempt to bring the EWCS one step further into policy evaluation by adding all the information into a single number which allows for 'worse-better' judgments (Tangian 2005, p. 9).

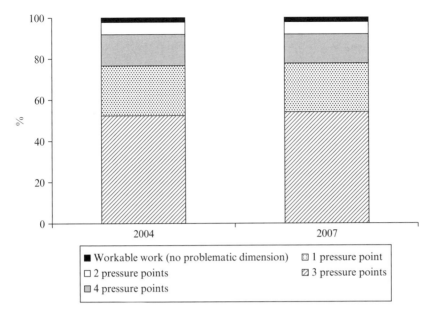

Source: Authors' analysis from Flanders Social and Economic Council (2009).

Figure 4.17 *The evolution of workability rate in Flanders according to the QWF indicators (2004–2007)*

Assuming that the questionnaire of the EWCS itself reflects a model of job quality, the author does not develop any new model. He just uses nearly all of the questions, 109 items in total (excluding those that are obviously not indicators of job quality in any way, such as socio-demographic information), grouping them in ten dimensions and constructing an aggregated index. The dimensions are: physical work environment (10 variables), health (24 variables), time factors (8 variables), stressing factors (15 variables), independence (8 variables), collectivity (3 variables), social environment (22 variables), career prospects-training (2 variables), work–life balance (10 variables) and subjective evaluations (7 questions).

Although these ten dimensions are little more than headings for the questionnaire, the fact that they are all equally weighted but are based on different numbers of items introduces a clear arbitrary element in the construction of the index. For instance, each of the three variables that constitute the dimension 'collectivity' have much more influence in the final score than any of the 22 variables that constitute the dimension social environment; but why is 'getting assistance from colleagues' so much more important than the 'ability to discuss working conditions with superiors'? The inclusion of the variables in the different dimensions is also often unclear: for instance, it is not obvious why the 'ability to discuss working conditions with superiors' is within the dimension of social environment, 90% of which is composed by questions on violence and harassment, rather than within the dimension 'collectivity', which includes three variables all related to work organization at the level of the individual worker ('getting assistance from colleagues', 'rotating tasks with colleagues' and 'working in a team').

The main problem with this composite indicator is that it relies too much on the EWCS questionnaire, assuming that the structure of the questionnaire itself reflects a model of job quality (Tangian 2005, p. 16), which is not really the case. As discussed earlier, even if the EWCS is loosely based on a model of job quality, the inclusion or not of different items, the importance assigned to the different aspects of job quality and so on, are not the systematic result of any theoretical model. The EWCS questionnaire was constructed by a process of political and scientific consultation, and there are several different reasons why specific items can be included or not: in some cases, they were included because it was considered important to cover those areas for policy purposes, in other cases for scientific purposes, in other cases simply to keep consistence with time trends or for other reasons. For instance, it is common practice in surveys such as this (and the EWCS is no exception) to include relatively redundant questions in order to double-check the validity of responses associated to some complicated items: following the approach of Tangian, those areas would receive double weighting.

Nevertheless, although Tangian's approach is relatively weak in its theoretical grounding (in the construction and justification of the model), it is technically sophisticated, discussing with great detail the statistical methodology followed for constructing the index as well as some potential alternatives and their implications. Every methodological decision is well explained and documented in extensive annexes to the papers.

In order to illustrate Tangian's approach, Figure 4.18 shows the overall scores of individual countries on his composite index. It is important to note that, with a few small differences, the rankings are quite similar to those of other indices, for instance the EJQI or the composite indicator presented in the 2008 *Employment in Europe* report. Northern European countries are at the top and Southern European countries at the bottom, with Continental Europe in the middle. The UK comes slightly lower than in other indicators and Germany slightly higher, but this may be partly due to the fact that the relative position of those two countries seemed to change relatively quickly between 2000 and 2005.

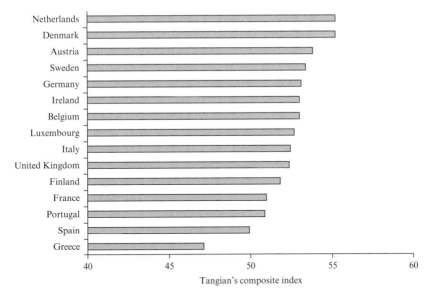

Source: Tangian (2005, p. 479).

Figure 4.18   Tangian's composite index, overall scores by country

4.1.15.   Ritter and Anker's Good and Bad Jobs Index (GBJI)

Joseph A. Ritter and Richard Anker (2002), though working as research-ers at the ILO, have developed an index of job quality not based on the concept of decent work, but on subjective indicators of work satisfaction. They use data from the 2001 ILO People's Security Surveys (IPSS), which allows derivation of scores at the individual level and avoids the inclusion of ad hoc dimensions linked to the distribution of an attribute (like gender gaps), in contrast with other measures proposed by the ILO staff. Their indicator is computed entirely from the responses of workers to a specific survey, so it is very different from the decent work indices reviewed above. Six dimensions related with both results and procedures are considered: labour income, social benefits, interest of the job, autonomy at work, opportunities of improving skills and opportunities of advancement. Workers report their satisfaction in each dimension, from 1 to 5. The job quality index is computed simply by adding the scores of all dimensions, so all of them receive the same weight in the index. Therefore, the index proposed by Ritter and Anker is always between 6 and 30.

The index is applied to five middle-income countries (Argentina,

Table 4.12   Average job satisfaction in selected middle-income countries according to the GBJI

	Labour income	Social benefits	Interesting job	Autonomy	Opportunities of improving skills	Opportunities of advancement	Total job satisfaction
Argentina	2.9	2.9	3.6	3.5	3.1	2.9	18.8
Brazil	2.8	2.8	3.7	3.4	3.2	2.8	18.6
Chile	2.7	3.0	3.7	3.6	3.3	3.2	19.8
Hungary	2.6	2.3	3.8	3.7	2.9	2.7	18.0
Ukraine	2.5	2.5	3.4	3.1	3.1	2.8	17.4

Source: Authors' construction from Ritter and Anker (2002).

Brazil, Chile, Hungary and Ukraine) and, according to the authors, total satisfaction tends to be highly correlated with some objective indicators of job quality (for example, income, safety at work and unionization). The indicator, though mainly focused on job attributes, is multi-purpose, since it comprises indicators such as social benefits, with the problems described in detail above. The results from the application of the index (Table 4.12) reveal very small differences between countries, showing once more the problems of using workers' satisfaction as an indicator of job quality.[11]

4.1.16.   Duncan Gallie's Employment Regimes and the Quality of Work

Duncan Gallie (2007), at Oxford University, suggests a set of dimensions to be evaluated in order to assess the evolution of job quality across countries and over time. His proposal comprises the five following dimensions: skill level, degree of task discretion or autonomy, opportunities for skill development, job security and the extent to which jobs are compatible with work–family balance. Furthermore, Gallie also recommends taking into account the issue of work pressure in the context of work–family conflict and that of pay in the context of changing skill profiles. These worker-oriented dimensions are not aggregated, so what he proposes is in fact a system of indicators. At least in principle, the goal is to base the measurement of job quality on objective indicators, explicitly ruling out subjective measures such as job satisfaction. Gallie's proposal is more a set of basic guidelines to evaluate job quality than a system of indicators in itself.

4.1.17. Tilly's Assessment of Job Quality

Chris Tilly (1996), from the Department of Policy and Planning at the University of Massachusetts, proposes seven dimensions in order to assess the evolution of job quality in the United States: wages, fringe benefits, due process in discipline (protection from arbitrary disciplinary action), hours flexibility, permanence, upward mobility and control over the work process. The author relies on both quantitative and qualitative secondary sources in order to evaluate the evolution of job quality in these seven dimensions. This system of indicators is clearly worker-oriented, including not only static measures of job quality but also a dynamic one (upward mobility, discussed on the basis of longitudinal studies). The author claims that a substantial deterioration of job quality is observed in the United States during the last few decades. Apart from the difficulties of applying the index to European countries (especially regarding the problems behind the inclusion of fringe benefits, see section 3.2), the main shortcoming of this index is that it derives entirely from the analysis of secondary data (so that no comparisons between population subgroups can be carried out).

4.1.18. Green's Capabilities Approach

The proposal of Francis Green (2006), Professor of Economics at the University of Kent, starts by taking a step backward and rethinking the concept of job quality from a theoretical perspective. Green's concept of job quality draws from the well-known Amartya Sen's approach to freedom, based on the concept of capabilities (Sen 2000). Sen highlights the importance of persons' capabilities, understood as the ability to be or do what people want to be or do. For example, according to this approach, doing a given activity is considered inferior to choosing and doing such activity. Applying this approach to job quality, Green suggests to evaluate the capabilities that are afforded to workers in the job to achieve well-being (dependent on the set of wages and other reward conditions) and achieve agency goals (the extent to which the job enables the individual to pursue personal goals). The author does not propose an explicit and concrete system of measuring job quality, but suggests six dimensions that should be included when carrying out such a task:

- Skills (because of their intrinsic value and their utilization, as it allows people to address a wider range of activities and they are a means for achieving self-fulfilment).
- Work effort (as long as it is linked to stress and other health-related issues).

- Personal discretion of workers over their job tasks and other forms of participation in workplace decisions.
- Pay (including indicators of fairness of remuneration, which is mostly a subjective measure).
- Risks and security (both in terms of health safety and job stability).
- Job satisfaction and indicators of affective well-being at work.

In principle, Green's proposal does not aim to construct an aggregate index, but it is intended to be a system of indicators. This worker-oriented approach is complex and not very cohesive, since it includes both subjective and objective dimensions and both process and results variables.

In sum, Green's approach is more theoretically grounded than most of the other proposals discussed here. Although it does not attempt any kind of aggregation (and therefore, there are no straightforward conclusions from the comparative analysis), the range of issues covered is relatively wide and balanced. His approach is clearly worker-oriented, which is also an important advantage. On the downside, it leaves out some important areas of job quality (such as working time, for instance) and includes job satisfaction as a component of job quality.

4.1.19. Index of Characteristics Related to the Quality of Employment (ICQE)

This indicator is proposed by Kirsten Sehnbruch (2004), at the Center for Latin American Studies at the University of Berkeley. The ICQE starts recognizing the limitations of existing indicators of the *quantities* of employment (for example, unemployment rate) and presents a new job quality indicator again inspired on Sen's capabilities approach. Sehnbruch extensively discusses the wide scope afforded by the capabilities approach; however, for simplicity, the index is centred on the Chilean labour market and only five dimensions are included: income, social security coverage, contractual status, employment stability and professional training received. Each dimension only comprises a variable with three possible outcomes (0, 1 or 2 points). Then, the score of each dimension is added up for each individual and divided by five: all dimensions are equally weighted in the final index. Finally, four categories for job quality are created from the average score (very low, low, medium and high-quality job). The process of aggregation is briefly summarized by Figure 4.19. The author illustrates the application of the index using an ad hoc survey of Santiago de Chile (the capital of the country), whose main results are reproduced in Figure 4.20.

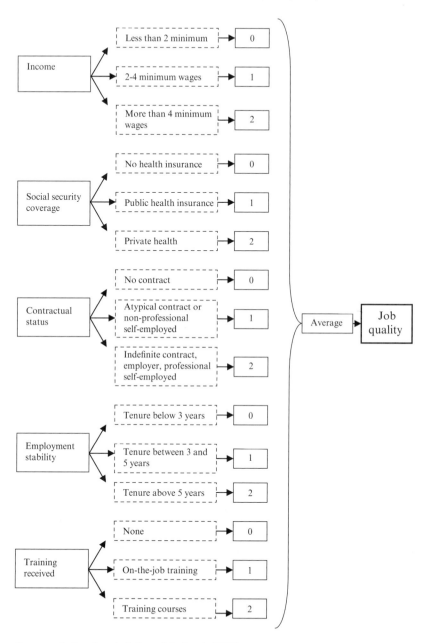

Source: Authors' analysis from Sehnbruch (2004).

Figure 4.19 Construction procedure of the ICQE

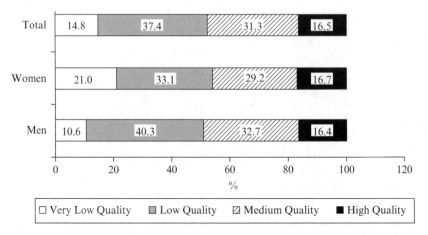

Source: Authors' analysis from Sehnbruch (2004).

Figure 4.20   Job quality in Santiago de Chile according to the ICQE

4.2.   COMPARATIVE SUMMARY AND CONCLUSIONS

In this chapter, we have reviewed over 20 recent proposals for measuring job quality, from international and institutional indicators to proposals made by individual academics. The main characteristics of these indicators are summarized by Tables 4.13 and 4.14, following the principles discussed in Chapters 2 and 3 of this book. Each proposal has its own strengths and weaknesses, which are summarized in Table 4.15.

We can draw several conclusions from this review. The main conclusion is that, despite the current availability of several indices of job quality, there is still a need at the EU level of a worker-oriented, individually-constructed and theoretically sound job quality indicator in order to measure, compare and monitor job quality in the different Member States, as required by the objectives of the European Employment Strategy. Some of the existing indicators are excellent, some others are not so good, but all of them have some shortcoming that makes it still necessary to devote resources to the development of a better index. In the following pages, we try to offer an overall perspective of the advantages and shortcomings of the measures reviewed in this chapter.

First, eight of the indices reviewed are not really (or not strictly) measures of job quality, as they comprise dimensions associated to other issues such as labour market access, a Gini index of disposable income, the illiteracy rate

Table 4.13 List of acronyms, complete names, sources and databases of the reviewed indices of job quality reviewed

Acronym	Complete name	Scope	Source	Databases
Laeken	Laeken indicators of job quality	European Union	European Commission (2008)	ECHP, ELFS, SILC
EJQI	The European Job Quality Index	European Union	Leschke, Watt and Finn (2008)	ELFS, EWCS, SILC. AMECO, ICTWSS
EWCS	European Working Conditions Survey	European Union	Parent-Thirion *et al.* (2007)	Itself a data source
GJI	Good Jobs Index	Middle-income and developing countries	Avirgan, Bivens and Gammage (2005)	ILO databases
DWI-1	Decent Work Index-1	Developed and developing countries	Ghai (2003)	ILO databases
DWI-2	Decent Work Index-2	Developed and developing countries	Bonnet, Figueiredo and Standing (2003)	ILO databases
DWI-3	Decent Work Index-3	Developed and developing countries	Anker *et al.* (2003)	ILO databases
DWI-4	Decent Work Index-4	Developed and developing countries	Bescond, Châtaignier and Mehran (2003)	ILO databases
QEI	Quality of Employment Indicators	Canada, US and Europe	Brisbois (2003)	EWCS, ERNAIS
IJQ	Indicators of Job Quality	Canada	Jackson and Kumar (1998)	GSS, SWA
SQWLI	Subjective Quality of Working Life Index	Czech Republic	Vinopal (2009)	Ad hoc survey
DGBI	DGB Good Work Index	Germany	Mussmann (2009)	Ad hoc survey
WCI	Austrian Work Climate Index	Austria	Preinfalk, Michenthaler and Wasserbacher (2006), Michenthaler (2006)	IFES omnibus survey (dedicated module)

Table 4.13 (continued)

Acronym	Complete name	Scope	Source	Databases
IQL	Indicators of Quality of the Labour Market	Spain	Caprile and Potrony (2006), Toharia, Caprile and Potrony (2008)	NSI, MLI
QWF	Quality of Work in Flanders	Flanders (Belgium)	Flanders Social and Economic Council (2009)	Ad hoc survey
Tangian	Tangian's proposal	European Union	Tangian (2007)	EWCS
GBJI	Good and Bad Jobs Index	Middle-income countries	Ritter and Anker (2002)	IPSS
ICQE	Index of the characteristics related to the quality of employment	Chile	Sehnbruch (2004)	Ad hoc survey

Notes: ECHP = European Community Household Panel; ELFS = European Labour Force Survey; SILC = Statistics on Income and Living Conditions; EWCS = European Working Conditions Survey; AMECO = Annual Macroeconomic Database of the European Commission; ERNAIS = Ekos Rethinking North American Integration Survey; GSS = General Social Survey; SWA = Survey of Work Arrangements; IFES = Institut für empirische Sozialforschung; NSI = National Statistics Institute; MLI = Ministry of Labour and Immigration; IPSS = ILO People's Security Surveys

Source: Authors' elaboration.

or standard macroeconomic indicators. This problem is especially evident in the case of the ILO's decent work indices and the Laeken indicators. On the other hand, the EJQI, the EWCS, the SQWLI, the QEI, the DGBI and the WCI and the individual academic proposals avoid this problem. In addition, most of the indices include some measure of social security, which is problematic when making cross-country comparisons because of the existence of different welfare regimes with very different roles for the private and the public sector (for a detailed discussion, see Chapter 3).

Second, some dimensions highlighted as important in the social sciences literature (see Chapter 2) are absent in many indicators; this particularly applies to work intensity, an omission largely conditioned by the absence of other sources of information apart from the EWCS, whose periodicity is not annual. Only those indices using this specific survey avoid this limitation – in our view, quite relevant. In addition, there are some important proposals

Table 4.14 Summary of the main indicators of job quality

Indicator	Type of indicator				No. of. . .		Type of variables						Individual data	Periodicity
	Multi-purpose	Worker-oriented	System	Aggregate	Dimensions	Variables	Subjective	Objective	Results	Procedures	Static	Dynamic		
Laeken	X		X		10	25		X	X	X	X	X	NO	Annual
EJQI		X	X	X	6	17	X	X	X	X	X		NO	Annual
EWCS		X	X		4	Many	X	X	X	X	X		YES	Every 5 years
GJI	X		X	X	5	16		X	X	X	X		NO	Single exercise
DWI-1	X		X	X	4	9		X	X	X	X		NO	Single exercise
DWI-2	X		X	X	7	67		X	X	X	X		NO	Single exercise
DWI-3	X		X		11	37		X	X	X	X		NO	Single exercise
DWI-4	X		X	X		8		X	X	X	X		NO	Single exercise
QEI		X	X		5	11	X	X	X	X	X		NO	Single exercise, with occasional updates

143

Table 4.14 (continued)

Indicator	Type of indicator				No. of...		Type of variables						Individual data	Periodicity
	Multi-purpose	Worker-oriented	System	Aggregate	Dimensions	Variables	Subjective	Objective	Results	Procedures	Static	Dynamic		
IJQ	X		X		7	27	X	X	X	X	X	X	NO	Single exercise
SQWLI		X	X	X	6	18	X		X	X	X		YES	Single exercise
DGBI		X	X	X	3	31	X	X	X	X	X		YES	Annual
WCI		X		X	4 (16)	25	X	X	X		X		YES	Semesterly
IQL	X		X	X	8	38		X	X	X	X	X	NO	Annual
QWF		X	X	X	2	10	X		X	X	X		YES	Every 3 years
Tangian		X	X	X	10	109	X	X	X	X	X		YES	Single exercise
GBJI		X	X	X	1	6	X		X		X	X	YES	Single exercise
ICQE		X	X	X	5	15		X	X	X	X		YES	Single exercise

Source: Authors' analysis.

144

Table 4.15   *Strengths and weaknesses of the main indicators of job quality*

Indicator	Strengths	Weaknesses
Laeken	Objective variables Inclusion of dynamic variables Comparability	Some dimensions are missing Multi-purpose No aggregation Unable to cover distributional issues
EJQI	Worker-oriented Comprehensiveness Objective variables Some discussion on weighting	Some weighting issues are discretional Unable to cover distributional issues
EWCS	Comparability Worker-oriented Most comprehensive set of indicators Objective variables Comparability Individual-based	No aggregation
GJI	Objective variables Comparability	Some dimensions are missing Multi-purpose Discretional weighting Unable to cover distributional issues
DWI-1	Objective variables Simplicity Comparability	Some dimensions are missing Multi-purpose Discretional weighting Unable to cover (most) distributional issues
DWI-2	Objective variables Comparability	Some dimensions are missing Multi-purpose Discretional weighting Unable to cover (most) distributional issues
DWI-3	Objective variables Comparability	Some dimensions are missing Multi-purpose No aggregation Unable to cover distributional issues
DWI-4	Objective variables Comparability	Some dimensions are missing Multi-purpose Discretional weighting Unable to cover distributional issues Striking ranking of countries

QEI	Worker-oriented
	Comparability
	Comprehensive
	  analysis of non-
	  wage job attributes
		Some dimensions are missing
		No aggregation/ discretional weighting
		Job satisfaction and objective variables
		  included at the same time
		Unable to cover (most) distributional issues

Table 4.15   (continued)

Indicator	Strengths	Weaknesses
IJQ	Comprehensiveness Inclusion of dynamic variables Comparability	Multi-purpose Job satisfaction and objective variables included at the same time Unable to cover (some) distributional issues
SQWLI	Worker-oriented Comprehensiveness Individual-based	Exclusively based on subjective indicators Some weighting issues are controversial Limited comparability (ad hoc survey)
DGBI	Worker-oriented Comprehensiveness Objective variables Individual-based	Discretional weighting Limited comparability (ad hoc survey)
WCI	Worker-oriented Comprehensiveness	Multi-purpose Discretional weighting Limited comparability (ad hoc survey) Unable to cover distributional issues
IQL	Comprehensiveness Comparability Inclusion of dynamic variables	Multi-purpose Job satisfaction and objective variables included at the same time Discretional weighting Unable to cover (most) distributional issues
QWF	Worker-oriented Individual-based	Some dimensions are missing No aggregation Job satisfaction and objective variables included at the same time Limited comparability (ad hoc survey)
Tangian	Worker-oriented Comprehensiveness Objective measures Individual-based Comparability	The foundations of its weighting procedure are wrong
GBJI	Worker-oriented Comparability Inclusion of dynamic variables	Some dimensions are missing Multi-purpose Discretional weighting Exclusively based on subjective indicators
ICQE	Worker-oriented Objective measures Individual-based	Some dimensions are missing Multi-purpose Limited comparability (ad hoc survey)

Source: Authors' elaboration.

– the Laeken indicators, the DWI-1, the QEI and the QWF – that make no reference to wages, which is clearly a serious omission.

Third, apart from those proposals only aiming at sketching some relevant dimensions, there are five indices that yield no aggregate measure of job quality, but only present a system of indicators. By proceeding in that way, they avoid setting – and justifying – weights for the different dimensions. However, as we have extensively discussed, this cannot be seen as a positive feature of an indicator, as it means the overall evaluation of the results can be quite ambiguous (the different dimensions can yield contradictory results), while each observer will anyway use their own value judgments to draw their own conclusions from the results of the different dimensions.

Fourth, the number of dimensions and measurement variables varies greatly across the indicators, from six variables (the GBJI) to more than a hundred (the EWCS and Tangian's proposal based on it). In most of the cases, aggregation is done on the basis of equal weights, usually without any explicit or theoretically sound explanation, though sometimes variables are carefully classified into different dimensions in advance. There are two exceptions to this rule: the SQWLI weights for the importance given by each worker to each attribute, and Tangian considers that the importance of a dimension depends on the number of questions included in the EWCS about it. The first approach, though quite original, has the potential problem of the lack of independence between real and desired job attributes, an issue that has been discussed in this book (see Chapter 2). The second one is likely to lead to wrong conclusions because (as argued in our review of this index) the number of questions is unrelated to the relevance of each dimension in a survey. Our review indicates that much more effort of justification and documentation is needed with regard to the aggregation of the different job attributes and dimensions.

Fifth, in this book we have commented in detail on the problems of using job satisfaction as a component of job quality. It should be mentioned that only two of the indices reviewed – the QWF and the SQWLI – are based solely on subjective variables. Another one (the DGBI) relies on subjective dimensions and workers' subjective evaluations of 'objective' job attributes (noise, working time, etc.). But several indices (for instance, the QWF and the SQWLI) include job satisfaction as elements of the index, within measures of the attributes of jobs, which has the problem of using input and output indicators simultaneously, thus counting certain attributes twice.

Sixth, many measures present methodological problems when trying to deal with distributional aspects. We have argued that, rather than including within the index measures of gaps within a specific area (which is not an aspect of job quality, but of its distribution), it is preferable to present separately the index scores for specific or problematic subgroups of the working population. This approach is more consistent with gender mainstreaming principles, as sex differences are retained throughout the index rather than assigned to a single dimension. In this respect, it is worth mentioning that some of the indices reviewed here (the EJQI, the IJL and the IQL) present their results disaggregated by gender as a matter of course. In fact, the best way to deal with this problem in an effective way is to design indicators that can be computed at individual level, that is, that allow comparing job quality for specific subgroups of workers. Eight of the indices reviewed in the previous subsection – the ECWS, the SQWLI, the DGBI, the WCI, the QWF, Tangian's proposal, the GBJI and the ICQE – have this desirable characteristic.

Seventh, periodicity, authorship and data sources are usually inter-related. Those indicators backed by institutions tend to be more regular than those authored by individual researchers. While institutional indices often use aggregate data derived from surveys, in the case of academic proposals it is not uncommon to find indicators computed using micro-data and therefore allowing the calculation of indices by subgroups. Finally, it is obvious that if the results are based on surveys, regularity is extremely conditioned by the periodicity of the surveys on which measures are based. In order to avoid these kinds of limitations, many proponents opt to use only labour force surveys or aggregate labour market data that can be obtained on a regular basis.

Eighth, the considerable consistence of the rankings of job quality suggests that the differences in job quality across Europe are so important and consistent that any indicator which aggregates information from a sufficiently large number of relevant variables is likely to produce consistent results. Of course, this does not mean that it is not important to develop a sound theoretical framework for a composite indicator on job quality in Europe: this is necessary to be able to interpret properly the results, to make sense of any abnormality that may appear, and to give meaning to the whole exercise. With these ideas in mind, in the next chapter we lay out a concrete proposal for measuring job quality, which will be applied to the 27 Member States of the European Union in the subsequent chapter.

NOTES

1. This aspect was not part of the Employment Guidelines of 1997 for Member States on labour market policies, which prioritized employability, entrepreneurship, adaptability and equality of opportunities, making no reference to the quality of jobs created.

2. It could be argued that high levels of productivity would be related to high levels of job quality (as in the High Performance Workplace Theory), but in any case productivity would be only a proxy variable of wages.

3. For instance, the UK shows a similar position in the index of Davoine *et al.* (2008); the report of the Fourth European Working Conditions Survey also shows this country in a good position in many individual indicators, see Parent-Thirion *et al.* (2007).

4. According to ILO, decent work involves promoting 'opportunities for women and men to obtain decent and productive work, in conditions of freedom, equity, security and human dignity' (87th International Labour Conference Report, June 1999).

5. The Global Policy Network (www.gpn.org) is a network of union-friendly research institutions in 50 countries around the world, more than half of them based in the developing world.

6. See Lara and Rubio (2006) for an application of the index to El Salvador.

7. The Canadian Policy Research Networks (www.cprn.org) is a non-profit research organization based in Canada. Reports and statistical information are updated roughly every six months, and disseminated through the website www.jobquality.ca.

8. The idea of weighting using the importance given by workers to different job attributes was firstly proposed by Jencks *et al.* (1988) for the United States.

9. Following the same methodology as the Austrian WCI, since the summer of 2009 an Austrian Occupational Health Monitor has been published. Parallel to this new project, a new set of questions for workers in managerial positions have been added in order to produce an Austrian Management Monitor.

10. The Centro de Iniciativas e Investigaciones Europeas en el Mediterráneo (CIREM, Centre for European Initiatives and Research in the Mediterranean Region) is a private not-for-profit foundation created in 1989 dedicated to applied research and consultancy in the field of social sciences. For more information, see www.cirem.org.

11. A similar approach, based on a different database (a survey on workers' satisfaction from the International Social Survey Program), is presented by Clark (2005).

5. The construction of a European job quality index

5.1. INTRODUCTION

In this chapter, we put our own ideas and recommendations into practice, constructing our own proposal of a job quality index for the European Union. To construct such an indicator, we follow the key principles outlined in previous pages:

1. The index should be based on a clear definition of job quality, and the elements included in the index should not go beyond the boundaries of such concept. We use the operational definition proposed earlier (see Chapter 1): job quality refers to the characteristics of jobs that have a direct impact on the well-being of workers. Such broad definition restricts considerably the type of information that a multidimensional job quality index should summarize: it should be restricted to information about the attributes of jobs, not of the workers that hold them (even if the information is reported by the workers themselves); it should not include contextual information (on institutional settings, unemployment levels, etc); and it should refer to results rather than procedures (unless such procedures have themselves a direct impact on the well-being of workers).

2. The selection of attributes to be measured, and the principles used for aggregating the information, should be based on a properly justified theoretical model. For this purpose, we draw from the literature review carried out in Chapter 2: our model of job quality has five dimensions that broadly correspond to the five main traditions of study of job quality (or the impact of job attributes on the well-being of workers) in the Social Sciences. There is only one broad area of job quality reviewed in the previous chapter but not included in the model (because unfortunately the EWCS does not cover it): participation and industrial democracy.[1]

3. The index should be calculated at the individual level in order to allow analysing the situation of specific groups of workers. The data used should be highly harmonized across countries to make the results

really comparable at international level. In order to fulfil both purposes, we use data from the 4th EWCS, which is without any doubt the best existing data source on job quality at the European level (and quite probably at a worldwide scale as well), although it has important limitations in terms of the size of the sample and periodicity.[2] With the single exception of participation at the workplace, the EWCS contains variables on virtually all the areas of job quality identified in the literature review and is, therefore, adequate for our purposes.

4. Finally, we should produce an aggregated index with which we can make an unambiguous evaluation of job quality for any subgroups of workers, but that is also decomposable in terms of its dimensions, components and indicators, so that we can make sense of any observed difference to a high level of detail.

These are our goals for this chapter, which includes eight sections following these introductory remarks. In the next section, we discuss the general structure of the index and the principles followed in its construction, while in the subsequent five sections, we describe the construction of each dimension from the individual variables of the EWCS, evaluating their properties and the plausibility of the results obtained. Then in section 5.8, the overall index of job quality is presented, evaluating its distribution and results for a representative set of workers' categories. We conclude with a few final remarks and reflections on this attempt at constructing a Job Quality Index for the EU.

5.2. GENERAL STRUCTURE OF THE INDEX

Figure 5.1 presents the overall structure of the index, including the weight assigned to each component and subcomponent, and listing the individual variables from the EWCS used for constructing them. It is not necessary to give further explanations about this structure, because we have already devoted a full chapter for this purpose (Chapter 2).

The index comprises five dimensions: pay, intrinsic job quality, employment quality, health and safety and work–life balance. In the baseline formulation of the Job Quality Index, each dimension receives the same weight (20 per cent) and the aggregation is carried out using a weighted geometric average. In the next chapter we present the results of a sensitivity analysis performed in order to assess if the indicator is robust to other sorts of weighting and aggregation methods.

The following pages discuss the logic behind the construction of each

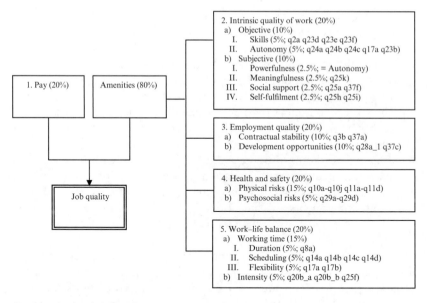

Source: Authors' elaboration.

Figure 5.1   The structure of the Job Quality Index

component, presenting the underlying variables and the specification used. We also look at the structure of correlations between the variables used for each dimension, which are supposed (unless otherwise stated) to capture essentially the same thing but from different angles: hence, we expect them to be positively correlated, though not so much as to be redundant. Finally, we focus on the scores of the main indicators of each component for five non-exclusive categories of the working population: all workers, employees, self-employed, construction workers, workers in hotels, restaurants and catering (**HORECA**), workers in the health sector, professionals and machine operators. The purpose of such exercise is not analytical, but illustrative and evaluative: by looking at the overall scores for these six disparate categories, we shall be able to make a quick assessment of the plausibility of results, trying to spot potential problems in the construction of each component. The actual analysis of the results of our index for different subgroups of the European working population is carried out in the following chapter.

Before getting into a detailed discussion of each component of the index, we should make some clarifications regarding the principles followed in its construction:

1. As already mentioned, there is only one dimension which was part of the literature review of Chapter 2, but that is not included in the operational model of Figure 5.1: participation and industrial democracy. The reason is simply the lack of relevant information in the EWCS. In future editions of the survey, such dimension may be covered, and hence the model may be expanded to cover such extra dimension; but for the moment, it is simply not possible.

2. The index is constructed by aggregating variables from the EWCS, which are selected according to their correspondence to the model shown in Figure 5.1. Whenever possible (that is, when there are several variables measuring the same underlying concept from different angles, we favour the use of more than one variable for each individual indicator/component in the model, aiming to increase the robustness of measurement: but because we are using a survey that was not specifically designed for this matter, this is not always possible.

3. Except in the case of pay, the original variables were consistently recoded into a metric of 0–100, according to a normative logic of how desirable in terms of job quality each job attribute is. Zero is the least desirable outcome, 100 the most desirable, and any existing intermediate values are graded accordingly. Because the answer categories of each variable vary considerably, there are different recodifications applied. For instance, the exposure to physical risk factors is measured in the EWCS with a 'Nordic' scale of relative time, going from 'Never' to 'Always', with such intermediate categories as 'One quarter of the time', 'Half of the time', etc. Because a physical risk is a bad thing for job quality, 'Never' is coded as 100 (that is, most desirable), 'Always' as 0 (least desirable), and the rest according to the relative time interval (so 'one quarter of the time' becomes 75). Another example: a series of dichotomous variables measuring autonomy in different areas of work (methods of work, order of tasks, etc.), is coded as 100 if the person has autonomy in such area, or 0 if she does not. In general (as it is stated in detail in the following pages), the coding of variables into a 0–100 normative job quality metric is sufficiently 'natural' as to be almost self-explanatory, although there are some possible exceptions that are explicitly addressed.

4. Besides such recoding into a 0–100 normative metric, we do not apply any further manipulation to the original variables. In particular, we do not standardize the original variables using Z-scores, a procedure that is sometimes followed when constructing this kind of composite index. Such standardization expresses the scores of each variable in standard deviation units, which means that the degree of dispersion of the original variables is also homogenized. Instead, we opt for making

the coding normatively meaningful, and hence a value of 100 means the presence of a positive attribute (or the absence of a negative one) and a value of 0 the opposite. If we express the variables in standard deviation units, we immediately lose such normative meaning. And furthermore, by homogenizing the spread of the different variables, we would be losing also information on the actual distribution (in absolute terms) of the different attributes. For instance, as will be shown in the following pages, the psychosocial component of the index has in general very positive values and very little dispersion: this is because there is a consistently low level of reporting of psychosocial risks. If we standardized this variable, because the level of dispersion is very low, values that are in fact very close to the average (even if they are the most distant of all) would appear as very far away and we would get the impression that there is more variation on the degree of exposure to psychosocial risks than there really is. So we prefer to keep the original variables as they are, even if this means that this particular component of the index has very little variability and therefore contributes very little to the variability of the overall score: we believe this procedure to be fundamentally correct, as long as it simply reflects the fact that there is very little dispersion in the exposure to psychosocial risks (as measured by the EWCS).

5.   Unfortunately, not all variables used for constructing the index have values for all individuals. In other words, for some respondents of the 4th EWCS, some of the elements displayed in Figure 5.1 are missing, either as a result of a refusal to answer a particular question or because the information was not relevant for a particular category of worker. Possible solutions to this problem include: leaving out all respondents for which there is missing information, calculating the index using the information available for each individual (even if the model is in some cases incomplete) or imputing the missing information using a specialized computer algorithm. The first solution (eliminating the cases with missing values) is not a reasonable option, as it would mean leaving out of our analysis nearly half of the EWCS sample (more than 40 per cent of cases have at least one missing value in any of the 47 variables used for constructing the index), and obviously biasing our results in a totally uncontrollable way. The other two solutions are more reasonable, but have also some problems. The second solution (using the available information for each individual for the calculation of the index) means that the underlying model of job quality can differ between individuals (because in each case, the model depends on the available information). When the missing values were the result of logical filters in the questionnaire (for instance, the question on type

of contract is not asked to the self-employed), we have used this solution: after all, in this case it makes sense that the model of job quality
changes for such particular dimension, since the information that is
missing would be irrelevant anyway. The third solution (imputing
the missing values) has the problem of being based in an ultimately
hypothetical model, which requires making some relatively arbitrary
assumptions. Nevertheless, it is useful when there is a key variable for
which there is a high percentage of missing values and these missing
values are likely to be biased. We have used this strategy in only one
case, but a very important one: the variable on pay. This variable has
nearly 15 per cent of missing values: had we used the second approach
(model based on available information), for nearly one in six workers
the job quality model would have totally excluded the pay dimension.
We use an ordered *logit* imputation model, under the assumption that
pay depends on sex, occupation, age, employment status and working
hours, within each European country (the model was computed separately for each country). The imputed values tend to be higher than
the average, because the categories of workers that are most likely
to refuse answering to this question tend to be at higher layers of
employment.

6. The aggregation of information within each dimension of the index
    is mostly done by arithmetically averaging the scores of individual
    variables following the hierarchical structure shown in Figure 5.1.
    In most cases, components that are at the same hierarchical level are
    assumed to be equivalent, and therefore receive equal weights within
    their branch (there are some exceptions, explained in detail in the fol-
    lowing pages). Within dimension 4, each individual receives the score
    that corresponds to the highest risk that she faced at work (as it is dis-
    cussed later, to average risks makes no sense in this context), although
    there is a final averaging aggregation of the two subcomponents of
    this dimension as well.

7. Finally, the aggregation of information at the highest level is carried
    out by geometrically averaging the five dimensions into the overall
    index score. Using a geometric rather than an arithmetic average in
    this final stage of the construction of the index has two important
    advantages for our purposes: first, the contribution of each dimension
    to the overall index is not linear, but decreasing (that is, an increase
    in a dimension from a low initial value produces a larger expansion
    of job quality than the same increase from a high initial value); and
    second, the contribution of each dimension depends on the values of
    all the other dimensions (that is, even if the sum of scores is the same,
    a job with more balanced values in the five dimensions would have

a higher quality than a job with very high values in two dimensions but very low in the other three). What this means is that our index of job quality assumes decreasing returns for the different work and employment attributes, and imperfect substitutability among the different attributes (with penalization for significant imbalances between them). A more detailed discussion of the theoretical implications of this type of final aggregation is presented in section 5.8 of this chapter.

As we can see on the left-hand side of Figure 5.1, the five top-level dimensions are split into two categories: on the one hand, we have the pay dimension; on the other, we have the other four dimensions, which are all grouped under the heading 'amenities'. Such twofold categorization derives from the theory of compensating differentials which was originally proposed by Adam Smith and which is still the canonic theory on job quality in orthodox economics (see Section 2.3.1 of Chapter 2 in this book). According to this framework, pay plays a special function in the determination of job quality as the main compensating mechanism for the disagreeableness of work, reflected here in the other four dimensions of job quality. In fact, our model of job quality is closer to the multidimensional approach of the sociological tradition (with pay being just one of five dimensions of job quality) than to the binary approach of the theory of compensating differentials (which would require assigning a special salience to pay as a universal compensating mechanism); but the binary categorization of the top-level dimensions shown in Figure 5.1 is useful to illustrate the links between our model and this important economic approach to job quality. An alternative classification of the five areas (not shown in Figure 5.1) would include the dimensions of pay and employment quality within the general heading of 'employment', intrinsic quality of work and health and safety within the heading of 'work', and health and safety somewhere in between.

5.3. PAY

What kind of indicator on pay do we need for an index of job quality? Pay is the monetary compensation for work, and its importance derives mainly from the access to resources it grants (although secondarily it may be used as a proxy for the social valuation attached to each job). Therefore, in the context of an international analysis like the one we carry out here, it is important to take into account the wide differences in living standards across Europe: that is, we should not use exchange rates to put all pay levels within the same metric, but some type of purchasing power equivalence.

We thus aim to work with a continuous measure of pay expressed in comparable units, adjusted for purchasing power differentials.

However, the variable of pay included in the 4th EWCS is, first of all, not really a continuous variable. In general purpose surveys, the questions on pay routinely get very high rates of non-response: in many countries, pay is very sensitive information, which some people are reluctant to give. Using broadly defined pay intervals to be pointed at in a card rather than asking directly for an amount of money tends to yield better results in terms of response rates, and many surveys (including the 4th EWCS) opt for this alternative. In the survey, those pay intervals were broadly aligned with the boundaries between the pay deciles in each country, using information obtained from the European Earnings Structure Survey (see Fernández-Macías 2006). So rather than a continuous variable, what we have is an ordinal variable classifying each respondent into one of ten categories of pay: but as we know the amount of money which is associated to each point in this scale, we can use it for defining the distances between the categories. So in essence, we can use the pay variable of the 4th EWCS as a pseudo-continuous variable (with only ten categories, but known distances between them). The main disadvantage of this type of variable is that it incorporates less variability than the real distribution of pay, but it should be a reasonably good approximation (and the response rates obtained were surely higher than if the question had been more direct).

Drawing on the original income bands of the 4th EWCS, we proceed to harmonize the information to make it internationally comparable, and to standardize it in order to use it as an input variable for our index. First, the non-euro currencies are transformed into euros; second, they were adjusted to purchasing power differences using Eurostat conversion factors[3]; and finally, they were rescaled to a 0–100 range, subtracting to each value the minimum value and dividing it by the distance between the minimum and the maximum. To get an idea of the results of this process, Figure 5.2 shows the range of this pay variable before it was rescaled to 0–100 (so the units express euros in purchasing power parity, PPP): the grey bars show the distance between the highest and the lowest values (first and tenth deciles), and the line in the middle of the bar shows the middle value (fifth decile) in each country. This chart clearly illustrates the wide differences between countries in terms of the purchasing power granted by labour compensation: all the values of the nine countries with lowest wages (all of them Eastern Member States) are below the lowest decile of the five countries with highest wages (Luxembourg, the UK, Denmark, Ireland and Sweden). These differences are all captured in the pay component of the index: because the normalization method used is just a rescaling of the original variables, the relative distances between pay

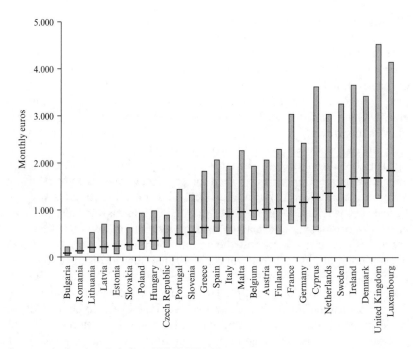

Source: Authors' analysis from EWCS 2005 micro-data.

Figure 5.2   Highest, lowest and middle pay intervals in PPP

levels shown in Figure 5.2 are kept intact in the variable (the only difference being the scale, which would go from 0 to 100 rather than from 0 to
5000 euros in PPP).

It is very important to understand that this variable does not only capture
differences in income levels between countries: because respondents are
positioned within a comparable 10-point scale, we can compare their individual positions nationally and internationally. For instance, although
wages in Spain are generally much lower than wages in Luxembourg, the
highest deciles in Spain are above the median wages in Luxembourg. The
spread between the highest and lowest decile in each country (the size of
the bars in figure 5.2) is in fact a measure of wage inequality: as is well
known, the UK has the largest spread, followed by Luxembourg, Cyprus
and Ireland; and it is much lower in Sweden or Denmark.[4]

After the mentioned normalization to a 0–100 scale, the distribution of
the first dimension of our model of job quality is shown as a histogram in
figure 5.3.[5] As could be expected, the distribution of pay is strongly skewed
to the left-hand side of the chart: the median value in the sample is around

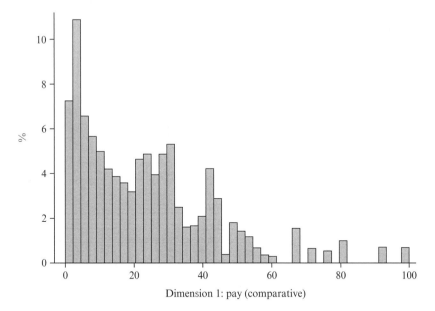

Source: Authors' analysis from EWCS 2005 micro-data.

Figure 5.3 Distribution of the comparative pay dimension

25, and more than 90 per cent of people are below 50 in this dimension. This not only reflects the well-known universal skewness of the distribution of wages, but the fact that we are putting together labour markets as widely different in their pay levels as shown previously in Figure 5.2. Also, the type of normalization applied to the original variable tends to emphasize such skewness: all values have been rescaled to the difference between the maximum and minimum value, and therefore the scores of this dimension reflect the proportion that each wage level represents over the highest decile in the UK, which is very high indeed (more than 4500 euros a month in PPP, according to this data). So the results are perfectly plausible, and do reflect the (striking) differences in pay levels across Europe, even after adjusting for PPP.

The variable whose distribution is shown in Figure 5.3 is perfectly adequate for the comparison of the pay dimension of job quality across the EU, and in the following chapter it is used intensively for such purpose. But if we are not interested in doing international comparisons, but on the distribution of job quality at the individual level or for the whole of the EU workforce, then the comparative pay indicator whose construction we have just outlined is not really adequate. Put simply, it is so sensitive to the

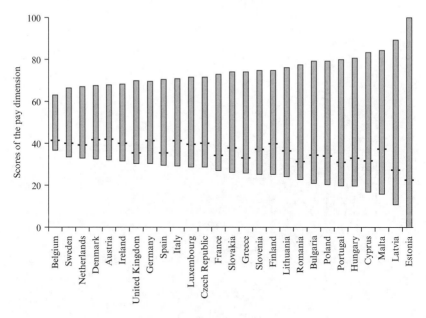

Source: Authors' analysis from EWCS 2005 micro-data.

Figure 5.4 *Highest, lowest and middle pay intervals in the national pay dimension*

differences in average pay levels across countries that any individual-level analysis based on such variable will be totally biased by those country level differences. To deal with this problem, we construct a secondary pay indicator which eliminates the country differences, positioning each individual in one of 10 positions that correspond to the income deciles in each country. The spread of these positions in each country is a measure of inequality (broadly corresponding to the distance in euros between the lowest and highest income decile in each country): the distance between the values of 0 and 100 in this non-comparative pay dimension (from now on, we will call it national pay dimension) correspond to the distance between the lowest and highest decile in the country where this distance is larger (which is Estonia), with the spread of the values in the other countries being proportional to this most unequal country. The results are shown in Figure 5.4, which are analogous to the results shown in Figure 5.2 for the comparative pay dimension. We can see that this new variable does not reflect the country differences in average pay levels (it places each worker within each country's pay structure), but it does reflect the differences across countries in the levels of pay inequality (the lowest levels of

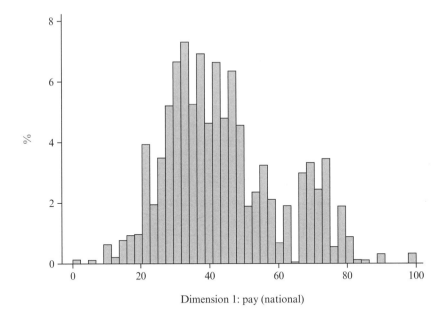

Dimension 1: pay (national)

Source: Authors' analysis from EWCS 2005 micro-data.

Figure 5.5   Distribution of the national pay dimension

inequality in workers' compensation according to this variable would be in Belgium, Sweden, the Netherlands and Denmark, and the highest in Estonia, Latvia, Malta and Cyprus). Figure 5.5, on the other hand, shows a histogram of the distribution of this variable for the whole European working population according to the EWCS: if we compare it to Figure 5.3, we can see that this new variable is not skewed to the bottom as the comparative pay variable, but rather centred around the median values in each country. We use this national pay dimension when the objective of the analysis is not the international comparison.

Finally, Table 5.1 shows the values in the comparative and national pay dimensions for eight different categories of workers. As argued earlier, the intention of these quick profiles is not analytic (in the next chapter we perform a detailed analysis of the index and the top-level dimensions), but purely illustrative and evaluative: to check whether the results look plausible. In the case of the pay dimension, which is based on a single variable (the other four dimensions draw from several EWCS variables each), this exercise is exceedingly simple, even though we have two versions of this dimension (one for comparative purposes and the

Table 5.1 *Average values of the pay dimension for different types of workers*

	Total	Self-employed	Em-ployee	Construc-tion	HOR-ECA	Health sector	Profes-sionals	Machine operators
Pay dimension (compara-tive)	29.1	30.9	29.0	31.1	26.4	30.9	36.1	23.6
Pay dimension (national)	45.6	50.1	44.9	49.0	42.6	44.9	52.4	43.9

Source: Authors' analysis from EWCS 2005 micro-data.

other for individual-level analysis). The differences in pay for occupational levels are generally higher than for sectors: the value of professionals in our pay indicator is 50 per cent higher than the value of machine operators (with a smaller difference in the national pay dimension), whereas the differences in the three illustrative sectors shown in table 5.1 are considerably smaller (around 20 per cent between HORECA and construction). It may seem surprising that the overall value for construction is slightly higher than for health, but if we look at the internal differences by occupational levels (not shown here), we see that this results from the bigger dispersion of pay within the health sector.[6] The difference between the average values for self-employed and employees is very small, but the dispersion is much larger for the former. Finally, the mean for all workers (with little interest on its own) is around 29 (and roughly 46 for the national version of the pay dimension). Overall, the distribution of the pay indicator and its values for our illustrative set of categories of workers seems plausible.

5.4. INTRINSIC QUALITY OF WORK

This dimension derives from a humanistic concept of work as purposeful and conscious human activity: not only as a means to provide the resources necessary for survival, but as a form of human expression, realization and fulfilment. In Chapter 2, we argued that the roots of these ideas in the Social Sciences lie in the Marxist concept of alienation, and that this debate has been dominated by two main approaches: an objectivist one, focused on skills and autonomy, and a subjectivist one, focused on the perception of alienation and self-estrangement. Following this argument, the 'intrinsic job quality' component of our index has two sub-components, each of them accounting for half of its total score.

The formulation of the 'objective' sub-component of intrinsic job quality we used here can be traced back to the classic work of Braverman (1974). It has two main elements: skills and autonomy. The concept of skills we use here is atypical in the sense that it refers to jobs and not workers: so instead of 'the ability to use one's knowledge effectively and readily in execution or performance' (Merriam-Webster 2010), we refer to the requirements associated to each job in terms of skills. For measuring this concept, we use the four broad skill levels of the International Standard Classification of Occupations (ISCO): by design, those skill levels correspond to the four levels of formal education of the International Standard Classification of Education (Elias and Birch 1994). But to widen the concept to non-formal skill requirements, we have made the ISCO classification to account for only half of the skills indicator, the other half being based on the respondents' own assessment about the monotony, complexity and learning requirements of their jobs. Box 5.1 shows the variables composing this skills indicator, as well as the values assigned to each individual item. Box 5.1 also shows the operationalization of autonomy, the other element defining objective intrinsic job quality. Autonomy refers to the degree of freedom or discretion that the worker has within her job: this concept is naturally measured at the job level, and the variables available in the EWCS permit an adequate operationalization. Following Breaugh (1985 and 1999), we identify three different facets of autonomy: methods, scheduling and criteria. As Box 5.1 shows, we have two variables for *methods* (whether the respondent can choose or change the order of tasks and methods of work), two for *scheduling* (whether the respondent can choose or change the speed of work, and whether he can decide on the work schedule), and one for *criteria* (whether the respondent has to assess by herself the quality of her own work).

For the operationalization of a subjective approach to intrinsic job quality, we draw from the classic model proposed by Blauner (1964) for measuring alienation at work. Although this model may seem outdated, it is still very much in use, despite its Marxist roots, it is in practice akin to work psychologists' studies on job satisfaction (see Edgell 2006: 36). To empirically measure alienation, Blauner identified four different dimensions: powerlessness, meaninglessness, social isolation and self-estrangement. Although the EWCS does not include all the variables used by Blauner in his original study, it includes several variables that fit such concepts rather closely (after all, Blauner himself had to adapt his concepts to variables from pre-existing surveys for his original study). In

---

BOX 5.1   INTRINSIC JOB QUALITY – OBJECTIVE COMPONENT

a) Skills (50%)

– Q2A What is the title of your main paid job? By main paid job, we mean the one where you spend most hours. (50%) ISCO1-ISCO2 (100), ISCO3 (67), ISCO4-ISCO8, ISCO10 (33), ISCO9 (0).
– Q23 Generally, does your main paid job involve, or not . . .? (50%)
  D – monotonous tasks – Yes (0), no (100).
  E – complex tasks – Yes (100), no (0). [skill_3]
  F – learning new things – Yes (100), no (0).

b) Autonomy (50%)
METHODS (33%)

– Q24 Are you able, or not, to choose or change. . .?
  A – your order of tasks – Yes (100), no (0). [aut_1]
  B – your methods of work – Yes (100), no (0). [aut_2]

SCHEDULING (33%)

– Q24 Are you able, or not, to choose or change. . .?
  C – your speed or rate of work – Yes (100), no (0). [aut_3]
– Q17A How are your working time arrangements set? [aut_4]
  1 – They are set by the company / organization with no possibility for changes (0)
  2 – You can choose between several fixed working schedules determined by the company (33)
  3 – You can adapt your working hours within certain limits (e.g. flexitime) (67)
  4 – Your working hours are entirely determined by yourself (100)

CRITERIA (33%)

– Q23 Generally, does your main paid job involve, or not . . .?
  B – assessing yourself the quality of your own work – Yes (100), no (0). [aut_5]

BOX 5.2   INTRINSIC JOB QUALITY – SUBJECTIVE COMPONENT

a) Powerfulness (25%)
= autonomy in box 5.1

b) Meaningfulness (25%)
- Q25 For each of the following statements, please select the response which best describes your work situation.
  - K – You have the feeling of doing useful work – Almost always (100) Often (67) Sometimes (33) Rarely (16) Almost never (0).

c) Social Support (25%)
- Q25 For each of the following statements, please select the response which best describes your work situation.
  - A – You can get assistance from colleagues if you ask for it – Almost always (100) Often (67) Sometimes (33) Rarely (16) Almost never (0).
- Q37 How much do you agree or disagree with the following statements describing some aspects of your job?
  - F – I have very good friends at work – Strongly agree (100), Agree (75), Neither agree nor disagree (50), Disagree (25), Strongly Disagree (0).

d) Self-fulfilment (25%)
- Q25 For each of the following statements, please select the response which best describes your work situation.
  - H – At work, you have the opportunity to do what you do best – Almost always (100) Often (67) Sometimes (33) Rarely (16) Almost never (0).
  - I – Your job gives you the feeling of work well-done – Almost always (100) Often (67) Sometimes (33) Rarely (16) Almost never (0).

---

total, nine EWCS variables are used for constructing this sub-component, as shown in Box 5.2. The normative direction of the concepts is inverted with respect to Blauner's proposal, because otherwise this sub-component would not be coherent with the rest.[7]

The first component of Blauner's model, powerfulness, is in fact so close to the idea of autonomy that we opt to use directly the same indicator we constructed in the previous step. It may seem surprising to use the same indicator twice, but in fact this only means that we are giving it more weight in the final score. The model shown in Figure 5.1 is constructed by reviewing the most important traditions discussing job quality in the Social Sciences: if the same indicator plays an important role in two distinct important traditions, and for different reasons, it makes perfect sense to include it twice and thus give it twice the weight on the index score.[8] What could be argued, though, is that even if the underlying concept is basically the same, the previous sub-component is supposed to deal with autonomy from an objective perspective (and therefore, in principle, independently from the workers' perceptions) whereas the autonomy within Blauner's model refers to the subjective perception of latitude at work. The problem is that the EWCS, being a workers' survey, only includes measures of autonomy which are based on workers' own assessment. Hence, we have to rely on the same (subjective, or at least based on perceptions) variables for measuring autonomy in both cases. It seems reasonable enough to assume that in practice, the difference should be small.

The EWCS contains a few items measuring perceptions of meaningfulness, social support and self-fulfilment at work which seem adequate approximations to Blauner's concepts. These are 'soft' concepts, rather vaguely defined even in their original formulation, and it is fair to say that they may be more problematic than other more 'factual' variables in the context of an international survey like the EWCS. In any case, they should serve as a subjective approximation to the idea of intrinsic job quality. For meaningfulness, we include a single variable measuring whether the respondent feels she is doing useful work. For social support, two variables are used: one on whether the respondent feels he or she can have assistance from colleagues if needed, the other on whether she has good friends at work. Finally, the measure of self-fulfilment (which is the most vaguely defined concept of all, but which we take to mean something very similar to Veblen's 'instinct of workmanship', Veblen (1898)) is based on the perceptions of being able to do at work what the respondent does best, and whether the respondent has the feeling of 'work well-done'.[9]

Table 5.2 shows the pair-wise correlations between the 14 variables used for constructing the dimension of intrinsic job quality. In general, most correlation coefficients are moderate (between 0.10 and 0.20). They are generally higher (in many cases above 0.40 or 0.50) between variables included in the same component (which was to be expected considering that they are different measures of the same thing: for instance, a job involving complex tasks tends to require learning new things, their correlation being 0.42). There are three variables whose correlations with the rest are clearly lower: the level of monotony of the job, and the two

Table 5.2   Correlations among intrinsic job quality variables

	Objective variables related to skills				Objective and subjective variables related to autonomy					Subjective variables				
	ISCO level	Non monotonous tasks	Complex tasks	Learning of new things	Order of tasks	Methods of work	Speed of work	Working time schedule	Use of own criteria	Meaningfulness	Assistance from colleagues	Friends at work	Opportunity to do your best	Feeling the work well-done
Objective variables related to skills														
ISCO level	1.000													
Non monotonous tasks	0.181	1.000												
Complex tasks	0.260	0.049	1.000											
Learning of new things	0.275	0.109	0.421	1.000										

167

Table 5.2 (continued)

	Objective variables related to skills				Objective and subjective variables related to autonomy					Subjective variables				
	ISCO level	Non monotonous tasks	Complex tasks	Learning of new things	Order of tasks	Methods of work	Speed of work	Working time schedule	Use of own criteria	Meaningfulness	Assistance from colleagues	Friends at work	Opportunity to do your best	Feeling the work well-done
Objective and subjective variables related to autonomy														
Order of tasks	0.205	0.103	0.161	0.188	1.000									
Methods of work	0.224	0.138	0.181	0.207	0.568	1.000								
Speed of work	0.157	0.085	0.134	0.168	0.507	0.540	1.000							
Working time schedule	0.197	0.099	0.098	0.074	0.330	0.281	0.265	1.000						
Use of own criteria	0.153	-0.014	0.238	0.284	0.171	0.172	0.157	0.120	1.000					

Subjective variables													
Meaning-fulness	0.146	0.155	0.169	0.217	0.162	0.200	0.177	0.113	0.163	1.000			
Assistance from colleagues	0.066	0.029	0.105	0.174	0.041	0.033	0.049	-0.126	0.053	0.153	1.000		
Friends at work	0.055	0.049	0.040	0.085	0.038	0.026	0.033	-0.062	0.054	0.191	0.273	1.000	
Opportunity to do your best	0.157	0.098	0.117	0.145	0.257	0.214	0.239	0.204	0.170	0.415	0.131	0.170	1.000
Feeling the work well-done	0.114	0.159	0.132	0.178	0.175	0.193	0.188	0.127	0.164	0.642	0.157	0.199	0.512	1.000

Source: Authors' analysis from EWCS micro-data.

variables measuring social support (support from colleagues and having good friends at work). In the case of monotony, such low level of correlation may signal that although monotony and skill deployment at work are surely related issues, monotony is not a direct component of skills. But even if we are not sure about where to locate it in our model, it is such a key concept for intrinsic job quality from an objective perspective that we opted to leave it in. In the case of the two variables measuring social support, the case for leaving them in is even stronger: even if it is relatively uncorrelated to the other elements of intrinsic job quality, it is obviously a desirable job attribute that fits into this component, as it is reflected in the literature. In any case, an important thing to note in Table 5.2 is that nearly all correlation coefficients are positive, which means that all the job attributes included in the table tend to go together. There is only one exception: schedule flexibility and social support are negatively correlated, which seems quite plausible considering that working with people does involve some limitation of the degree of autonomy in the timing of work. So in general, the structure of correlations between the source variables of the EWCS fits reasonably well the assumptions of our model.

Figure 5.6 shows the distribution of scores for the second dimension of our index according to the EWCS. Contrary to the pay indicator, our indicator of intrinsic job quality is skewed to the right-hand side of the chart, with a median value of around 67, only 22 per cent of cases below the value of 50, and an interquartile range that roughly goes from 52 (percentile 25) to 79 (percentile 75). If we take the overall values of our dimensions as an evaluation of job quality for the whole of the EU working population (which, to some extent, they are: although as usual, these indices are better used for comparisons than for absolute evaluations), we could say that European jobs are much better in terms of their intrinsic qualities (according to the evaluations made by workers themselves) than in terms of pay. This, again, seems reasonably plausible, and consistent with previous research on intrinsic job quality and job satisfaction.

Table 5.3 shows the average values of the intrinsic job quality dimension, each of its components, and their sub-components for our list of illustrative categories of the working population. The first column shows the average score for all workers. In general, the scores are higher for the subjective than for the objective intrinsic job quality indicators: particularly, the values are lower for skills than for the other sub-components. This, of course, results from the way each component has been constructed and the source variables specified. The skills measure is largely based in ISCO levels, and there are a relatively large proportion of workers with mid-low values in such variable. Most of the other variables are of a very

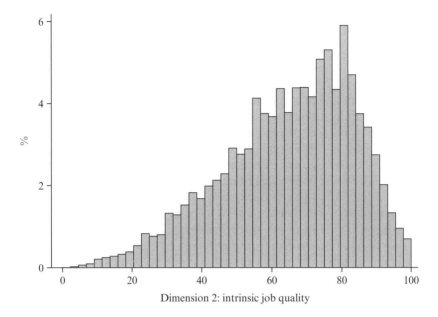

Source: Authors' analysis from EWCS 2005 micro-data.

Figure 5.6   Distribution of the intrinsic job quality dimension

subjective nature (in fact, they are close to measures of job satisfaction, though specific), and tend to have quite positive replies and hence quite high scores in the index. It is a well-established finding of the socioeconomic literature that job satisfaction measures tend to receive surprisingly positive answers, and to have a rather low variance (see Muñoz de Bustillo and Fernández-Macías 2005).

Looking at specific groups of workers, we can see that the self-employed exhibit higher scores than employees in both the objective and subjective components of this dimension, especially in the autonomy subcomponent, as could be expected. Workers in hotels, restaurants and catering (HORECA) have rather low values, especially in the objective component (skills and autonomy), while workers in the health sector have quite high scores in the subjective component, particularly with respect to meaningfulness and social support. Professionals have very high scores in all components and subcomponents of intrinsic job quality, especially in skills and autonomy, while machine operators and assemblers have very low values in general, especially in autonomy and self-realization (this core group of industrial workers still fits Braverman's classic arguments about

Table 5.3 Average values of the intrinsic quality dimension and its components for different types of workers

	Total	Self-employed	Employee	Construction	HORECA	Health sector	Professionals	Machine operators
Dimension 2: intrinsic job quality	64.3	74.9	62.3	64.2	58.5	70.2	78.7	51.3
Intrinsic objective job quality	59.1	72.8	56.5	58.1	50.5	66.2	81.4	41.3
Skills	55.7	60.9	55.0	53.7	43.7	69.4	90.0	39.3
Autonomy	62.4	84.7	58.0	62.4	57.3	63.0	72.8	43.3
Intrinsic subjective job quality	69.5	76.9	68.1	70.4	66.5	74.1	76.0	61.3
Powerfulness	62.4	84.7	58.0	62.4	57.3	63.0	72.8	43.3
Meaningfulness	77.0	83.1	75.9	78.6	70.9	86.7	84.4	70.7
Social support	68.4	57.0	70.9	69.1	70.6	72.7	70.8	67.6
Self-fulfilment	70.4	82.2	68.1	71.8	67.6	74.1	75.9	64.1

Source: Authors' analysis from EWCS 2005 micro-data.

the degradation of work in the twentieth century). All these results seem plausible and within expectations.

5.5. EMPLOYMENT QUALITY

If the previous component conceptualized job quality from the perspective of the *human* contents of work, this one looks at jobs as relationships between agents in the labour market. Our model differentiates two main components of employment quality: contractual stability and development opportunities. The first element tries to measure the stability of the contractual bond between employer and employee, the second the opportunities that the current job affords the worker in terms of training and career development. Box 5.3 provides details on the variables and scoring used for constructing this component.

Type of contract accounts for half the indicator of contractual stability: the desirable outcome is having an indefinite contract, which is coded as 1, whereas any other type of contract (fixed-term, temporary agency, apprenticeship or no contract) is coded as 0. Although it seems undisputable that having an indefinite contract is (*ceteris paribus*) more desirable in terms of job quality than having any of the other types of contract specified in question about the kind of contract, the dichotomous coding used is certainly an oversimplification with respect to the underlying idea of contractual stability. On top of this, we must bear in mind that the 'indefiniteness' of an indefinite contract is not the same across all of Europe (because of the very important differences in labour regulation), and therefore this variable on its own probably misrepresents to some extent the degree of stability of the labour relation across countries. For these reasons, we include a second variable (that accounts for the other half of the indicator of contractual stability) that measures the *perception* of stability: this variable is more nuanced (it is measured as a scale with five ordered values) than the previous one, and it should be less affected by the mentioned institutional differences. Also, this variable is asked to all workers, whereas the previous one is asked to employees only: this way, we can have a value of employment stability for the self-employed as well.

The second element of employment quality (development opportunities) is also based on two different variables, and again one is factual and the other a perception. The first one is a dichotomous variable measuring whether the respondent has received training provided by the employer (or herself if self-employed) in the previous twelve months; the second one, a variable holding the level of agreement of the respondent to the statement 'my job offers good prospects for career advancement'.

BOX 5.3   EMPLOYMENT QUALITY

a) Contractual stability (50%)
– Q3B What kind of employment contract do you have? (50%)
An indefinite contract (100); a fixed-term, temporary agency, apprentice or no contract (0).
– Q37 How much do you agree with the following statements describing some aspects of your job? (50%)
A – I might lose my job in the next 6 months – Strongly agree (0), Agree (25), Neither agree nor disagree (50), Disagree (75), Strongly Disagree (100).

b) Development opportunities (50%)
– Q28 Over the past 12 months, have you undergone training paid for or provided by your employer, or by yourself if you are self-employed? – Yes (100), no (0). (50%)
– Q37 How much do you agree or disagree with the following statements describing some aspects of your job? (50%)
C – My job offers good prospects for career advancement– Strongly agree (100), Agree (75), Neither agree nor disagree (50), Disagree (25), Strongly Disagree (0).

Table 5.4   Correlations among employment quality variables

	Type of contract	Subjective job security	Training	Development opportunities
Type of contract	1.000			
Subjective job security	0.219	1.000		
Training	0.069	0.081	1.000	
Perspectives on career advancement	0.046	0.138	0.182	1.000

Source: Authors' analysis from EWCS 2005 micro-data.

Table 5.4 shows the pair-wise correlations between the four variables that make this second dimension of the index. The correlation between the variables forming each component is moderate (around 0.20), and the correlation between the variables of different components low (.05 to

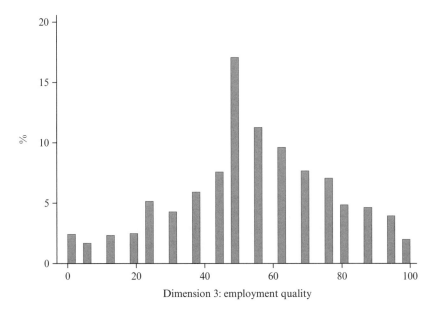

Source: Authors' analysis from EWCS 2005 micro-data.

Figure 5.7 Distribution of the employment quality dimension

0.14). All correlations go in the same direction, and generally seem to fit reasonably well the model assumptions.

Figure 5.7 shows a histogram with the distribution of scores of this third dimension of our index for the whole of the EU working population according to the EWCS. The values of this dimension are less skewed to the left or right of the distribution than in the two previous cases, although there are slightly more cases above than below the mean, which is approximately 55. But what may seem most unusual in Figure 5.7 is that this dimension is not distributed as a more or less continuous variable, as was the case for the two previous dimensions: instead, the cases are concentrated on a limited set of discrete values, corresponding to the relatively few and separated bars in the histogram. This type of distribution is the result of the way the dimension was constructed: we only used information from four variables, two of them dichotomous, hence the limited range of possible outcomes. In principle, a more continuous variable would have been preferable (if the EWCS had had more than four relevant variables for this dimension), because an implicit assumption is that the underlying concept that we are trying to measure (employment quality) is itself continuous: but this is a very minor problem as long as the values do reflect the level of employment quality of the different jobs (even if less precisely). We can try to check this by looking at the values for a representative set of workers' categories, which is done in Table 5.5.

As we can see in the first column of Table 5.5 (which represents all workers), the stability component tends to be higher than the development one, because of the way both indicators were constructed. Most European workers (86 per cent) have an indefinite contract, while just one-third of European workers received training in the last 12 months: as these variables account for half of each component, and they are coded as dichotomous variables (with 100 being the positive outcome), the score of stability tends to be higher than that of development opportunities.

Because the self-employed do not have an employment contract as such, they have no value in that variable and as Table 5.5 shows, their score in this component is entirely dependent on the other variable (perceived employment stability, which is generally higher than for employees). And although the self-employed did answer the question on training (which is in this case paid for by themselves, whereas for the rest of the working population it refers to training paid for by the employer), their values are much lower than for employees: but this is partly compensated by a perception of higher development opportunities for this group of workers. Regarding the three sectors included in Table 5.5, workers in construction and HORECA have low scores in stability and very low values (especially HORECA) in development opportunities, whereas health workers are above average in both components of this second dimension of our index. In terms of occupations, professionals have very high values in both components, whereas operators are near average in terms of stability but very low in development opportunities. These scores look generally plausible and according to expectations.

5.6.   HEALTH AND SAFETY (RISKS)

The fourth dimension of the index deals with environmental factors with a potential negative impact on the physical and psychological health of workers: in other words, with risks. The total score of the dimension is calculated by averaging the scores of two components: physical and psychosocial risks, which receive a score of 75 per cent and 25 per cent respectively. This unequal weight reflects the importance of both types of risks in the health and safety literature, and also the fact that the former are much better measured in the EWCS than the latter.

For assigning a score to each worker in the component of physical risks, the method of aggregation of information from the individual variables is different from the method followed in other components of our index.

Table 5.5   Average values of the employment quality dimension and its components for different types of workers

	Total	Self-employed	Employee	Construction	HORECA	Health sector	Professionals	Machine operators
Dimension 3: employment quality	55.1	53.5	55.7	51.8	43.7	60.5	64.4	48.8
Contractual stability	76.8	83.3	75.6	72.6	64.1	79.0	81.9	74.5
Type of contract	77.5	0.0	77.5	72.9	53.3	78.2	83.5	80.0
Subjective job security	75.4	83.3	73.9	70.8	68.5	79.5	80.5	68.6
Development opportunities	34.2	27.2	35.9	31.5	24.4	42.4	47.4	23.5
Training	26.1	12.2	29.1	18.5	11.9	40.8	40.9	16.4
Perspectives on career	42.9	43.3	43.0	45.3	37.2	44.5	54.3	30.9

Source: Authors' analysis from EWCS 2005 micro-data.

BOX 5.4   HEALTH AND SAFETY

a) Reported exposure to physical risks (50%)

[All variables use the Nordic scale, and are equally coded in the following way: Always (0), almost always (10), three quarters of the time (25), half of the time (50), one quarter of the time (75), almost never (90), never (100). The individual receives the score that corresponds to the higher level of exposure.]

– Q10 Please tell me, using the following scale, are you exposed at work to. . .?

A – Vibrations from hand tools, machinery, etc.

B – Noise so loud that you would have to raise your voice to talk to people

C – High temperatures which make you perspire even when not working

D – Low temperatures whether indoors or outdoors

E – Breathing in smoke, fumes (such as welding or exhaust fumes), powder or dust (such as wood dust or mineral dust) etc.

F – Breathing in vapours such as solvents and thinners

G – Handling or being in skin contact with chemical products or substances

H – Radiation such as X rays, radioactive radiation, welding light, laser beams

I – Tobacco smoke from other people

J – Handling or being in direct contact with materials which can be infectious, such as waste, bodily fluids, lab materials, etc

– Q11 Please tell me, using the same scale, does your main paid job involve. . .?

A – Tiring or painful positions

B – Lifting or moving people

C – Carrying or moving heavy loads

b) Psychosocial risks (50%)

[The individual receives a score of 0 if exposed to two or more of these risks, 25 if exposed to one, 100 if exposed to none.]

– Q29 Over the past 12 months, have you or have you not, personally been subjected at work to. . .?

A – threats of physical violence
B – physical violence from people from your workplace
C – physical violence from other people
D – bullying/harassment

Rather than averaging the level of exposure to the different physical risks, we take the highest level of exposure to any of the risks as the value that determines the score of each individual.[10] The reason is that each one of the risks (listed in Box 5.4) can on its own have a serious impact on the health of the worker, and in most cases it is almost impossible to be exposed to more than one or two of them simultaneously: hence, if we would average the levels of exposure of each individual to all of them, the resulting scores would be misleadingly low. Therefore, in the physical risks component, an individual gets a score of 100 (most desirable) when she is *never* exposed to *any* of the risks listed in Box 5.4 (which is the case for around 13 per cent of workers according to the EWCS), a score of 0 (least desirable) when she is *all the time* exposed to *at least one* of the risk factors (around 23 per cent of the working population), and the intermediate values correspond to the highest level of exposure to any of the risks listed in box 5.4 (so if a worker is exposed 75 per cent of the time to radiations, she gets a value of 25, etc.).

The second component, psychosocial risks, is constructed differently, because the relevant EWCS variables are not measured on the same type of Nordic scale, but as dichotomous variables holding a value of 100 if the individual suffered one of the situations shown in Box 5.4 over the previous year. This is very unfortunate, because it is impossible to construct an indicator of psychosocial risks which is really comparable to the indicator previously constructed for physical risks. The reported levels of exposure to the four psychosocial risks shown in Box 5.4 are extremely low: the maximum level is for threats of violence, and it is below 6 per cent for the whole European sample. Hence, we have to resort to a relatively ad hoc coding, in which the individual receives a value of 0 (most undesirable) if she reports exposure to at least two of the psychosocial risks, a value of 25 if the individual reports exposure to just one psychosocial risk, and a value of 100 if the individual reports no exposure to any of the psychosocial risks. Despite this rather generous coding, almost 90 per cent of the working population receives a value of 100 in this component of risks, only 5 per cent a value of 25 and 5 per cent a value of 0.

For inspecting the correlation between the physical factors, rather than looking at the full matrix of correlations for the 13 original variables, we carry out a principal components analysis, whose results are displayed in

Table 5.6   Results of the factor analysis of the variables related to exposure to physical risks

	Factor 1	Factor 2	Factor 3	Uniqueness
Vibrations	0.63	0.41	−0.15	0.42
Noise	0.66	0.39	−0.13	0.40
High temperatures	0.69	0.23	0.04	0.47
Low temperatures	0.71	0.05	0.04	0.49
Smoke	0.50	0.60	−0.09	0.38
Vapours	0.20	0.80	0.04	0.33
Chemical products	0.11	0.74	0.21	0.40
Radiation	0.03	0.51	0.24	0.68
Tobacco	0.30	0.26	0.05	0.84
Infectious materials	0.01	0.34	0.70	0.39
Tiring positions	0.66	0.06	0.29	0.48
Moving people	0.08	−0.06	0.82	0.32
Heavy loads	0.70	0.07	0.26	0.44
Variance explained (%)	23.9	18.2	11.3	
Cumulative variance explained (%)	23.9	42.2	53.5	

Source: Authors' analysis from EWCS 2005 micro-data.

Table 5.6. Principal components analysis is a data reduction method that generates a set of new variables (factors) which are linear combinations of the original variables and which successively account for as much variability of the original variables as possible. It is the correlation between the original variables which makes it possible to construct these summarizing factors: hence, we can use this method to study the structure of correlations between the 13 physical risk variables more succinctly. In Table 5.6, the rotated loadings of the first three factors are shown: as can be seen in the two lowest rows of the table, these three factors account for more than 50 per cent of the variance of the 13 original variables (the first factor for 24 per cent, the second for 18 per cent, and the third for 11 per cent).

The rotated factor loadings (which show basically the correlation between each of the original variables and the generated factors rotated to show clearer patterns) allow us to identify what each factor stands for. The first factor is associated with work of an intensely physical nature (moving heavy loads, tiring positions), which takes place outdoors (high and low temperatures) and with mechanical tools (vibrations, noise and smoke). Overall, these are the risks traditionally associated with agriculture, construction and some industrial sectors. The second factor seems to reflect exposure to chemical risks, typical of some types of industrial occupations: this factor is highly correlated with breathing in vapours (such as solvents or thinners), smoke, fumes and handling chemical materials; it is also moderately correlated with vibrations and noise. Finally, the third factor seems to summarize the types of risks exposure usually associated with caring jobs in the health sector: moving people, contact with infectious materials, and to a lesser extent radiation and chemicals. The final column of Table 5.6 shows the *uniqueness* of each variable, which summarizes the degree of non-correlation between each variable and the three factors extracted. The most *unique* variables (that is, the most uncorrelated to the factors and therefore, to the other variables) are breathing in tobacco smoke and exposure to radiation: these risks tend to happen in isolation, whereas the other mentioned risks are more likely to happen simultaneously in some particular types of employment.

Table 5.7 shows the structure of correlations between the four individual variables used for constructing the psychosocial component, and we have also added for illustrative purposes the three factors generated by the principal components analysis of the 13 physical risks discussed earlier. There is a fair degree of correlation between the exposure to the four psychosocial risks shown in Table 5.7: in particular, those suffering threats were also likely to suffer violence from coworkers and other people outside work. There is a rather low correlation between the psychosocial and the physical risk factors: only those who are exposed to the physical risks usually associated with care professions are also likely to be more exposed to psychosocial risks (especially threats and violence).[11]

The distribution of scores of the resulting fourth dimension of our index is shown in Figure 5.8, as a histogram. The shape of this diagram is considerably different from that of the previous dimensions: it is not only a very bumpy distribution, but it is clearly bimodal (with the two most frequent values being 25 and 100). Although the most frequent value is 25 and the median 43, there are more values above than below 50, so that the overall mean is 53.8. Overall, the implicit assessment of job quality with respect to health and safety made by indicator is slightly more negative than for the two previous dimensions, though less negative than for pay.

Finally, Table 5.8 shows the average scores for the same set of representative worker categories discussed in previous sections. The first column shows that the scores of psychosocial risks are much more positive than those of physical risks, because as we discussed earlier, the reported levels of exposure are really much lower in the former case. There are few differences between employees and the self-employed on both components, so there is not much to comment there. Much more telling are the differences across the three

Table 5.7   Correlations among health and safety variables

	Physical risks			Psychosocial risks			
	Intense physical risks (1st factor)	Chemical risks (2nd factor)	Risks in caring jobs (3rd factor)	Threats of violence	Violence from work-mates	Violence from others	Bully-ing
Physical risks							
Intense physical risks (1st factor)	1.000						
Chemical risks (2nd factor)	0.000	1.000					
Risks in caring jobs (3rd factor)	0.000	0.000	1.000				
Psychosocial risks							
Threats of violence	0.041	−0.009	0.139	1.000			
Violence from workmates	0.056	0.027	0.142	0.412	1.000		
Violence from others	0.040	−0.020	0.145	0.586	0.228	1.000	
Bullying	0.071	0.024	0.056	0.287	0.166	0.222	1.000

Source: Authors' analysis from EWCS 2005 micro-data.

representative sectors shown in Table 5.8. Construction workers face the higher levels of physical risks (that is, their score is lower, at 22.9), and health workers the lower (score of 35.1). But the scores are totally inverted when we look at psychosocial risks: health workers suffer them considerably more often than construction workers. A similar contrast (even more pronounced) can be observed between professionals and operators.

   Table 5.8 also shows the scores for each of the physical factors (just shown for illustrative purposes) and each of the psychosocial risks. The highest levels of exposure, in general, are for the risks related to intensely physical work (the first factor): but there are important differences by groups of workers, from 51.2 for construction workers to 68.3 and 68.5 for health workers and professionals. The exposure to chemicals is higher in

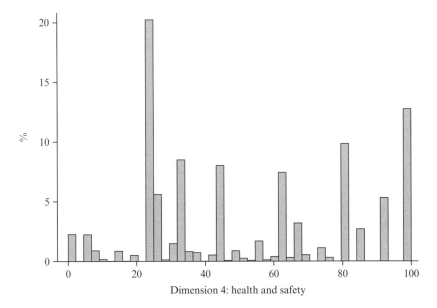

Source: Authors' analysis from EWCS 2005 micro-data.

Figure 5.8   Distribution of the health and safety dimension

construction workers and operators (near 70 in both cases). And confirming that the third factor refers to physical risks associated with caring jobs, its highest levels of exposure are by far for workers in the health sector (61 in health against 78.9 in construction or 77.6 in HORECA, for instance). All psychosocial risks show very low levels of exposure (and hence, high scores in terms of job quality), for almost all groups: only the health sector displays relatively lower scores, with workers in this sector reporting higher exposure to threats of violence and bullying. All these results look plausible and within expectations.

5.7.   WORK–LIFE BALANCE

The fifth and final dimension of our job quality index is work–life balance. The key work characteristic for this dimension is, without any doubt, the organization of working time: in particular, the duration, scheduling and flexibility of working hours. A secondary aspect which is also mentioned in the specialized literature is the intensity of the work effort. The weight assigned to each of these two components within the dimension of

Table 5.8   Average values of the health and safety dimension and its components for different types of workers

	Total	Self-employed	Em-ployee	Construc-tion	HOR-ECA	Health sector	Profes-sionals	Machine operators
Dimension 4: health and safety	53.8	52.2	54.0	40.6	42.3	46.1	64.9	38.5
Physical risks	41.6	38.5	42.2	22.9	27.8	35.1	57.0	20.8
Intense physical risks	61.7	59.9	62.1	51.2	58.8	68.3	68.5	53.7
Chemical risks	71.4	72.5	71.2	67.7	73.6	70.9	72.0	68.9
Risks in caring jobs	77.3	77.3	77.3	78.9	77.6	61.0	76.0	79.9
Psychosocial risks	90.4	93.2	89.7	93.7	85.6	78.8	88.7	91.4
Threats of violence	94.0	95.1	93.7	96.3	90.8	83.6	92.3	94.2
Violence from workmates	98.2	99.5	97.9	98.1	98.7	93.9	98.2	98.5
Violence from others	95.7	95.7	95.6	98.1	92.5	88.6	95.2	95.3
Bullying	94.9	97.3	94.4	97.0	91.5	91.3	94.2	95.5

Source: Authors' analysis from EWCS 2005 micro-data.

work–life balance is unequal, trying to reflect the relative importance that each of them receives in the literature: working time accounts for 75 per cent of the dimension, and intensity for 25 per cent.

Box 5.5 provides details on the construction of this dimension of the index. The working time component has three sub-components. The duration of work is based on the standard question on the number of hours usually worked in the main paid job on a normal week. For standardizing the values of this variable (to rescale it to our 0–100 desirability scores), rather than using the max-min method on the original continuous variable, we have opted for generating five categories of working hours and then manually assign scores within the 0–100 range to each category. The reason is that although working hours is in theory a continuous variable, in practice (as a result of regulations and cultural norms) it behaves as a discrete or categorical variable. In other words, workers do not really have the chance to choose any number of hours of work, but a few discrete options such as working full-time or part-time: for this reason, the variable is in many cases better specified in intervals (Creedy and Kalb 2005). This also allows us to use a non-linear metric for the coding of hours of work. Working less than 20 hours a week is the most desirable outcome and hence receives a value of 100; working between 20 and 38 (a long part-time or a short full-time) receives a value of 75; the standard 40 hours a week (plus or minus two hours) receives a value of 50; long full-time hours between 42 and 48 receives a value of 25; and very long hours (in principle, not even allowed by European legislation) above 48 a week receive a value of 0. Considering the often disadvantaged conditions of employment of part-time workers, it may seem surprising that working less than 20 hours is considered as the most desirable outcome in this component of our index: but we must bear in mind that this is just one indicator within a composite index that includes many other job quality measures. If part-time workers have worse employment conditions, that will be accounted for by the employment quality dimension. Each attribute has to be evaluated on its own, and working less hours is, *ceteris paribus*, better than working more hours.

The second subcomponent of working time is scheduling. The idea behind the specification of this subcomponent is that working outside 'normal' hours is undesirable because it interferes with social and family life. We have four variables measuring the extent to which the respondent works at nights, evenings, Saturdays and Sundays: in each case, the outcomes have been coded as 100 if the respondent never works on such atypical schedules, 0 if they always (or very often) do, and a gradation for the values in between, as shown in Box 5.5. The overall score of this subcomponent is, as usual, the average of such four variables.

Finally, the third subcomponent of working time is flexibility/control.

BOX 5.5   WORK–LIFE BALANCE

a) Working time (75%)
a.1. Duration (25%)
- Q8a How many hours do you usually work per week in your main paid job?

  0–20 hours (100), 20–38 (75), 38–42 (50), 42–48 (25), 48–168 (0).

a.2. Scheduling (25%)
- Q14A Normally, how many times a month do you work at night, for at least 2 hours between 10.00 pm and 05.00 am?

  Never (100), 1–5 (75), 6–10 (50), 11–20 (25), more than 20 (0).
- Q14B And how many times a month do you work in the evening, for at least 2 hours between 6.00 pm and 10.00 pm?

  Never (100), 1–5 (75), 6–10 (50), 11–20 (25), more than 20 (0).
- Q14C And how many times a month do you work on Sundays?

  Never (100), 1 (75), 2 (50), 3 (25), 4 or 5 (0).
- Q14D And how many times a month do you work on Saturdays?

  Never (100), 1 (75), 2 (50), 3 (25), 4 or 5 (0).

a.3. Flexibility/control (25%)
- Q17A How are your working time arrangements set?
    1 – They are set by the company/organization with no possibility for changes

      If schedules change regularly (according to variable q17b), coded as (0).

      If schedules do not change (according to variable q17b), coded as (25).
    2 – You can choose between several fixed working schedules determined by the company/organization (50)
    3 – You can adapt your working hours within certain limits (75)
    4 – Your working hours are entirely determined by yourself (100)

b) Work intensity (25%)
- Q20B And, does your job involve. . .? *[Nordic scale, same code as in box 5.4]*

A – Working at very high speed
B – Working with tight deadlines
– Q25 For each of the following statements, please select the response which best describes your work situation. . .
    F – You have enough time to get the job done – Almost always (100) Often (67) Sometimes (33) Rarely (16) Almost never (0).

The idea here is that the more control the worker has of her own work schedule, the better she will be able to adapt it to her non-work commitments (and vice versa). So the most desirable outcome (receiving a score of 100) is having total control over one's working times, and the less desirable (score of 0) is having schedules which not only are imposed on the worker, but which change regularly.

With respect to the second component of the work–life balance dimension, which, as mentioned, receives one fourth of the weight, it was constructed by averaging three variables that measure work intensity from slightly different angles: whether the respondent works at very high speed, with tight deadlines, and whether she has enough time to get the work done (see Box 5.5).

Table 5.9 shows the pair-wise correlation coefficients between the variables used for the construction of the work–life balance dimension of our index. The duration and scheduling of working time are positively and moderately correlated, as happens with most variables within our index (in most cases, the desirable and undesirable work attributes tend to go together). But the correlation between the flexibility/control indicator and the other two working time indicators goes in the opposite direction, and although it is not very high, it is significant. This is important, because it is one of the few cases in which we find a *compensation* rather than an *accumulation* between different work attributes: generally, jobs that have very long and unsocial schedules (and therefore, a low score in those two indicators) tend to involve a higher degree of flexibility and control by the worker (and a high score in this third indicator), and vice versa. This involves some kind of trade-off, and means that the aggregated variability of the working time component is lower than the variability of the three indicators used for constructing it: averaging values which go in opposite directions, we end up with more middling scores. This is perfectly correct and fitting the logic of our index: it simply reflects the fact that there is, in this particular case, compensation between positive and negative attributes. But as we have already seen, there are very few

Table 5.9   Correlations among work–life balance variables

	Working time			Work intensity		
	Duration	Scheduling	Flexibility	Speed of work	Tight dead-lines	Enough time to do the work
Working time						
Duration	1.000					
Scheduling	0.347	1.000				
Flexibility	−0.162	−0.123	1.000			
Work intensity						
Speed of work	0.140	0.127	0.085	1.000		
Tight deadlines	0.154	0.074	0.049	0.622	1.000	
Enough time to do the work	0.072	0.024	0.058	0.243	0.258	1.000

Source: Authors' analysis from EWCS 2005 micro-data.

cases of compensation between different job attributes: instead, the predominant mechanism seems to be one of accumulation of good and bad attributes.

The rest of Table 5.9 is less noteworthy. There is a rather high correlation between the three variables measuring intensity, as could be expected considering that they are really three different ways of measuring the same thing. The correlation between working time and intensity is less strong, though significant in the case of work duration. It is interesting to note that those working longer hours also tend to feel that they have tight deadlines and work at high speed.

Figure 5.9 presents the distribution of the fifth dimension of our index. This is the dimension whose distribution is closest to normality, although with a slight skewness to the right-hand side. The average value is 59, the median is 59.5, and the interquartile range roughly goes from 49 to 69.

The average scores for our representative categories of workers (shown in Table 5.10) look rather plausible, and quite interesting in some cases. The contrast between employees and self-employed illustrates the trade-off between flexibility and duration/scheduling mentioned earlier: whereas the self-employed (as expected) have extremely high values in terms of control of their working time, they have very low values (the lowest in the table) for duration and scheduling. But the overall value for self-employed

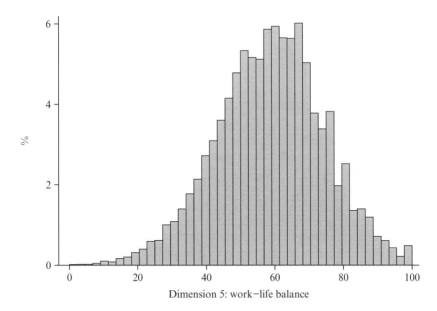

Source: Authors' analysis from EWCS 2005 micro-data.

Figure 5.9   Distribution of the work–life balance dimension

and employees are relatively similar (61.8 *versus* 58.3), because in both cases the positive and negative attributes (which are inverted) compensate each other. There are no significant differences in terms of intensity between employees and self-employed workers.

The profiles of the three representative sectors are also fitting to expectations. In terms of sectors, the worst overall scores are for HORECA, the best for health workers. HORECA have low values in two of the three working time indicators (long and unsocial schedules), near average values in the third one (so there is not much compensation in this case), and below average values in two of the three intensity indicators. Construction workers have good scores in terms of schedules, but they are slightly below average in duration, control and intensity. Health workers have good scores in duration, slightly above average in intensity and slightly below in control and scheduling. Finally, it is interesting to see that the lowest values for control of the whole table are for operators, a category that is slightly below average in most other indicators of work–life balance.

Table 5.10 *Average values of the work–life balance dimension and its components for different types of workers*

	Total	Self-employed	Employee	Con-struction	HORECA	Health sector	Profes-sionals	Machine operators
Dimension 5: work–life balance	59.1	61.8	58.3	56.1	49.9	60.3	62.6	51.2
Working time	58.7	61.4	57.9	57.7	48.4	60.7	62.6	50.0
Duration	51.9	31.7	55.4	40.9	47.5	63.3	56.4	43.4
Scheduling	78.7	63.2	81.8	86.0	50.7	76.2	82.0	75.7
Flexibility	45.2	86.1	36.5	45.5	46.0	42.7	49.1	30.7
Work intensity	60.2	62.9	59.5	51.4	54.4	59.2	62.5	54.9
Speed of work	57.8	58.6	57.4	48.0	44.0	55.6	64.8	49.1
Tight deadlines	55.5	56.9	54.9	42.9	50.6	57.3	57.5	47.0
Enough time to do the work	67.5	73.0	66.3	62.8	69.0	64.9	65.3	68.6

Source: Authors' analysis from EWCS 2005 micro-data.

5.8.   THE OVERALL JOB QUALITY INDEX

As briefly explained earlier, the overall job quality index is then calculated using the following weighted geometric mean formula:

$$EJQI = \prod_{i=1}^{n} X_i^{\alpha_i} \qquad [5.1]$$

where α_i is the weight given to each dimension X_i and $\Sigma_{i=1}^{n}\alpha_i = 1$.

The main disadvantage of using a geometric aggregation in the final stage of construction of the index is that its decomposition is not as obvious as with an arithmetically aggregated index. It is possible to do an additive decomposition of the index, but the dimensions have to be transformed into logarithms and the index exponentiated: this makes such decomposition less intuitive and therefore less useful.

On the other hand, the proposed aggregation method has very desirable properties for our purposes. The weighted geometric mean is formally equivalent to a modified Cobb-Douglas production function, a specific type of production function that is widely used in economics and whose properties are well-known.[12] In the context of job quality, the production function yields the level of job quality that corresponds to different combinations of amenities (the five dimensions of our index).

There are some properties of the Cobb-Douglas production function that are desirable for our purposes. The first one is the assumption of constant returns to scale. This property means that a variation of the same scale of every dimension of the index results in a variation of the overall index of exactly that same scale. In the second place, the marginal contribution of each component to overall job quality is decreasing, that is, other things being equal, an increase in a certain dimension of job quality produces a rise in job quality progressively less and less important. The last relevant feature of this function is that it implies that the production function of job quality is concave: if two different combinations of job attributes yield the same overall job quality, then any combination resulting from the weighted average of the original combinations leads to at least the same job quality. In other words, this property means that more balanced sets of amenities yield higher job quality than extreme combinations of job attributes (where some dimensions take very high and others very low values). At the same time, this feature implies that, other things being equal, in order to hold job quality constant, a reduction of the level of quality in a certain dimension requires a compensating larger increase in another. This increase has to be larger (in absolute terms) the more scant is the first attribute.[13]

As we have two versions of the pay dimension, there are two versions of

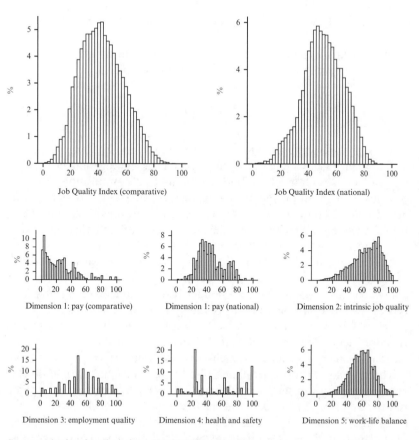

Source: Authors' analysis from EWCS 2005 micro-data.

Figure 5.10   Distribution of the Job Quality Index and its five dimensions

the index as well: one specifically designed for international comparisons and one designed for individual-level (non-comparative) analysis. Figure 5.10 shows the distribution of both versions of the index as histograms, and for reference we show again the histograms of each dimension below. Table 5.11 displays some summary statistics and Table 5.12 the pair-wise coefficients of correlation between both versions of the index and their dimensions. The scores of the comparative index lean slightly to the left-hand side of the chart (both the mean and the median are slightly below 50), and their distribution looks relatively normal and continuous (the skewness and kurtosis statistics in Table 5.11 show that the distribution of the index is quite close to normal, more than any of the individual

Table 5.11 Descriptive statistics of the Job Quality Index and the five dimensions

	Mean	Standard deviation	Coefficient of variation	Skewness	Kurtosis	5th percentile	25th percentile	50th percentile	75th percentile	95th percentile
Job Quality Index (comparative)	45.7	15.3	0.34	2.58	0.03	20.8	35.0	45.5	56.7	71.3
Job Quality Index (national)	51.6	14.1	0.27	2.83	−0.20	26.7	42.4	51.6	61.9	74.4
Dimension 1: pay (comparative)	29.1	20.4	0.70	4.94	1.18	3.0	14.3	26.8	39.8	67.0
Dimension 1: pay (national)	45.6	15.6	0.34	2.28	0.54	24.4	32.9	41.7	55.9	72.9
Dimension 2: intrinsic job quality	64.3	19.2	0.30	2.70	−0.54	28.5	52.0	66.7	79.6	91.6
Dimension 3: employment quality	55.1	22.2	0.40	2.92	−0.26	12.5	43.8	56.3	68.8	93.8
Dimension 4: health and safety	53.8	29.9	0.56	1.69	0.20	10.9	25.0	43.8	81.3	100.0
Dimension 5: work – life balance	59.1	15.7	0.27	3.05	−0.17	32.5	49.0	59.6	69.3	84.8

Source: Authors' analysis from EWCS 2005 micro-data.

Table 5.12   Correlations between the Job Quality Index and the five dimensions

	Job Quality Index (comparative)	Job Quality Index (national)	Dimension 1: pay (comparative)	Dimension 1: pay (national)	Dimension 2: intrinsic job quality	Dimension 3: employment quality	Dimension 4: health and safety	Dimension 5: work-life balance
Job Quality Index (comparative)	1.000							
Job Quality Index (national)	0.923	1.000						
Dimension 1: pay (comparative)	0.658	0.411	1.000					
Dimension 1: pay (national)	0.500	0.468	0.674	1.000				
Dimension 2: intrinsic job quality	0.528	0.576	0.260	0.294	1.000			
Dimension 3: employment quality	0.601	0.634	0.279	0.255	0.353	1.000		
Dimension 4: health and safety	0.613	0.695	0.135	0.114	0.192	0.172	1.000	
Dimension 5: work-life balance	0.402	0.426	0.065	−0.031	0.202	0.056	0.328	1.000

Source: Authors' analysis from EWCS 2005 micro-data.

dimensions). Comparing the distribution of the index with its five building dimensions, we see that it represents a fair summary of them, although the fact that we have used a geometric method for aggregating the information from the five dimensions means that it is a summary that emphasizes certain aspects of them. In particular, the geometric aggregation penalizes having low values in any of the dimensions, and hence it gives more prominence in the final overall scores to dimensions 1 and 4, because their values are lowest and their dispersion highest (as shows the column with the coefficients of variation in Table 5.11).

This is also reflected in the pair-wise correlations between both versions of the index and the dimensions of Table 5.12: the comparative index is most highly correlated with the pay dimension (0.658), followed by the health and safety and employment dimensions (around 0.6), and finally by the intrinsic job quality (0.528) and the work–life balance dimensions (0.402). In the case of the national version of the index, as the systematic country differences are eliminated from the first dimension, the dimension that has a larger influence on the overall index scores is health and safety (0.695) followed by employment quality (0.634).

Table 5.12 also allows us to inspect the correlations between the dimensions among themselves, which has significant interest on its own. With a single exception, all the coefficients of correlations are positive, which means that at the level of the dimensions, there is more accumulation than compensation of positive and negative job attributes (we must remember that in our detailed analysis of the components of each dimension, we only found two clear cases of compensation, between flexibility and duration of working time, and between flexibility and social support). The five dimensions of the index seem to cluster in two different groups, highly correlated among themselves but not so much across: pay, intrinsic job quality and employment quality are quite highly correlated (around 0.3–0.35), as are health and safety and work–life balance (0.328), but the correlations between the former and the latter are below 0.2. Work–life balance, in particular, has nearly no correlation with pay and employment quality (and a very moderate correlation with intrinsic job quality), which probably reflects some kind of trade-off that we have already mentioned in previous pages: some workers with very long and unsocial schedules (and hence low values in the work–life balance dimension) have very good conditions of pay, employment and intrinsic rewards from work, and vice versa. We discuss these patterns in more detail in the next chapter.

Finally, Table 5.13 shows the scores of the index and the five dimensions for our representative categories of workers, for a final evaluation of the plausibility of our results. The mean score of the comparative index for the EU27 as a whole is 45.7, with highest values for the intrinsic

Table 5.13   Average values of the Job Quality Index and its dimensions

	Total	Self-employed	Employee	Construction	HORECA	Health sector	Professionals	Machine operators
Job Quality Index (comparative)	45.7	47.2	45.6	43.3	37.4	46.2	54.9	36.5
Job Quality Index (national)	51.6	54.1	51.3	48.6	42.3	51.1	60.9	43.2
Dimension 1: pay (comparative)	29.1	30.9	29.0	31.1	26.5	30.9	36.1	23.6
Dimension 1: pay (national)	45.6	50.1	44.9	49.0	42.6	44.9	52.4	43.9
Dimension 2: intrinsic job quality	64.3	74.8	62.3	64.2	58.5	70.2	78.7	51.3
Dimension 3: employment quality	55.1	53.5	55.7	51.8	43.7	60.5	64.4	48.8
Dimension 4: health and safety	53.8	52.2	54.0	40.6	42.3	46.1	64.9	38.5
Dimension 5: work–life balance	59.1	61.8	58.3	56.1	49.9	60.3	62.6	51.2

Source: Authors' analysis from EWCS 2005 micro-data.

job quality dimension (64.3), above 50 for the other three dimensions of amenities (employment quality, health and safety and work–life balance), and a much lower value of 29.1 for the dimension of pay (we have already discussed at length the differences in the distribution of scores for the five dimensions). The self-employed receive a slightly higher score than employees, with most of the difference coming from the intrinsic job quality dimension (as we saw earlier, most of this difference is explained by the difference in autonomy levels). Of the three illustrative sectors shown in Figure 5.13, the lowest value is for workers in Hotels, Restaurants and Catering (HORECA), which receive an overall value of 37.4, with very low scores in employment quality, work–life balance and pay. Workers in the health sector have rather high scores in terms of intrinsic job quality and employment quality, whereas construction workers have higher scores in terms of pay. The job quality score of professional workers is 50 per cent higher than the score for operators and assemblers: and although the difference in favour of professionals appears in all five dimensions, it is highest in health and safety (nearly double), pay and intrinsic job quality. This final set of illustrative results look plausible and within expectations.

5.9.   SOME FINAL REMARKS

Once we have constructed our Job Quality Index for the EU, we can go back to the objectives we set ourselves in the introduction to this chapter and try to evaluate to what extent our index fulfils such objectives.

First, is our Job Quality Index clearly delimited? Are all the areas of information covered relevant for the underlying concept of job quality? We believe they are, to a larger extent than most of the indices evaluated in Chapter 4. The fact that the selection of relevant job attributes was based on an extensive literature review, and the use of a wide-ranging working conditions survey (the EWCS), ensured that the coverage of our index was reasonably exhaustive (with the exception of participation in the work-place, which is unfortunately absent from the EWCS). And we have been very strict in leaving out issues which may be related, but are not attributes of job quality: in particular, we have not included in our index informa-tion related to the worker rather than the job (such as job satisfaction or employment history), nor information related to the labour market (such as unemployment levels) or the institutional environment (such as labour regulation or unemployment benefits). Such restraint does not only ensure that our index is strictly about job quality, but in fact it shall facilitate evaluating the links between all those secondary elements and job quality at a later stage.

That said, we have to acknowledge that there is some degree of una-voidable *contamination* of some of those alien elements in our index. Although we have tried to leave job satisfaction out of our index, some of the variables used for constructing it are strongly subjective in nature, and therefore in practice relatively similar to job satisfaction (in particu-lar, some of the variables included in dimension 2, intrinsic job quality). Such 'subjective' contamination (which is at odds with our concept of job quality, focused on the attributes of jobs, and therefore unrelated to the subjectivity of individual workers) is unavoidable when constructing an index based on a workers' survey, as is the case here. The other alterna-tive would involve doing some type of external evaluation of job quality (by specialized surveyors measuring job quality attributes on site, for instance), which would have problems on its own and is obviously imprac-tical. There is also some degree of contamination of the institutional environment in our index: to the extent that the institutional environment affects the responses of workers, the differences across countries may partly reflect them. For instance, countries with a high degree of institu-tional protection against workplace risks may paradoxically reveal higher levels of exposure, because workers are more aware of them (for instance, this is almost certainly happening with psychosocial risks, as mentioned earlier). This is also very difficult to avoid in an international index such as this one: the cultural and institutional differences across countries tend to permeate the index in one way or another, even if the objectives of the index are defined in more or less institutionally-neutral terms. These minor problems of contamination of alien elements in our index should be taken into account when its results are analysed.

Second, is our Job Quality Index based on a clear and coherent model, which guides the selection of attributes and the logic of aggregation of information? We believe it is, to a larger extent than most of the propos-als reviewed in the previous chapter. Rather than coming up with a new model of job quality, we opted for building a model based on a review of the main arguments found in the Social Sciences with respect to the impact of jobs on the well-being of workers. Such review provided an extensive list of relevant attributes to be included in our index, as well as some type of conceptual structure that was used for constructing the model shown earlier in figure 5.1, and which provided some logic for the aggregation of different pieces of information into an overall index. In that sense, our index of job quality is transparent in its construction, grounded in a long tradition of research (which facilitates the interpretation of results) and meaningful in its structure and components.

That said, it must be acknowledged that there is some degree of un-avoidable arbitrariness in the selection of elements and in the allocation of weights to the different pieces of information, even in a more or less theoretically-grounded index as ours. Our literature review did provide us with a list of concepts to be covered: but the actual operationalization of such concepts into the variables used for the index is not obvious, and therefore involves making decisions which can always be challenged. The need to confine our choices to an existing questionnaire, however good, makes this problem even larger (the clearest example being the need to leave out a full dimension because of lack of information in the EWCS questionnaire). The weights assigned to each variable, indicator, component and dimension in their aggregation are also at most loosely suggested by the literature review. Nevertheless, it would be completely naïve to expect that any model of job quality can unambiguously determine the areas to be covered and the logic to be followed for the aggregation of information: rather than that, we should aim at a reasonably transparent selection and aggregation of information, that provides a justification for each important decision so that it can be challenged in its own terms. We believe that our index fulfils such goals.

An important decision with respect to the operationalization of concepts into variables and indicators is the logic followed for recoding the original variables into a homogeneous metric so that they can be aggregated. For constructing our index, we decided to avoid the usual practice of standardizing into Z-scores, and proposed a transformation of the original values into a 0–100 range according to their meaning in terms of job quality. This was a risky decision, which can be criticized for bringing even more arbitrariness into the index. But we believe that the Z-score standardization (or any derivation) would imply even more problems for our purposes: most importantly, it involves homogenizing the variability of the different job quality attributes, and therefore distorting the real differences in such variability, which is crucial information in this case. For instance: most people have similarly high scores in the psychosocial component of the fourth dimension (health and safety), while the physical component has much more variability. If we standardize both components, we end up with two variables with an apparently similar variability: the existing small differences in the psychosocial components would be magnified, and both components would contribute similarly to the variability of the aggregated health and safety dimension. In our view, this amounts to a misrepresentation of the distribution of job quality. If the component of psychosocial risks has a low variability, the index should reflect that, because it means that psychosocial risks have in general a low impact on the overall distribution of job quality. Hence, we opted for a method of standardizing the variables that respected their original variability. An implication of this choice is that the resulting index has a lower degree of variability than otherwise (because some of its components have a low variability that has been left intact), which makes the analysis slightly more difficult, but the results slightly easier to interpret (as they have a more direct meaning).

Third, can our Job Quality Index be computed at the individual level to do analysis by subgroups? Is the information sufficiently harmonized across countries to do meaningful comparisons? The use of the EWCS to construct our index ensured that both goals were fulfilled to a larger extent than most of the indices reviewed in the previous chapter. Our index was fully constructed at the individual level, which not only enables the analysis by subgroups, but also the evaluation of the micro-level interaction between the different job attributes (for instance, whether there is compensation or accumulation of good and bad job attributes). But the source used imposes some restrictions as well: the EWCS has a relatively small sample at the country level, which means that, in practice, our capacity to deepen the analysis to very specific subgroups at the country level is limited. In this sense, it would be more than desirable that in future editions the EWCS expands its sample size at the country level to at least five or ten thousand respondents, which would boost its analytic potential. With respect to the comparability of information in the EWCS, we can be certain that it is one of the most harmonized surveys at the European level, but this does not mean that there are no problems in this respect. We have already mentioned that differences in the cultural and institutional contexts can contaminate the answers to some questions, so that they not only reflect differences in the job attributes but also in how such attributes are socially constructed (we exemplified such effect with the differences in the reported levels of psychosocial risks across Europe). The only solution to this problem, again, is to be careful when analysing the data, and keep a critical eye on possible cultural effects in the responses to some variables.[14]

Finally, does our Job Quality Index provide a clear and unambiguous evaluation of job quality for any type of subgroup of the working population? Is it possible to decompose the overall score transparently, to identify the attributes which are behind any difference found? Our index has been generated by aggregation, following a nested structure that makes it very easy to decompose any observed difference to a very detailed level (from the overall scores to the dimensions, then to the components and subcomponents, then to the indicators and finally to the original variables from the EWCS). The final index, which allows clearly and unambiguously evaluating and ranking the job quality of any subgroup of workers, has been computed through a geometric rather than an arithmetic aggregation. This gives the final index some desirable properties: most importantly, the contributions of the different dimensions to the overall score are decreasing rather than linear, and the contribution of each dimension is not independent from the contribution of the other four (the index takes into account the interaction between them).

Our Job Quality Index for the European Union is, therefore, reasonably close to the objectives we set ourselves in the beginning of this chapter, following our own recommendations from previous pages. But the real test of its value, nevertheless, will be carried out when we use it for evaluating the quality of jobs across the European Union, which is the main task of the next chapter.

NOTES

1. It is important to note that, following our definition, these job attributes would only be included in our model insofar as they have a direct impact on workers' well-being (for communicational/expressive reasons, for instance), but not as a tool for improving job quality. Although in our view, it is undisputable that workers' participation and political action at the workplace has historically been one of the main drivers of the improvement of job quality, it is a determinant and not a component of job quality as such (except, as mentioned earlier, as an element of workers' autonomy and communicational possibilities). In any case, the EWCS does not cover this very important aspect of work and employment, so we are forced to leave it out of our model.
2. For a review of the characteristics of the EWCS see Section 3.3 of Chapter 3.
3. See http://epp.eurostat.ec.europa.eu/portal/page/portal/purchasing_power_parities/int roduction.
4. Of course, this is not intended to be a measure of inequality, and as such it is problematic: in particular, it is very conservative compared to others, because it only compares the values of the highest and lowest deciles, ignoring the disparities which exist within the deciles, which are in fact enormous in the top category.
5. As in the rest of the analysis, the data has been weighted to make it representative of the employed population in the European Union of 27 members.
6. In construction, half of the people are in the category of craft workers, with a value of around 33 in the pay indicator. In health, one-fourth of the workers are professionals (doctors, with a value of approximately 38), another third technicians (nurses, with a value of 26) and another third service and support workers (with values ranging from 17 to 25).
7. Powerlessness thus becomes powerfulness, meaninglessness meaningfulness, social isolation social support and self-estrangement self-fulfilment.
8. In fact, it is not twice the weight, but one and a half times the weight. The overall weight of autonomy in the job quality index is 7.5 (5 per cent in the previous component, 2.5 per cent in this one).
9. Some of the variables used in this component, as shown in box 5.2, had a coding problem in the original EWCS questionnaire (which was simply the result of a mistake): the missing values of their response scales ('always' and 'never') were not included in the answer cards. We can assume that the people that would have given those answers chose instead the closest values ('almost always' and 'almost never'), so we have given those items the values of 0 and 100 in the scores.
10. Only if the individual is equally exposed to more than one risk do we combine (multiply) their values (for instance, if the exposure is 50 to two risks, the value assigned to the individual is lower, 25).
11. The factors generated by principal components analysis are totally uncorrelated among themselves (orthogonal).

12.   The simplest Cobb-Douglas function, when there are only two inputs, capital (K) and labour (L), is written as $Y = AK^{\alpha}L^{1-\alpha}$, where A and α are constants. If $A = 1$, the Cobb-Douglas function would be a weighted geometric mean of the quantity of inputs. A generalized Cobb-Douglas function would be $Y = A\Pi(X)_i 0^{\alpha_i}$, where $\Sigma\alpha_i = 1$ and X_i denotes the input I, with a weight α_i.

13.   This function has an additional – and much more technical – property: it has a constant elasticity of substitution (equal to unity). The constant elasticity of substitution measures the ease with which one production factor can be substituted by another holding the output constant. Formally, this measure is the ratio between the proportional change in the ratio of two inputs and the ratio of their marginal productivities (which here can be interpreted as the marginal contribution of each dimension to overall job quality). If the elasticity of substitution is high, then a percentage change in the marginal contribution of each dimension will lead to a large percentage change in the mix of dimensions embedded in the preferred job. Particularly, the worker would choose a job with a larger weight of the amenity whose return increased.

14.   It could be argued that, to some extent, it does not matter whether the evaluations given by workers to the job attributes across countries are affected by these cultural differences, because after all, what affects people's well-being is not necessarily the reality as such (what is the reality as such, anyway?) but the way such reality is experienced, which is mediated by social norms and cultural values.

6. Making concepts work: job quality in Europe

6.1. INTRODUCTION

Previously in this book we have discussed the principles and methods to be followed for constructing a job quality index for purposes of international comparisons. By way of illustration, in Chapter 5 we presented our own proposal of a European Job Quality Index (JQI), taking advantage of the existence of an excellent statistical source for this matter in the EU, the European Working Conditions Survey (EWCS). In this chapter, we continue with this illustration by presenting the empirical results of our indicator across the EU, trying to answer the type of questions which such an index should be able to answer. First, we use this index for evaluating job quality in the different European countries, which is the most obvious interest of an index of this kind. This analysis includes the study of the role played by the different dimensions of the overall aggregate job quality index as well as robustness analysis to see the effect on the index of changes in the weighting and aggregation method chosen. Second, we shift the unit of analysis to jobs rather than individuals or countries, to evaluate the differences in job quality of different sectors and occupations. Third, we explore the distribution of job quality within the countries of the sample and evaluate the differences in job quality between genders and age groups. Then, we take advantage of the multidimensional nature of our index to study the interrelation between the different job quality attributes at the individual level, trying to answer the important question of whether there is compensation or accumulation between these job quality attributes. Finally, we compare the results of our index to the results of a simpler index of satisfaction with working conditions, a way to test the external validity of our proposal as well as an evaluation of the determinants of job satisfaction.

Although we hope that this chapter will convince the reader that our proposal constitutes a fully-fledged job quality index that can be used for comparative purposes in the EU, and could eventually feed the policy process, we present it as an illustrative or a preliminary proposal, mostly because of the limitations imposed by the data used for its construction.

As discussed in Chapter 3, the EWCS is an excellent source that covers most of the areas that a job quality index should include, and does so in a highly comparable manner. But its small sample size makes it still unsuitable for policy purposes, because it does not allow breaking down the overall figures by subgroups of the working population at the country level (which is of crucial interest for a social indicator: without such knowledge, it is extremely difficult to design effective and targeted policies). What we do in this chapter, then, is just scratching the surface of what a job quality index could do: we evaluate the broad differences in job quality at the country level and, by pooling the data of the 27 EU countries together (because at the national level the sample size is too small for any analysis), we discuss the distribution of job quality for specific subgroups for the whole of the EU, which is what a job quality index should be able to do at the country level. The EWCS has some other disadvantages that emphasize the preliminary nature of our proposal: its coverage of the pay dimension is limited and somewhat defective, it lacks information on one important dimension of job quality (participation and interest representation) and its periodicity is too sparse. As already mentioned in the previous chapter, it would be desirable that either the EWCS is expanded to cover these gaps, or that it is subsumed into its big brother, the European Labour Force Survey (a source with a large sample size and excellent methodological properties, but very weak at present in its coverage of job quality attributes).

On the other hand, although for the reasons mentioned our Job Quality Index is preliminary and illustrative, it is a real proposal: we believe that the structure of its underlying model and the principles followed in its construction (including the coding of the original variable and the method followed for aggregating the information) are fundamentally sound and valid, and that they could be used as a basis for a future European Job Quality Index constructed with more adequate data. We hope that this chapter, at least, serves as an illustration of the potential that such an index could have to better design and evaluate European employment policies.

6.2. JOB QUALITY ACROSS EUROPE

We start this analytic chapter with the most obvious application of our job quality index: the evaluation of the existing differences in job quality across European countries. Such an evaluation has many potentially interesting implications for policy, as it involves comparing country performance in terms of the provision of good quality jobs (which can be put in relation with their performance in terms of the provision of jobs *of any type*, i.e., in terms of employment quantities), and should allow the identification of problematic countries and/or areas, as well as the identification of good practices and exemplary cases.

How much difference can we expect between European countries with respect to job quality? On the one hand, there are large differences in terms of economic development (per capita GDP) and economic structure that could be associated with large differences in job quality across Europe. On the other hand, the EU should itself be a force of convergence in this matter, because of the existence of a single market with free movement of labour and capital (which in theory would tend to equalize differences) and because of the explicit and conscious effort by European institutions to impose certain standards and harmonized conditions in this matter (as exemplified by the directives on working time, temporary contracts, health and safety, participation and consultation, etc.). So any large difference in the levels of job quality across countries can be understood as a failure of the European project, especially if such difference persists or even intensifies over time. In this sense, it is very unfortunate that it is not possible to construct retrospective time series with our job quality index (it will be possible in the future, using later waves of the EWCS) to be able to evaluate dynamically the differences in job quality across European countries. A second important preliminary consideration refers to the role played by structural differences: if the hypothetical differences in job quality result from the fact that the countries have different economic structures (for instance, some countries have a larger share of the employed population in agriculture, which tends to have specific conditions of work and employment), then they would not be as problematic as if there are systematic differences across countries in the quality *of the same type of jobs*. In the end of this section, we will try to address this issue, differentiating between a structural and an *idiosyncratic* component of the differences in job quality across countries.

6.2.1. Overall Differences in Job Quality Across Europe

Figure 6.1 presents what could be used as the headline result of our proposal: a comparison of the average level of job quality in each European country according to our index. The chart (a *sui generis* box-and-whiskers plot) represents the distribution of job quality in each country: the thick black bar in the middle of each country line represents the average level of our index; the box around it represents the interquartilic range (the distance between values of job quality in the 25th and the 75th percentiles in each country), and the whiskers represent the distance between the values

Measuring more than money

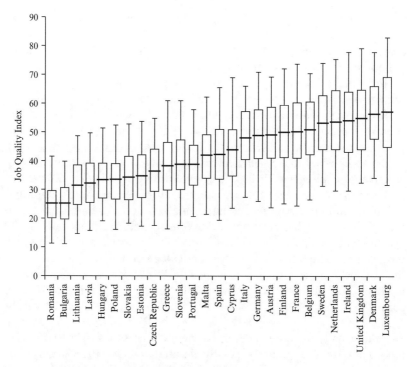

Source: Authors' analysis from EWCS 2005 micro-data.

Figure 6.1   European Index of Job Quality by country

of job quality of the 5th and 95th percentiles in each country. The countries have been sorted from low to high average job quality, left to right. The countries that occupy the bottom of the job quality ranking displayed in Figure 6.1 are all Eastern European countries that joined the EU in 2004 or later (the two most recent members, Romania and Bulgaria, occupy the very bottom of the list). Southern Europe goes next, with mid-low levels of job quality. Continental European countries generally have mid-high values, and the top positions are occupied by Nordic countries, the UK and Ireland. There are some outliers to these general patterns: the value of Slovenia puts it within Southern rather than Eastern European countries; Finland has slightly lower values than the other Scandinavian states; the Netherlands gets a value as high as the Nordics; and the very top of the list is occupied by a very special Continental country, Luxembourg. But despite these small inconsistencies, our job quality index does a surprisingly good job at discriminating the institutional clusters of countries that are well-known for European Social Scientists. Such 'welfare regimes' or 'institutional families' are coherently associated with clearly differentiated levels of job quality according to our index.

The average values of our index range from 25 (Romania) to 57 (Luxembourg), in a scale of 0 to 100. Does that seem like a plausible assessment of the scale of differences in job quality across Europe? Is job quality on average more than two times higher in Luxembourg than in Romania? It is difficult to tell, because we have no external source of information on job quality with which to compare and evaluate the external validity of our measure. To do some type of validation of our results, we will later compare the ranking that derives from our measure with the rankings of previous proposals of job quality indices, to see to what extent does our index deviate from them. We will also look at the individual components of the index (the five dimensions of job quality and their subcomponents), whose results can be interpreted more directly, to evaluate the plausibility of our overall results and understand them better. But first, we can try to put the differences in the country averages in the context of the differences within each country, which are also shown in Figure 6.1 (in the box and whiskers around the average value).

The important point here is that although the average values vary considerably across countries, there is an even larger within-country variation in the values of our index. It is interesting to observe the degree of overlap between the boxes that represent the interquartilic range within each country, which can be understood as a representation of the values of job quality for the bulk of the working population in each country (the 50 per cent of the people that are around the median value in our index). The upper bound of the box in all countries except Eastern Member States overlap with the lower bound of Luxembourg, the country with the highest overall level of job quality: hence, according to our approach there is a large proportion of the European working population with similar levels of job quality, with only Eastern Member States clearly falling behind. And although the proportion of people with levels of job quality comparable to Luxembourg are extremely low in most Eastern European countries, if our point of comparison is the Continental and Southern European countries that occupy the middle of the ranking in Figure 6.1, the levels of job quality are broadly comparable in most cases. The two countries that clearly stand out from the rest, with very low overall levels of job quality and a high concentration of values around such low averages, are Romania and Bulgaria: these countries are only comparable with the Eastern Member States with a lower level of job quality.

In the previous chapter, we discussed at length the difficulties associated with constructing a normative comparative measure of 'wage quality' across Europe (the first dimension of our index). We explained that, for cross-country comparisons, we would use an indicator of wage levels which takes into account the (wide) differences in purchasing power of wages across Europe: we believe that such an indicator is necessary to account for the differentials in the access to resources (and to live chances) granted by similar jobs in different countries, a necessarily important component into an index of job quality to be used for international comparisons. This approach has a problem, though: it incorporates into the index the differences in standard of living across Europe (differences in per capita GDP in PPP), which could be considered as an alien element with respect to a work-centred measure of job quality as the one defended here. Although we would not agree with such a criticism (differences in access to resources is a real element of the quality of jobs, even if such differences are partly explained by per capita GDP in each country), it seems reasonable to complement the results shown in the previous graph with another comparison of job quality across Europe excluding the wage component, and therefore without the mentioned (debatable) problem. As discussed in the previous chapter, a concept of job quality without the pecuniary element is akin to Adam Smith's concept of 'amenities' (those attributes of job that in the theory of compensating differentials must be compensated by wages), and hence we can call the index presented in Figure 6.2 an 'amenities' index (which is simply a geometric average of the four non-pecuniary dimensions of job quality).

The average values for this amenities index have a smaller range of variation across countries (from 44 to 61) than the job quality index (we must bear in mind that the only difference between both indices is the inclusion or not of the pay dimension in the geometric average). On the contrary, the within-country spread in the values of this index is larger, so all the interquartilic ranges overlap: what this would suggest is that the non-pecuniary levels of job quality are broadly comparable across Europe; in other words, that country is a variable that does not discriminate very well those aspects of job quality which are not pecuniary.

The ranking of countries according to this new index is more or less consistent with the overall job quality index presented earlier. Nevertheless, there are some very interesting differences. Some of the Southern European countries (especially Greece and Spain) become as bad as (or even worse) as Eastern European countries; Luxembourg, the UK and Ireland lose several positions, becoming mid-high rather than highest in the ranking; and Denmark, the Netherlands and Sweden improve considerably their scores, becoming the three best performers in Europe.

Therefore, the inclusion or not of the pay dimension does make a difference, even though the results with and without pay are broadly consistent.

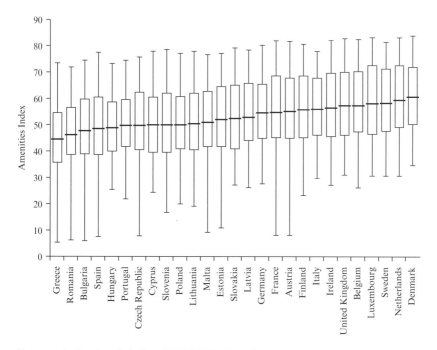

Source: Authors' analysis from EWCS 2005 micro-data.

Figure 6.2   Amenities Index by country

Figure 6.3 makes this point clearer by plotting the average scores of the pay dimension alone against the average scores of the amenities index (that is, a geometric average of the other four dimensions). We can immediately see that the spread of the pay dimension (in the horizontal axis) is much wider than that of the amenities index (scores of 2 to 55 against 44 to 61), and although the average values of both indices are highly correlated (the value of R^2 is 0.585), there are some important outliers (the value of amenities for Greece and Spain are much lower than expected according to their wage levels, while the opposite happens in Slovakia, the Netherlands and Denmark, for instance).

The pay dimension, therefore, adds a considerable amount of variability to our index at the country level, and it alters the positioning of countries to some extent. But, on the one hand, such changes seem rather plausible: because of the direct impact of GDP levels on it, the differences in pay across countries are likely to be wider than the differences in other job attributes, and our index should reflect that. In fact, the alterations to the ranking that result from introducing our comparative index of wages

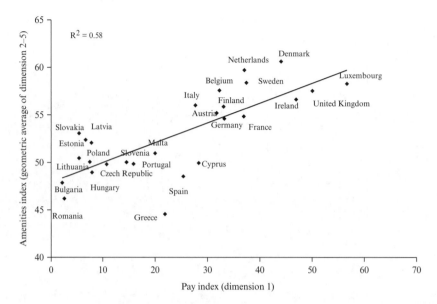

Source: Authors' analysis from EWCS 2005 micro-data.

Figure 6.3   Comparative pay index versus Amenities Index across Europe

probably fit better into our prior knowledge of European differences in
terms of the socioeconomic structure and institutional framework (which
are likely to be associated with systematic differences in job quality). On
the other hand, the decomposability of our index means that we can easily
check the consistency of results with and without the wage dimension:
although there are some differences in the positioning of specific countries,
the overall picture is broadly the same.

But how do the results of our index compare to other similar proposals for the measurement of job quality across Europe? Table 6.1 shows
the ordinal correlation (Spearman's rank correlation coefficient) between
the country rankings derived from our Job Quality Index, our Amenities
Index, ETUI's European Job Quality Index, the proposals made by
Tangian (for the EU15 and EU27), and the three proposals of operationalization of the ILO's Decent Work concept. All of these indices have been
thoroughly discussed in Chapter 4, so we will not go into any more details
here: our aim is only to evaluate the coherence between these different
proposals and our own. The country ranking of our JQI is very similar
to the ranking of ETUI's proposal (the correlation is 0.89, the highest
between any two indices in the table), which is quite reassuring considering

Table 6.1   Rank correlation between the country rankings of the different indices

	Our JQI	Our AI	EJQI (ETUI)	Tan-gian 1	Tan-gian 2	DWI-1 (Ghai)	DWI-2 (Bonnet, Figuei-redo and Standing)	DWI-4 (Bescond, Châtai-gnier and Mehran)
Our JQI	1.000							
Our AI	0.808	1.000						
EJQI (ETUI)	0.891	0.854	1.000					
Tangian 1	0.575	0.743	0.679	1.000				
Tangian 2	0.803	0.764	0.809	0.689	1.000			
DWI-1	0.429	0.517	0.657	0.574	0.385	1.000		
DWI-2	0.566	0.549	0.620	0.314	0.500	0.714	1.000	
DWI-4	0.588	0.679	0.787	0.573	0.525	0.955	0.692	1.000
No. of countries	27	27	27	15	27	17	14	17

Source: Authors' analysis from EWCS 2005 micro-data and Chapter 4.

that ETUI's proposal is certainly among the best available ones, and that this proposal draws on many data sources beyond the EWCS (see section 4.1.2 of Chapter 4 for a detailed account of the construction of this index). The second proposal by Tangian also has a rather high correlation with our JQI (0.80), while the first one (which only covered EU15) is only moderately correlated (0.58). The correlations between our JQI and the three indices based on ILO's Decent Work concept are also moderate (0.59, 0.43 and 0.57), but these indices also have relatively low correlations with the other proposals included in the table.

Table 6.2 shows the actual ranking positions of each country, so that we can inspect the discrepancies with some detail. In 19 of the 27 countries, the distance between our ranking and ETUI's is four or less positions, so the match is very high. The largest discrepancies are: Greece and Spain, which are seven positions higher in our JQI than in ETUI's, a discrepancy that disappears if we do not take into account the pay dimension (as shown in the column with our Amenities Index); Luxembourg (five positions higher in our index, also mostly the result of the pay dimension); Poland (five positions higher in our index, in this case the reason does not lie in the pay dimension but in the other four, that is, in the non-pecuniary

Table 6.2   Ranking of the EU countries according to different indexes of job quality

	Our JQI	Our AI	ETUI	Tangian 1	Tangian 2	DW Bescond	DW Ghai	DW Bonnet
Luxembourg	1	4	6	8	6		8	7
Denmark	2	1	1	2	1	2	2	2
United Kingdom	3	6	3	10	4	5	7	15
Ireland	4	7	8	6	3	13	12	11
Netherlands	5	2	2	1	2		9	8
Sweden	6	3	4	4	8	1	1	1
Belgium	7	5	7	7	5	6	6	6
France	8	11	11	12	17	3		4
Finland	9	9	5	11	7	4	3	3
Austria	10	10	9	3	9		4	10
Germany	11	12	14	5	10	7	5	5
Italy	12	8	15	9	18	14	11	12
Cyprus	13	20	13		11			
Spain	14	24	21	14	13	17	14	9
Malta	15	16	10		12			
Portugal	16	22	18	13	20	8	10	14
Slovenia	17	19	12		24			
Greece	18	27	25	15	27	16	13	
Czech Rep.	19	21	17		23			18
Estonia	20	15	16		21	10		
Slovakia	21	14	23		16	12		17
Poland	22	18	27		25	15		
Hungary	23	23	22		19			16
Latvia	24	13	19		15			
Lithuania	25	17	20		26	9		
Bulgaria	26	25	24		14			
Romania	27	26	26		22	11		

Source: Authors' analysis from EWCS 2005 micro-data and Chapter 4.

job attributes); Malta, Slovenia (five positions lower in our index, both for the wage component and for the rest according to our data), Latvia and Lithuania (five positions lower in our index mostly because of the pay dimension: if such dimension is excluded, these countries get a ranking position even higher than in ETUI's). If we look at the other indices, other countries whose position is more inconsistent are the UK and Ireland, which get a slightly higher position in our index (and, by the way, also in ETUI's proposal) mostly because of the impact of the higher relative wages in those countries.

Therefore, we can conclude that the country ranking that derives from our index is reasonably similar with that of previous proposals, especially with the measure that in our view is the best available, ETUI's one. The fact that our index, which was constructed at the individual level with the purpose of being able to analyse job quality for subgroups of workers, is highly consistent with a proposal which was specifically constructed for country comparisons and which draws from many different sources at the country level, is especially reassuring. We can take this as a test of the external validity of our approach.

6.2.2. A Deeper Look: the Dimensions and Components of Job Quality Across Europe

But the real richness of a multidimensional index such as the one we are proposing here is the capacity for a deeper understanding of the headline differences by breaking them down by dimensions and components. This will be done in this section, presenting the average scores of each country for the five higher level dimensions of our index and further differentiating into the eight second-level components. As our index has a nested structure, we could continue further down (until the level of 45 individual variables): but to get a broad understanding of the headline differences between European countries, the two higher levels suffice. We discuss each dimension separately, one by one, concentrating in patterns which differ from those of the overall index. Figure 6.4 represents the range of average values of each dimension and component across Europe (as a high-low line), as well as the values of five representative countries within that range (one from each European institutional family: Denmark for the Nordics, UK for the British Isles, France for the Continent, Spain for the South and Romania for the East). Table 6.3 includes the average values for each country, dimension and component. In this table, the countries have been sorted according to their values in the overall index (although we do not discuss the index in this section, as we already did it in the previous one), and we have included a pseudo-graphical representation of bars within each column of values to help the identification of significant deviations from the overall patterns (when the bars of a column differ significantly from the bars of the column representing the overall index).

Dimension 1 (pay): as can be seen in Figure 6.4, the range of average values in this variable is considerably wider than in any of the other dimensions of our index, as we discussed already in the previous section (the reason behind this wider range of variation is the differences in per

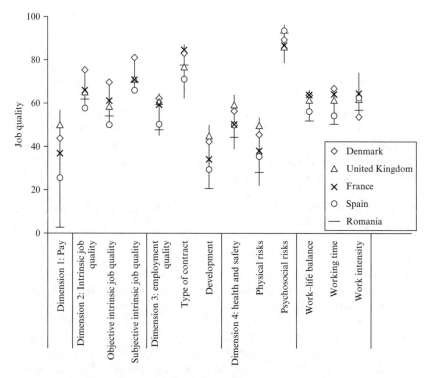

Source: Authors' analysis from EWCS 2005 micro-data.

Figure 6.4 Spread of average country values for comparative index,
dimensions and components

capita GDP in PPP, which have a strong effect in our comparative wage
indicator). Looking at Table 6.3, we can see that Luxembourg, the UK
and Ireland owe their very high position in the overall index to their very
high value in this dimension, as also mentioned in the previous section;
without this dimension, Denmark, the Netherlands and Sweden would be
the three top countries in terms of job quality. The value of Greece in this
dimension is also interesting, because it is higher than expected: without
the pay dimension, Greece would be much lower (indeed, as we saw with
the Amenities Index, it would occupy the bottom of the list). Most Eastern
European countries are very negatively affected by their position in this
particular component, much lower than the other ones. The low wage
levels associated to the recent transition to democratic capitalism in these
countries make job quality lower than it would otherwise be.

Dimension 2 (intrinsic job quality): as the figure shows, this is the

Table 6.3   Average values of the Job Quality Index, its dimensions and components by country

	Job Quality Index	Dimension 1: pay	Dimension 2: intrinsic job quality			Dimension 3: employment quality			Dimension 4: health and safety			Dimension 5: work-life balance		
			Overall	Objective intrinsic job quality	Subjective intrinsic job quality	Overall	Type of contract	Development opportunities	Overall	Physical risks	Psycho-social risks	Overall	Working time	Work intensity
Austria	48.9	31.7	68.9	64.6	73.2	60.1	80.4	40.9	52.7	40.0	90.7	58.0	59.6	53.4
Belgium	50.9	32.3	66.7	62.8	70.5	62.6	84.3	41.9	57.1	47.1	87.2	61.5	62.0	60.0
Cyprus	43.9	28.3	63.4	52.3	74.4	46.6	62.0	31.8	51.4	36.4	96.3	56.7	58.0	52.9
Czech Rep.	36.3	10.7	61.3	56.1	66.4	48.7	66.6	32.9	55.9	44.6	89.9	54.2	54.0	54.6
Germany	48.8	33.2	61.7	58.8	64.7	56.7	78.8	35.2	56.0	44.5	90.8	57.5	59.1	52.8
Denmark	56.4	44.1	75.5	69.8	81.1	62.5	83.0	42.4	56.4	45.5	89.3	63.6	66.9	53.7
Estonia	34.7	7.8	66.8	62.8	70.8	53.7	74.6	33.3	50.1	36.9	89.7	58.0	55.7	64.8
Spain	42.2	25.3	57.8	49.8	65.8	49.9	71.2	29.3	49.9	35.3	93.7	56.5	54.6	62.3
Finland	50.0	33.1	70.2	66.6	73.9	64.8	79.7	50.1	49.7	40.0	78.7	59.4	61.6	52.8
France	50.1	36.9	66.1	61.5	70.8	59.1	84.7	34.4	49.9	37.8	86.2	64.1	64.0	64.4
Greece	38.3	21.8	62.8	56.3	69.4	46.3	68.1	24.8	39.2	22.0	90.5	52.0	51.5	53.4
Hungary	33.3	7.9	62.6	55.6	69.5	48.7	73.3	24.2	46.4	29.9	95.9	54.7	53.1	59.5
Ireland	54.0	47.0	69.1	62.2	76.0	55.7	69.3	43.2	59.7	50.8	86.1	61.0	59.2	66.6
Italy	48.1	27.6	66.0	63.0	68.9	52.3	79.4	26.5	60.5	48.4	96.6	60.6	60.3	61.7
Lithuania	31.4	5.3	60.8	55.7	66.1	50.9	72.3	30.7	48.9	35.7	88.9	58.0	54.7	68.0

Table 6.3 (continued)

	Job Quality Index	Dimension 1: pay	Dimension 2: intrinsic job quality			Dimension 3: employment quality			Dimension 4: health and safety			Dimension 5: work-life balance		
			Overall	Objective intrinsic job quality	Subjective intrinsic job quality	Overall	Type of contract	Development opportunities	Overall	Physical risks	Psycho-social risks	Overall	Working time	Work intensity
Luxembourg	57.2	56.7	68.8	64.2	73.5	64.6	87.3	41.9	55.3	44.9	86.4	60.6	59.4	64.3
Latvia	32.3	5.4	67.1	61.0	73.2	52.7	75.6	30.3	51.4	37.7	91.6	57.2	51.9	73.1
Netherlands	53.6	37.0	71.2	68.2	74.3	57.3	76.4	38.3	60.8	53.4	83.0	66.3	67.7	62.1
Malta	41.9	20.0	71.9	65.6	78.1	52.8	64.5	41.6	48.7	35.0	89.9	54.3	54.0	55.3
Poland	33.3	7.4	64.5	56.8	72.3	49.5	67.0	33.0	48.9	34.2	92.6	55.8	52.0	67.2
Portugal	38.8	15.8	62.8	55.4	70.2	50.4	71.4	30.2	46.3	31.0	92.4	57.3	54.3	66.5
Sweden	53.2	37.4	74.0	70.0	78.0	62.2	79.5	45.1	53.5	41.7	88.9	61.3	64.1	53.0
Slovenia	38.7	14.6	64.2	59.4	68.9	54.8	71.6	38.0	46.3	31.5	90.6	53.6	52.9	55.7
Slovakia	34.2	6.7	58.8	53.0	64.5	55.3	76.1	34.8	55.8	43.6	92.5	53.7	50.7	62.9
UK	54.9	50.1	65.3	59.0	71.6	60.8	77.1	44.8	59.2	50.0	86.8	61.9	61.8	62.2
Bulgaria	25.3	2.1	59.2	50.1	68.2	44.9	68.8	22.4	51.2	36.2	96.0	56.2	50.1	74.5
Romania	25.1	2.6	61.9	54.0	69.8	47.6	77.8	20.6	44.2	28.0	92.5	51.8	50.2	56.9

Source: Authors' analysis from EWCS 2005 micro-data

dimension with highest overall scores, as a result of the aggregation of two components with generally high values and low cross-country variation. The three Nordic members of the EU, plus the Netherlands and Ireland, get the highest scores in this dimension (with very high values in both the objective and the subjective components), while in general Eastern and Southern Europe get the lowest values. The position of Spain and Germany with respect to this dimension of our index is unexpectedly low: Spain has the lowest value of the EU, while Germany gets the sixth-lowest place (mostly as a result of its very low score in the subjective component of intrinsic job quality, the second-lowest of the EU). Other countries whose score in this dimension differs significantly from their overall index are Latvia and Estonia (among the ten highest scores in this dimension), and the UK (the third-highest score in overall job quality, but the 14th position in terms of intrinsic job quality).

Dimension 3 (employment quality): this dimension, together with pay, has the lowest discrepancy with the overall index. The first component of this dimension, which measures contractual stability, has generally high values but a relatively high dispersion across Europe (62 to 87), while the component measuring opportunities for development has rather low values and an even higher dispersion (20 to 50). Although in general the values of this dimension go along those of the overall index, there are some interesting exceptions: the scores of Eastern European countries in employment quality are not as low as in other dimensions (although Bulgaria, Romania, Hungary, the Czech Republic and Poland do get quite low values), with Southern European countries getting the lowest position in this case (especially Greece, Cyprus and Spain).

Dimension 4 (health and safety): the scores of this dimension range from 40 to 60, as a result of the aggregation of two very different components. Physical risks, on the one hand, show a very wide range of variation across countries and generally low values (between 22 and 53). Psychosocial risks, on the other, have a very limited variation across countries and very high scores in general (between 80 and 95, the highest of all variables shown in Table 6.3). By far, the lowest values in this dimension correspond to Greece; Portugal, Slovenia, Hungary and Romania also get rather low values. As we shall see later, the values in this dimension, especially in its physical component, are strongly linked to the sector structure of the economy: those countries with a large proportion of employment in the agricultural/industrial sectors tend to have much larger levels of exposure to physical risks at work, while countries where services predominate (or even more, knowledge-intensive services) tend to have much lower levels of exposure to physical risks. Interestingly enough, the scores in psychosocial risks follow a completely different logic: in many ways, almost the *opposite* logic. To begin with, the scores in this component of our index are extremely high everywhere (in most countries, near or above 90): and the few countries with marginally lower scores in this component (never below 75) are not at all the countries with more exposure to physical risks or the countries with lower job quality in general, but the other way around. The lowest scores in this component (that is, the highest reported levels of psychosocial risks) are those of Finland, the Netherlands, Ireland and France; while the highest scores (above 95) correspond to Italy, Cyprus, Bulgaria and Hungary. The correlation between the average country scores in the overall job quality index and the psychosocial component is, in fact, negative and substantial (−0.56).

Dimension 5 (work–life balance): this dimension, which has the lowest range of variation at the country level of all five, from 51 to 66, results from the aggregation of two components that often go in opposite directions at the country level (we will later evaluate their behaviour at the individual level). For instance, Bulgaria, Latvia and Lithuania have very low scores in terms of working time but very high values in terms of work intensity (in other words, in those countries work schedules are long, unsocial and rigid, but the intensity of effort is relatively low); while the opposite happens in Finland, Germany or Sweden (with relatively short and flexible schedules, but very intense). There are exceptions, though, with bad conditions in both attributes: the worst case is Greece (the fourth-lowest score in terms of time, and the fifth-lowest in terms of intensity), but many Eastern European countries share such accumulation of negative attributes in terms of work–life balance. In general, while the country averages of the working time component of this dimension have a similar distribution as the overall job quality index, the intensity component goes in the opposite direction, with a negative correlation at the country level of −0.35.

So in general, the dimensions and components of the index tend to show a similar distribution at the country level as the overall job quality index, with the usual exceptions associated to national idiosyncrasies in terms of work culture or economic structures. In broad terms, the levels of job quality tend to consistently reflect an axis of socioeconomic development that puts at the top the Nordic countries, followed by the UK and Ireland, Continental Europe, the South and finally the Eastern European countries that joined the EU in its last two enlargements. But there are two components in our index which represent a significant exception to such general rule: psychosocial risks and work intensity tend to move in the opposite direction to the rest of the components and dimensions, and also to the mentioned axis of socioeconomic development. Therefore, these results seem to suggest that the higher socioeconomic development, the higher levels of reported psychosocial risks and intensity of the work effort. Both components are relatively recent additions to the literature on job quality, representing new forms of risks or negative work attributes generally associated with relatively advanced sectors and occupations, requiring higher levels of skills and qualifications, etc. The existence of these 'new' types of job quality attributes, that have a most negative impact precisely where and when the more traditional attributes are most positive, illustrates the nature of job quality as a 'moving target': an objective that will never be fully achieved, because new types of problems will always substitute for settled ones, and because, also with respect to job quality, expectations tend to expand with socioeconomic development.

6.2.3. Differences in the Employment Structure and Job Quality

We have seen in the previous pages that there are important differences in the levels of job quality across Europe, even if we do not take into account the differences in the standard of living that are captured by our comparative pay indicator (the non-pecuniary elements of our job quality index also varied systematically across countries, even if less widely). What we do not know yet is whether such differences are driven by systematic variations in the quality of jobs across Europe, or the result of differences in the economic structure. In other words: as EU countries have very different economic structures, even if each job had exactly the same quality across Europe, the overall levels of job quality would vary between countries. This is a very important question for policy purposes, because the same difference in the overall level of job quality between two countries has different implications if it simply results from the fact that their economic structures are different or if it results from the fact that the same jobs are systematically better or worse in one of the two countries. Some European countries are less economically developed than others, and this tends to be associated with a specific economic structure (higher share of employment in agriculture and industry, lower share in knowledge-intensive services): if the less developed countries have a lower overall level of job quality because of their higher share of 'lower quality jobs', then the best way to improve job quality may be to grow and modernize the economy; while if their lower level of job quality is unrelated to their economic structure, then it would be better to focus on the formulation of specific policies to improve the quality of jobs in those countries.

In this section, we will try to distinguish between the differences in overall job quality that result from structural differences and those that result from national *idiosyncrasies* in terms of job quality (by which we mean systematic differences across countries in the levels of job quality associated to the same jobs). For this, we will follow a methodology that has been proposed in recent years to study processes of structural change in labour markets and job quality over time (Wright and Dwyer 2003; Fernández-Macías and Hurley 2008; Goos *et al.* 2009). Such methodology, to which we can refer as the 'jobs approach', departs from a shift in the unit of analysis from individuals to 'jobs', defining the latter as specific occupations within specific sectors (using as a basis the international classifications of ISCO and NACE at the two-digit level). This way, the structure of employment in each country can be synthetically represented as a large matrix, in which each row is an occupation, each column, a sector and each cell, a job. These jobs matrices are internationally comparable (as long as the classifications of NACE and ISCO are comparable at the two-digit level, Elias 1997), so we can use them as a tool for comparing job quality levels and job quality structures across Europe. Basically, if the same jobs – that is, cells in the matrix – have more or less the same average level of job quality across countries, then the differences must be mostly the result of differences in the structure, and vice versa.

It must be noted that this *jobs approach* is very well suited for the analysis of job quality from the perspective adopted in this book. Although we have computed the index of job quality (and all its components) at the individual level in order to be able to break down the analysis for specific subgroups, in many ways its natural measurement level is the job rather than the individual worker, at least to the extent that job quality refers to the nature of jobs rather than the characteristics, expectations, etc. of the individuals performing them. But there are three reasons why we have not systematically adopted such an approach in all our analysis, opting instead for using it as a (very useful) complementary approach. First, although the operational definition of 'job' as the combination of ISCO and NACE at the two-digit level is extremely useful for comparative purposes, it is by no means a perfect operationalization of the idea of a *job* as a specific position in the employment structure, requiring specific skills and associated to specific opportunities for development, conditions of work and life chances. Second, because even if we would have a perfect operationalization of the idea of 'job', there would still be systematic within-job differences between workers, associated to career effects, discrimination or other factors, that we would want to capture and analyse. And third, because in any case, most statistical sources on job quality (including the EWCS, which we are using here) are based on interviews to workers, not on measuring the attributes of work at the job level and, hence, the unit of analysis is always ultimately the individual rather than the job. When we shift the unit to the job, what we actually do is to generate job-level averages of individual-level measurements.

In any case, we can use this approach to analyse how much of the variations discussed in the previous section can be explained by the structural composition of employment across European countries. The results discussed above are based on averaging within each country the values of the index and its components for all individuals: those country differences can be decomposed into a structural component and an idiosyncratic component, as explained earlier. One possible way of eliminating the effect of the idiosyncratic component is to generate a European average for each job, and recalculate overall level of job quality across countries assigning to each individual such homogeneous European value of job quality. Because these European averages of job quality are homogeneous, they eliminate the national idiosyncrasies, and hence all the remaining differences in job quality must be entirely the result of differences in the employment structure. The results of this test are shown in Figures 6.5, 6.6 and 6.7. For the overall job quality index, and for four of its five components, these figures show the original country averages and the country averages obtained when the idiosyncratic component is eliminated from the picture. For this test, we have used the national job quality index rather than the comparative one (that is, using the national pay dimension). The reason is that the differences in the comparative index are strongly associated to differences in per capita GDP, a constant multiplicative factor for each country that has nothing to do with the structural differences in job quality that we want to differentiate here. Hence, although we will use the national pay dimension, we will not discuss its results here (such dimension has no comparative value, as it has been calculated in relative national terms).

Because this exercise is focused on the differences in the average levels of job quality across the EU, and not the levels of job quality themselves, Figures 6.5, 6.6 and 6.7 express the average values of our index in terms of their difference with the overall EU average. For each country, we have two figures, which are represented by two bars: the black bar represents the difference between the original value of our index (the national version) and the overall EU average; the white bar below represents the difference between a hypothetical index calculated as if the same jobs had exactly the same value across Europe (such values correspond the European averages for each job) and the same overall EU average. In these graphs, the overall EU average acts as a yardstick: if the idiosyncratic component would be an important part of the differences in job quality levels across Europe, keeping constant the levels of job quality of the different jobs would reduce considerably those differences, and the white bar would be much smaller than the black bar.

As we can immediately see by looking at Figure 6.5 (which displays the results for the aggregate index), eliminating the idiosyncratic component and keeping just the differences that result from structural component does reduce considerably the original variability in the levels of job quality

Measuring more than money

Overall index

Source: Authors' analysis from EWCS 2005 micro-data.

Figure 6.5 *The relevant structural and idiosyncratic components in explaining the gap in job quality in EU countries with the EU average job quality (overall index)*

across Europe. In most cases, the size of the white bar is less than half that of the black bar, which means that the idiosyncratic component accounts for most of the original variability. The standard deviation of the only-structure country averages is nearly a third of the standard deviation of the

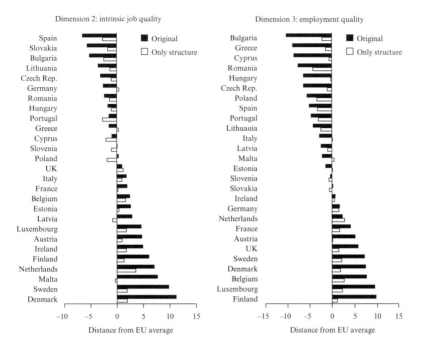

Source: Authors' analysis from EWCS 2005 micro-data.

Figure 6.6 *The relevant structural and idiosyncratic components in explaining the gap in job quality in EU countries with the EU average job quality (dimensions 2 and 3)*

original averages across Europe (4 versus 1.7): therefore, we can say that just around one-third of the original differences are the result of the different economic/employment structures, with the remaining two-thirds being the result of actual differences in the quality of (the same type of) jobs across Europe. The policy implications of these findings are very clear: according to our results, although economic development and structural change can still improve average job quality in some countries, the bulk of the problem lies in the fact that the quality of jobs (of the same jobs) is much lower in some countries than in others. It is not that some countries are relatively underdeveloped and have a higher proportion of bad jobs: it is that in some countries job quality as such is lower than in others. In our view, this provides strong support to the idea that European employment policies should broaden its traditional focus on growth and structural development, and aim directly at the improvement and harmonization of the conditions of work and employment across the EU.

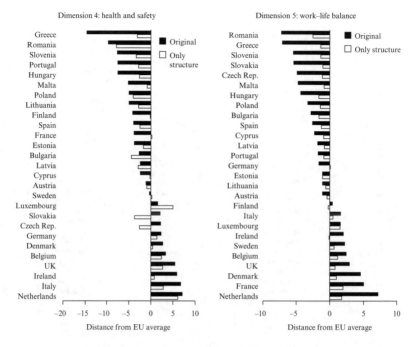

Source: Authors' analysis from EWCS 2005 micro-data.

Figure 6.7   *The relevant structural and idiosyncratic components in explaining the gap in job quality in EU countries with the EU average job quality (dimensions 4 and 5)*

The reduction in the difference between the country average and the EU average that results when eliminating the idiosyncratic component, nevertheless, is not the same across all countries: in some cases it is very large, in some (fewer) cases, relatively small. Inspecting each country in Figure 6.5, we can evaluate whether their individual positions in the aggregate job quality ranking are mostly the result of structural or idiosyncratic characteristics. At the top of our job quality ranking, we have some countries whose position depends almost entirely from having higher levels of job quality across the jobs spectrum, rather than from having an employment structure more abundant in good jobs: the clearest cases are Denmark, Finland, Austria and Sweden. These are, therefore, the countries that are doing better in terms of job quality, in a strict sense. Below the EU average, the countries that improve the most when we eliminate the idiosyncratic component are Greece, Cyprus, Hungary, Malta and Estonia: these are the countries where there is a bigger problem with respect to the quality of work and employment, independently of their economic structure.

Figures 6.6 and 6.7 include four more charts with a similar decomposition of the differences in each of the five components of the index. As explained earlier, we have used the national version of the pay dimension, so there is no interest in discussing its results across countries (it is not comparable). With respect to the other dimensions, dimensions 2 (intrinsic), 3 (employment) and 5 (work–life balance) reduce their cross-country variability in roughly the same amount as the overall index when we eliminate the idiosyncratic component, so we can extend our earlier arguments to them. In the case of dimension 4 (health and safety), the reduction in variability is considerably smaller (nearly two-thirds of the original variability remains after eliminating the idiosyncratic component), which suggests that in this particular case, the differences in the economic structure are more important than the differences in job quality as such. There are some countries where, in fact, taking only into account the structure would make the score in terms of health and safety even lower: for instance, in Slovakia, the Czech Republic, Bulgaria and Latvia. These are countries either with a very large share of employment in heavy industry (with traditionally harsher health and safety conditions) or with a large share of employment in agriculture, which probably explains such an anomalous result. Another surprising result is that of Luxembourg, where the score is much higher after eliminating the idiosyncratic component, which can be interpreted as showing that Luxembourg has a very large share of jobs that across Europe have a better than average health and safety condition (and vice versa).

The same 'jobs approach' can be used to answer another crucial policy question with respect to job quality in Europe: how many 'good' and 'bad' jobs are there in the different European countries? Or more precisely: what is the proportion of people working in jobs of different qualities? The difficulty for answering such question lies in the fact that it requires a homogeneous definition of good and bad jobs across Europe, something that we have partly achieved in the previous analysis by constructing an index of job quality which represents the average of our index within each combination of sector and occupation for all European countries. We can use such average European job quality index at the job level to define five categories of jobs, each holding 20 per cent of European employment and jobs of similar quality (from low to high). These five categories are, in fact, quintiles of job quality at the European level (five equally-sized groups of jobs which have been previously sorted by their quality). Then, we can study how many workers in each country fall in each of those five categories of jobs: this way, we should be able to easily evaluate how much employment falls into each of those categories in each country. In other words, how many people work in equally-defined very bad, bad, middling, good, and very good jobs.

This is done in Figure 6.8, using a stacked-bar representation of the distribution of employment in each country across the five EU-defined job quality quintiles. As in the previous case, the EU as a whole is used as a yardstick, a kind of centre of gravity that serves as a point of comparison of each national result. If a country would have exactly the same proportion of employment in the jobs of the different qualities, it would have an exactly even distribution of employment across the five quintiles (with 20 per cent in each category): the deviations from such patterns can be used as a way of evaluating each country's specificity. To simplify the interpretation of results, the countries have been sorted according to the proportion of employment in bad jobs (the summatory of the two lowest categories).

Unsurprisingly, there are wide differences across Europe in the distribution of employment across the five job quality quintiles. The differences are much larger for bad than for good jobs. In some countries, nearly two-thirds of employment is concentrated in bad jobs (including the two lowest quintiles), while in others there is little more than one-fourth of employment in those same bad jobs. On the other hand, the highest proportion of employment in good jobs in Europe is 53 per cent, and the lowest 20 per cent. If we take just the extreme quintiles, the contrast is even larger: the share of employment in very bad jobs in Romania is 5.7 times higher than in the Netherlands, while the share of very good jobs is only 3.4 times higher in Luxembourg than in Romania.

A comparison of the relative position of different countries in Figure 6.8 and that of previous sections (in which we simply looked at the average score of our job quality index) is quite instructive. Romania remains squarely at the bottom of the ranking, with an enormous proportion of employment in very bad jobs (nearly 50 per cent, when for the whole of the EU these very bad jobs account for just 20 per cent of employment) and a tiny proportion of very good and good jobs (9 and 11 per cent, respectively). The Netherlands has the lowest proportion of employment in very bad jobs (8.5 per cent) and the highest proportion of good jobs (adding together the two highest quintiles). Sweden has the lowest proportion of employment in bad jobs (adding the two lowest categories) and Luxembourg the highest proportion of very good jobs (31 per cent). There is some realignment in the regional categories with respect to the analysis done earlier for the average index scores. There are many Eastern European countries whose position improves considerably when we consider job quality with this new structural/distributional approach: especially, central-Eastern European countries such as Slovenia, Czech Republic and Hungary appear now around the middle of the European list (as well as Estonia). Southern

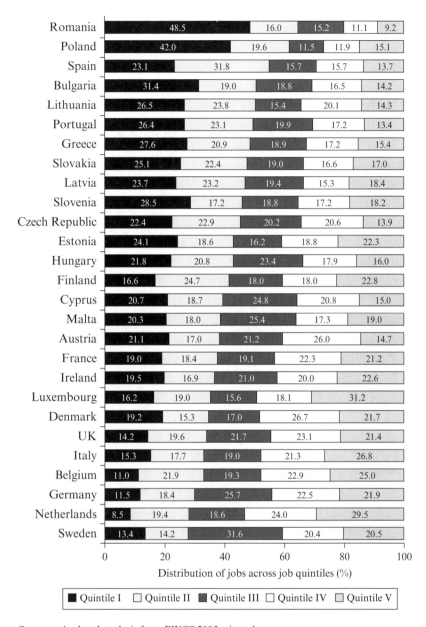

	Quintile I	Quintile II	Quintile III	Quintile IV	Quintile V
Romania	48.5	16.0	15.2	11.1	9.2
Poland	42.0	19.6	11.5	11.9	15.1
Spain	23.1	31.8	15.7	15.7	13.7
Bulgaria	31.4	19.0	18.8	16.5	14.2
Lithuania	26.5	23.8	15.4	20.1	14.3
Portugal	26.4	23.1	19.9	17.2	13.4
Greece	27.6	20.9	18.9	17.2	15.4
Slovakia	25.1	22.4	19.0	16.6	17.0
Latvia	23.7	23.2	19.4	15.3	18.4
Slovenia	28.5	17.2	18.8	17.2	18.2
Czech Republic	22.4	22.9	20.2	20.6	13.9
Estonia	24.1	18.6	16.2	18.8	22.3
Hungary	21.8	20.8	23.4	17.9	16.0
Finland	16.6	24.7	18.0	18.0	22.8
Cyprus	20.7	18.7	24.8	20.8	15.0
Malta	20.3	18.0	25.4	17.3	19.0
Austria	21.1	17.0	21.2	26.0	14.7
France	19.0	18.4	19.1	22.3	21.2
Ireland	19.5	16.9	21.0	20.0	22.6
Luxembourg	16.2	19.0	15.6	18.1	31.2
Denmark	19.2	15.3	17.0	26.7	21.7
UK	14.2	19.6	21.7	23.1	21.4
Italy	15.3	17.7	19.0	21.3	26.8
Belgium	11.0	21.9	19.3	22.9	25.0
Germany	11.5	18.4	25.7	22.5	21.9
Netherlands	8.5	19.4	18.6	24.0	29.5
Sweden	13.4	14.2	31.6	20.4	20.5

Distribution of jobs across job quintiles (%)

■ Quintile I   □ Quintile II   ■ Quintile III   □ Quintile IV   □ Quintile V

Source: Authors' analysis from EWCS 2005 micro-data.

Figure 6.8   Distribution of employed population across EU-defined job quality quintiles

European countries such as Spain and Portugal, on the contrary, fall into a considerably lower position from this new approach. And, on the other hand, some Continental European countries (especially, the Netherlands, Germany and Belgium) have a considerably better outlook in terms of this structural approach to job quality, while some Nordics (Finland especially, but also Denmark), Luxembourg and the British Isles get a lower position.

6.2.4.   The Robustness of the Index of Job Quality. A Sensitivity Analysis

The results presented in this chapter were obtained using a methodology involving non-trivial decisions on the normalization, weighting and aggregation procedures, which have been extensively discussed throughout the book. As we have argued in previous chapters, it is important to test whether any proposed measure is sensitive to changes in such methodological decisions. This section provides some evidence on the impact of such decisions on the JQI proposed in the book. Particularly, we assess the size of the changes in the relative position of countries in the index of job quality resulting from the following changes: (1) in the aggregation procedure, using an arithmetic mean instead of a geometric mean; (2) in the weight given to the different dimensions, departing from equal weighting and giving each dimension, in following rounds, a weight of twice the rest of the attributes (0.33 *versus* 0.17).

   In order to test the role played by the choices made in relation to the above-mentioned items, we perform 11 additional computations of job quality (five using the geometric mean and six using the arithmetic mean). The results of such analysis are briefly presented in Table 6.4, which shows the position of each country in the baseline analysis (using the original JQI) and the highest and lowest rank of each state across the alternative specifications of the index. The results obtained suggest that, with a few exceptions limited to some Eastern European countries and Portugal and Greece, the ranks of the countries is remarkably stable. This reassuring finding was to be expected considering the high correlation among dimensions that was detected in the analysis presented in Chapter 5.

6.3.   BRINGING DISTRIBUTIONAL ISSUES INTO PLAY

6.3.1.   Overall Distribution

As it has been extensively discussed in previous chapters, one of the advantages offered by a measure derived at individual level is the possibility of

Table 6.4   Results of the sensitivity analysis

	Rank in the original JQI	Highest rank attained in alternative formulations	Lowest rank attained in alternative formulations
Austria	11	10	12
Belgium	7	7	8
Bulgaria	27	25	27
Cyprus	13	13	14
Czech Republic	19	16	21
Denmark	2	1	3
Estonia	20	15	21
Finland	9	7	10
France	8	7	11
Germany	10	8	12
Greece	18	16	26
Hungary	22	21	25
Ireland	4	4	6
Italy	12	8	12
Latvia	24	16	24
Lithuania	25	22	25
Luxembourg	1	1	2
Malta	15	13	15
Netherlands	5	3	5
Poland	23	21	23
Portugal	16	16	21
Romania	26	26	27
Slovakia	21	18	22
Slovenia	17	16	20
Spain	14	14	18
Sweden	6	4	6
United Kingdom	3	2	4

Source: Authors' analysis from EWCS 2005 micro-data.

carrying out inequality analyses. In fact, if we think that inequality is an important topic and plays a relevant role in determining – by any channel – the welfare of a society as a whole, how job quality is distributed across the population should be a matter of concern.

An intuitive and appealing way of studying the distribution of job quality is the well-known Pen's parade (Pen 1971). This diagram, also known as the 'parade of dwarfs and giants', is a simple figure that can be obtained by plotting the value of the variable of interest (in our case,

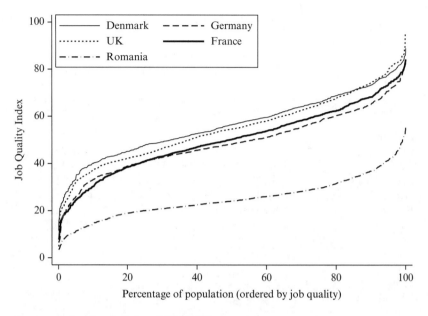

Source: Authors' analysis from EWCS 2005 micro-data.

*Figure 6.9   Pen's parade for job quality in Denmark, Germany, UK,
              France and Romania*

job quality) for each individual against the cumulative percentage of
individuals ranked by such variable. The figure looks like a parade where
the whole population marches after having been ordered by their height.[1]
Among others, this tool allows us to explore how job quality grows across
the distribution and to visualize how workers situated at different places
of the national distributions compare with other people from other countries. In order to illustrate the use of this tool, in Figure 6.9 we depict
the Pen's parade for job quality in Denmark, Germany, the UK, France
and Romania. We can draw interesting conclusions from looking at the
diagram. Firstly, job quality does not steadily grow across the distribution, but it increases slowly at the beginning and faster at the end (just
as it happens with income). In the second place, it allows to compare
countries across all the distribution of job quality and not only by looking
at the average, something especially important when lines cross. For
instance, though Denmark has (after Luxembourg) the highest level of job
quality, in the UK, just behind, workers located at the top of the national
distribution of job quality are in a better situation than their Danish
counterparts, while the opposite happens for individuals at the bottom.

Another example is provided by the comparison of France and Germany: as can be seen, the French workers with lowest levels of job quality in the country are worse off than their German colleagues, whereas this pattern reverses from roughly the 25th percentile on. Thirdly, looking at the distribution of job quality in Romania, we can see that the 10 per cent of the population with best jobs are in a better position, for example, than the 20 per cent of workers with the worst jobs in France. In sum, a glance at the distribution of job quality through the Pen's parade highlights the relevance of distributional issues.

In order to assess more formally the distribution of job quality, we compute the levels of inequality in terms of job quality using the Gini index. As it is well-known, this measure is bounded between 0 (total equality) and 1 (a situation of extreme inequality), the higher the index, the higher the inequality level.[2] Table 6.5, which shows the Gini index across the 27 EU countries, reveals, first, that the distribution of job quality is quite compressed, as indicated by the low values of the Gini index and, second, that such distribution does not vary very substantially across EU states. The pattern is quite similar to the one followed by average job quality: Nordic countries, jointly with the Netherlands, Italy and Belgium are placed at the top of the ranking (the most equal countries, with the lowest values for the Gini), whereas Mediterranean and Eastern European states are concentrated at the bottom, that is, they are the countries where job quality is more unequally distributed.

Without going into too many technicalities, the factors beyond the overall low dispersion observed are various. To begin with, we have to bear in mind the limitations of the database for capturing some of the dimensions, which are not originally derived from continuous variables. Secondly, the assumption of decreasing returns in the production function of job quality also leads to more compression (compared to other aggregation options as the simple average), especially if workers try to find jobs with a balanced structure of job attributes or if there is some kind of compensation among dimensions. In addition, in spite of the mentioned data shortcomings that might artificially lead to a reduction of dispersion, these levels of inequality – which are apparently low compared to widely known information on income or earnings distribution – also reflect the fact that the distribution of most of the non-pecuniary dimensions is more compressed than that of income. In fact, in most countries both legal regulations and social norms affect the distribution of non-monetary attributes in a very relevant way. In the fourth place, the dispersion observed in each dimension is remarkably low. The most disperse dimension is the fourth one, health and safety conditions, followed by the earnings dimension.

Another interesting point concerns the relationship between the mean

Measuring more than money

Table 6.5   Distribution of job quality in EU countries (Gini index)

	Overall job quality	Pay	Intrinsic job quality	Employment quality	Health and safety	Work–life balance
Austria	0.151	0.202	0.152	0.215	0.320	0.148
Belgium	0.144	0.169	0.164	0.192	0.307	0.141
Cyprus	0.169	0.284	0.167	0.283	0.324	0.153
Czech Republic	0.171	0.265	0.180	0.272	0.298	0.159
Germany	0.151	0.226	0.180	0.207	0.288	0.148
Denmark	0.133	0.207	0.105	0.205	0.288	0.130
Estonia	0.178	0.336	0.145	0.234	0.325	0.141
Spain	0.178	0.254	0.203	0.259	0.334	0.150
Finland	0.154	0.201	0.123	0.201	0.326	0.145
France	0.163	0.255	0.155	0.192	0.347	0.128
Greece	0.188	0.276	0.176	0.281	0.343	0.176
Hungary	0.158	0.304	0.171	0.230	0.322	0.157
Ireland	0.155	0.246	0.155	0.239	0.296	0.141
Italy	0.142	0.224	0.158	0.213	0.270	0.135
Lithuania	0.184	0.328	0.178	0.233	0.336	0.146
Luxembourg	0.160	0.254	0.140	0.180	0.326	0.133
Latvia	0.177	0.399	0.136	0.221	0.325	0.140
Netherlands	0.147	0.234	0.138	0.212	0.280	0.122
Malta	0.157	0.259	0.117	0.255	0.351	0.149
Poland	0.174	0.346	0.152	0.252	0.332	0.158
Portugal	0.159	0.293	0.162	0.221	0.331	0.133
Sweden	0.142	0.187	0.111	0.204	0.299	0.122
Slovenia	0.187	0.284	0.149	0.260	0.335	0.156
Slovakia	0.174	0.281	0.193	0.211	0.309	0.156
United Kingdom	0.150	0.279	0.177	0.205	0.300	0.148
Bulgaria	0.186	0.370	0.182	0.268	0.321	0.142
Romania	0.191	0.423	0.151	0.240	0.322	0.185
Unweighted mean	0.164	0.273	0.156	0.229	0.317	0.146

Source: Authors' analysis from EWCS 2005 micro-data.

and the dispersion of job quality at country level. As Figure 6.10 shows, there is a clear negative correlation between both variables; that is, the higher the average job quality, the lower the inequality in such variable. It is beyond the scope of this book to look at this issue in detail, but we

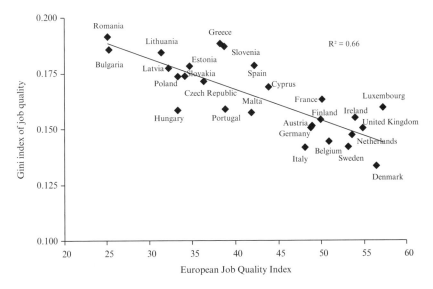

Source: Authors' analysis from EWCS 2005 micro-data.

Figure 6.10 *Relationship between average job quality and inequality of job quality across the EU*

can speculate about several possible explanations. For example, it is possible that in countries where job quality is high, the high employment and working conditions standards are established, to a large extent, across the board, without being reserved for a privileged minority.

A last way of illustrating the possibilities offered by an index that allows exploring dispersion is calculating 'correct' average values of job quality by the joint consideration of level and dispersion in a single index. As originally proposed by Sen (1976) for income, one might compute a sort of social welfare function where not only the average of the variable of interest but also its dispersion are taken into account in order to evaluate and compare how different populations rank regarding such variable. For simplicity, we use Sen's original proposal, consisting in computing a measure of average welfare by multiplying the average value of the variable of interest by one minus the Gini index of the variable. That is, we compute a modified JQI using the expression $\mu(1-G)$, where μ denotes the average job quality in a country and G represents the Gini index of job quality in the same state.[3] The ranks of countries derived using the original JQI and the modified JQI are presented in Table 6.6. As it is evidenced by the data, the changes in ranks are tiny. Nevertheless, such minor alterations

*Table 6.6   Ranks of countries using the original JQI and the inequality-
modified JQI*

	Rank according to the JQI	Rank according to the modified JQI
Luxembourg	1	2
Denmark	2	1
United Kingdom	3	3
Ireland	4	6
Netherlands	5	4
Sweden	6	5
Belgium	7	7
France	8	9
Finland	9	8
Austria	10	10
Germany	11	11
Italy	12	12
Cyprus	13	13
Spain	14	15
Malta	15	14
Portugal	16	16
Slovenia	17	17
Greece	18	18
Czech Republic	19	19
Estonia	20	20
Slovakia	21	21
Poland	22	23
Hungary	23	22
Latvia	24	24
Lithuania	25	25
Bulgaria	26	26
Romania	27	27

Source: Authors' analysis from EWCS 2005 micro-data.

are quite consistent with the popular perception of the performance of labour markets in Europe. For instance, Luxembourg and Ireland lose some positions, whereas Denmark, Sweden or the Netherlands climb up in the scale of job quality.

A final question that can be assessed by the proposed index is to what extent the dispersion of job quality among EU citizens is explained by inequalities between countries and within countries. This question can be answered straightforwardly using an additively decomposable inequality index. Although, unfortunately, this sort of exercise cannot be – perfectly – carried out using the Gini index, there are other measures (well-documented in the literature) that can play such role.[4] One obvious choice is the Theil index, which can be computed using the following expression:

$$T = \frac{1}{n}\sum_{i=1}^{n}\frac{q_i}{Q}\ln\left(\frac{q_i}{Q}\right) \qquad [6.1]$$

where n represents the number of workers, q_i denotes the job quality of worker i and Q is the average job quality. This index can be additively decomposed as follows:

$$T = T_{Between} + T_{Within} = \sum_{k=1}^{K}\frac{q_k}{Q}T_k + \sum_{k=1}^{K}\frac{q_k}{Q}\ln\left(\frac{q_k/Q}{n_k/n}\right) \qquad [6.2]$$

where the T_k denotes the Theil index for the country k, q_k, the average job quality of country k, n_k, the number of workers of country k and K represents the number of countries.

The results obtained from the application of this index indicate that 69.5 per cent of total inequality (as measured by the Theil index) is associated to inequality within countries, whereas only 30.5 per cent corresponds to average differences between countries.

6.3.2. Job Quality, Gender and Age

As argued thoroughly in previous chapters of this book, an index computed at the individual level gives the researcher the opportunity of exploring what happens to the weakest segments of workers in the labour market. In particular, this strategy allows assessing the situation of women and young workers in Europe. The results of our index of job quality by gender and age group are displayed by Table 6.7. These results are computed from the EU as a whole because of the problems of sample size commented on in previous chapters. Regarding gender, several interesting findings arise. First, there is no significant difference in overall job quality (at the highest level of aggregation). Second, the most relevant gap is in terms of pay in favour of men (more than eight points), while there are important differences against men in the case of health and safety and work–life balance. Third, scores of intrinsic job quality and employment quality are roughly equal for both sexes. In relation to age, in the table we compute the averages for three different age groups, namely, those aged less than 30 years old, those workers between 30 and 49 years old and, lastly, workers aged 50 years old or more. In this case the results are more clarifying, particularly,

Table 6.7   Average job quality by gender and age group

	By gender		By age group		
	Men	Women	Aged less than 30	Aged 30–49	Aged 50 and more
JQI	51.7	51.5	47.4	52.6	53.4
Pay	49.3	40.9	40.1	46.8	48.0
Intrinsic job quality	65.0	63.4	58.9	65.5	66.6
Employment quality	55.6	54.5	51.0	57.1	54.3
Health and safety	50.2	58.2	51.0	53.8	56.3
Work–life balance	56.6	62.1	57.5	58.4	62.1

Source: Authors' analysis from EWCS 2005 micro-data.

regarding young workers, since the scores of this group are systematically below those of middle-age and older workers. This is especially true in the dimensions of pay, intrinsic job quality and employment quality.

The results presented above, nevertheless, can be driven by differences in the sector of activity, the occupational level of workers or even the country considered. Therefore, it is convenient to repeat the analysis comparing similar workers, that is, making the comparisons between those workers in the same country, with the same schooling and occupational level and working in the same country and sector of activity. This task can be straightforwardly accomplished using a multivariate analysis: particularly, we regress job quality (the overall index or the index computed for a specific dimension) on the gender, age, education, experience, tenure, occupational level, sector of activity and country of residence. All the variables, apart from experience and tenure, are introduced in the regression using dummies. The variables of interest are gender, which is introduced in the specification through a fictitious variable for women, and age group, whose effect is also studied using dummies, particularly, considering workers aged between 30 and 49 as the reference category and including two dummy variables for workers below 30 years old and those aged 50 or more. The results of the regression (estimated by Ordinary Least Squares) are displayed in Table 6.8, which only presents the coefficients estimated for the variables of interest (being a female or a young worker). Such coefficients have to be interpreted as deviations from the reference category

Table 6.8   The effect of being a woman and a young worker on job quality

	Women	Workers aged less than 30
Overall job quality	−1.294 ***	−2.301 ***
	(0.313)	(0.459)
Pay	−7.386 ***	−2.582 ***
	(0.334)	(0.430)
Intrinsic job quality	−2.044 ***	−2.015 ***
	(0.418)	(0.565)
Employment quality	−2.272 ***	−1.497 *
	(0.519)	(0.798)
Health and safety	3.385 ***	−3.058 ***
	(0.746)	(0.974)
Work–life balance	4.066 ***	−0.628
	(0.378)	(0.526)

Note: The table displays the estimated coefficients for being a female worker or worker aged less than 30 from regressing job quality (the overall index or the index of a specific dimension) on education, experience, tenure, occupation, sector of activity, country, gender (a dummy variable for women) and age group (a dummy variable for workers aged less than 30 and another one for those aged 50 or more). Standard errors are presented between parentheses.
*** significant at 1%; ** significant at 5%; * significant at 10%.

Source: Authors' analysis from EWCS 2005 micro-data.

(male workers or middle-age workers) once controlling for education, occupation, sector of activity, tenure and country of residence.

These results are similar to those obtained in the descriptive exercise presented above, though with some significant deviations. On the one hand, there are differences against women in the overall index, intrinsic job quality, employment quality dimensions and, especially, in terms of pay. On the other hand, female workers seem to enjoy a higher level of job quality in aspects related with the health and safety and work–life balance. Probably, the 'advantage' in terms of health and safety can be explained by the existence of tasks with different, less demanding physical requirements mostly performed by women. In the case of work–life balance, the results probably are partly explained by the higher share of female part-time workers, and the implications of such form of work from the work–life balance perspective. In any case, it is more than probable that the leading position of women in terms of job quality in the work–life balance dimension does not translate in a higher overall well-being as women disproportionately assume most responsibilities of child (and other dependants) care. With respect to young workers, this group enjoys lower job quality than workers between 30 and 49 years of age in all dimensions except work–life balance, where no difference is found. Again, the higher gap is detected in the case of pay, intrinsic job quality and employment quality.

A final comment corresponds to the magnitude of the differences. As evidenced by the results presented in Tables 6.7 and 6.8, differences by gender and age are not very large if measured in raw points of the index. However, if we consider the low dispersion of the job quality variables (the standard deviation ranges from roughly 14 points in the case of the overall job quality index to approximately 30 points in the case of the work–life balance dimension), the differences found are certainly non-negligible. For instance, the gender gap in terms of wages accounts for more or less 0.5 standard deviations, and the gap between young and middle-age workers in the case of intrinsic job quality rises up to almost 8 per cent of the average job quality in such dimension or more than 0.25 standard deviations.

6.4.   DO GOOD JOBS CONCENTRATE ALL AMENITIES?

Another question we would like to address in this chapter is how the different attributes of job quality are distributed across the working population. More precisely, we are interested in assessing whether the characteristics defining a job as 'good' are concentrated in the same workers/jobs or whether, in contrast, jobs combine positive and negative attributes, as we would expect if there were some kind of compensating devices at work in the labour market. In order to do so, we compute the correlation between the different dimensions of job quality at the worker level controlling for different observable characteristics. These measures of correlation (which we already used in Chapter 3) are called *partial correlations*. In Table 6.9 we present the partial correlation coefficients between all pairs of different components of job quality, computed in three different ways. In the first calculation, we only control for country, aiming to determine whether, in raw terms, there is correlation among the different dimensions of job quality. The second specification, presented below, uses as additional controls worker's human capital endowment, measured by educational level, experience and tenure. The aim of this second calculation is to assess if, once we control for human capital, workers tend to face an accumulation or a compensation among different job attributes. The final set of partial correlation coefficients controls additionally for occupation and sector of activity, with the objective of assessing if, even when dealing roughly with the same types of jobs, we can still observe an accumulation of job amenities or disamenities.

Table 6.9   Partial correlation coefficients among the different dimensions of job quality

	Control: country				
	Pay	Intrinsic job quality	Employment quality	Health and safety	Work–life balance
Pay	1.000 ***				
Intrinsic job quality	0.263 ***	1.000 ***			
Employment quality	0.152 ***	0.276 ***	1.000 ***		
Health and safety	0.059 ***	0.071 ***	0.111 ***	1.000 ***	
Work–life balance	−0.128 ***	0.175 ***	0.060 ***	0.306 ***	1.000 ***

	Controls: country + education, experience, tenure				
	Pay	Intrinsic job quality	Employment quality	Health and safety	Work–life balance
Pay	1.000 ***				
Intrinsic job quality	0.196 ***				
Employment quality	0.138 ***	0.225 ***			
Health and safety	0.042 ***	0.016 **	0.087 **		
Work–life balance	−0.144 ***	0.193 ***	−0.045 ***	0.294 ***	1.000 ***

	Controls: education, experience, tenure, country + occupation, sector				
	Pay	Intrinsic job quality	Employment quality	Health and safety	Work–life balance
Pay	1.000 ***				
Intrinsic job quality	0.140 ***	1.000 ***			
Employment quality	0.129 ***	0.206 ***	1.000 ***		
Health and safety	0.024 ***	0.010	0.059 ***	1.000 ***	
Work–life balance	−0.117 ***	0.186 ***	−0.054 ***	0.259 ***	1.000 ***

Notes: *** significant at 1%; ** significant at 5%; * significant at 10%.

Source: Authors' analysis from EWCS 2005 micro-data.

The first set of results, controlling for country of residence, indicate that the correlations are statistically significant and positive in all cases, with the exception of the correlations between pay and work–life balance, and employment quality and work–life balance (a result observed also for the US: Golden 2001). These results suggest that most jobs do not combine high scores in some dimensions and low scores in others: quite on the contrary, the results show that most jobs tend to accumulate either good or bad attributes to a certain extent. From the perspective of the theory of compensating differentials reviewed in Chapter 2 this result could be interpreted as the existence of a preference (by workers) for jobs implying a balanced structure of amenities and disamenities rather than jobs with extremely high values in some positive dimensions/attributes but also very low values in other dimensions/attributes. In that sense, these results could be coherent with the production function of job quality presented in Chapter 2, and standard neoclassical assumptions on individuals' preferences. The negative correlation between work–life balance and pay, apart from other factors, is associated to the negative relationship between working hours, especially part-time work and atypical time schedules and pay. In the former case, lower hours imply lower take-home pay, a clear case of compensating differentials. In the second case, atypical hours often have a wage premium (night-shift, for example), often regulated by collective agreements or labour law.

The second set of estimations reveals that when we control for human capital variables most correlations decrease in value. However, in all cases, the signs of the correlations remain the same. This suggests that, after controlling for country, education, experience and tenure levels, most job attributes are positively correlated. Though our calculations do not take into account important individual unobservable characteristics (field of study, cognitive and non-cognitive abilities, etc.), this finding can be interpreted as a proof against the theory of compensating differentials. If the theory applied, even imperfectly, we should find non-positive correlations among different amenities. That is, even controlling for human capital endowments, good attributes tend to bunch together in the same jobs while disamenities concentrate in other jobs.

The last part of the table presents the partial correlations obtained when further controlling for occupation and sector of activity (plus the other variables mentioned above). The results are pretty much the same, although it is worth mentioning that the correlations weaken in all cases (disappearing in the case of health and safety and intrinsic job quality). We could interpret the persistence of positive association among amenities as an evidence of the existence of good and bad jobs even within the same type of occupation and sector of activity. This means that, even within a given type of job (defined as the combination of occupation and activity), there are remarkable differences in quality. This result might be, at least partially, statistically driven, as it is quite possible that the two digit disaggregation of activity and occupation performed might be not fine enough to isolate similar jobs. But it might also reveal than not all firms pay the same attention to job quality; for instance, some firms might be more rigorous with health and safety standards, allow more autonomy to their employees, offer different opportunities of training, etc. In any case, both the second and third sets of estimations suggest the existence of segmented labour markets, where good jobs might be rationed and are not accessible for all workers, even if they have similar levels of human capital.

6.5.   JOB QUALITY AND JOB SATISFACTION

In Chapter 2, we discussed the possibility of using a simple index of job satisfaction as an alternative method of measuring job quality. Despite its obvious advantages (most importantly, the simplicity of its measurement with a direct question to the workers concerned), we argued that it is not an adequate measure of job quality for comparative purposes because of its opacity and because of the existence of psycho-social confounding factors that result in an index whose behaviour was too often inconsistent with any reasonable expectation. For these reasons, we opted for the construction of a model based on a review of the main theoretical and empirical findings of the specialized literature, whose results we are discussing in this chapter.

Since we now have our multidimensional model-based index, an interesting question is how our results compare to the results obtained with a simpler job satisfaction-based alternative. The fact that we have individual-level data means that we can compare the scores obtained by each alternative for individual workers. Unfortunately, the EWCS does not include the standard general question on job satisfaction which is most often used as an indirect measure of job quality. Instead, there is a *sui generis* question on satisfaction with working conditions, which is probably (and we present below some evidence of this) a better question in itself (being much more specific and its interpretation less ambiguous), but which does not let us evaluate in strict terms how our index compares with the standard job satisfaction approach. Nevertheless, this section should serve as an approximation.

Figure 6.11 shows the distribution of our index and the distribution of responses to the EWCS question on satisfaction with working conditions. As can be gauged by the chart on the bottom of the figure, the question

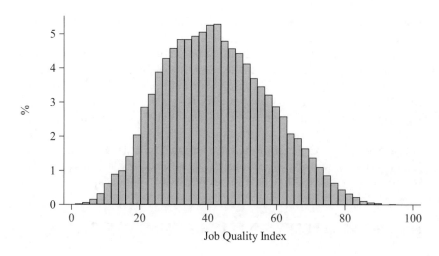

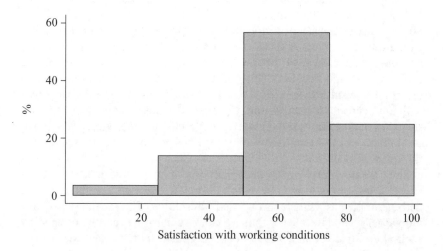

Source: Authors' analysis from EWCS 2005 micro-data.

Figure 6.11   *Our comparative job quality index versus an index of*
                satisfaction with working conditions

on satisfaction with working conditions has only four answer categories,
ranging from 'not at all satisfied' to 'very satisfied'. We have changed the
scale of these categories from 1–4 to 0–100, to make its results comparable to our index. The first thing that can be noted from this simple comparison is the vast difference in the level of detail obtained from the two

Table 6.10   Correlation between job satisfaction and the comparative job quality index

	Correlation coefficient
Comparative job quality index	0.443 ***
Dimension 1 – pay	0.241 ***
Dimension 2 – intrinsic job quality	0.335 ***
Dimension 3 – Employment quality	0.303 ***
Dimension 4 – Health and safety	0.291 ***
Dimension 5 – Work–life Balance	0.245 ***

Notes: *** significant at 1%; ** significant at 5%; * significant at 10%.

Source: Authors' analysis from EWCS 2005 micro-data.

approaches. While the histogram on the top of Figure 6.11 clearly shows a continuous distribution that can position each individual with some precision within a continuum of job quality outcomes, the second histogram can only discriminate between four broad categories. The richness of the picture given by the chart on the top is obviously much bigger than that of the chart on the bottom.

And this is just looking at the surface, at the highest level of aggregation of the index. But one of the key advantages of using a multidimensional approach is that we can go beyond the overall result and look at the partial pictures given by its components and subcomponents. Our index has a nested structure, with five dimensions, eight components, nine subcomponents and 45 individual variables: to understand better the results at any of these levels, we can break it down into the scores of its components, which enhances considerably our capacity to understand and interpret the results. This is illustrated by Table 6.10, which shows the correlation between the index of satisfaction with working conditions, the comparative job quality index and its five higher-level dimensions. The highest level of correlation is between satisfaction with working conditions and the overall job quality index: a coefficient of 0.443, which is relatively high but not so much as to suggest that they are simply two different ways of measuring the same thing. In other words, as we said earlier, the distribution of the satisfaction index seems to reflect not only the quality of each job, but other things as well (according to the specialized literature, these other things include expectations and the adaptive capacity of each worker). Still, the fact that the highest correlation is with the overall index suggests that the index of satisfaction with working conditions reflects a subjective evaluation of the job as a whole, rather than any specific aspect of it. Still, looking at the coefficient of correlation for each dimension, we can see that some of them seem to be more important than others in the subjective evaluation of working conditions: the lowest coefficients are for the dimensions of pay and work–life balance, which for many workers may not even be part of the idea of working conditions; the highest correlation is for the dimension of intrinsic job quality (which incorporates some relatively subjective variables whose correlation with a subjective evaluation of working conditions was to be expected), but the correlations are relatively high as well for the dimensions of employment quality and health and safety. Overall, it is reassuring to see that there are no big surprises in these results: all the coefficients are positive and strong enough as to be significant, yet not as much as to suggest that with a simpler satisfaction-based measure we could have achieved the same results.

A final point to be made in this respect concerns the country-level comparison of the average scores for the two indices. In Chapter 2, we saw that one of the problems of using job satisfaction as an indicator of job quality for comparative purposes was the fact that the distribution of average national scores did not seem to reflect neither a range of variation nor a country ranking which fitted any reasonable expectation. Figure 6.12 plots the average level of job satisfaction (this time, based on the standard general question) according to the 2005 International Social Survey Program (ISSP) against the average score of our comparative job quality index based on the 2005 EWCS. Only 16 countries are shown, because the ISSP does not cover the whole of the EU. To facilitate the comparison, the values of the ISSP job satisfaction index have been rescaled to 0 to 100 (originally it was scaled from 0 to 10). The contrast between the pictures given by the two approaches to job quality is enormous. Whereas the national scores of our index ranges from 25 to 57, the average values of the ISSP job satisfaction index range from 65 to 76. But what is more important is the actual positioning of countries in the two indices. In the ISSP index of job satisfaction, Bulgaria and Portugal are above Sweden, Belgium and France, to mention just some surprising examples. The positioning of countries according to the ISSP job satisfaction index and according to our comparative job quality index are completely different, despite the fact that both indices were carried out the same year and that both should to some extent reflect the same underlying realities of work around Europe. Anyone acquainted with quality of employment across Europe can probably tell, without much doubt, that the scores of our index look more plausible.

Part of the problem results from the use of such a general job satisfaction question as the one included in the 2005 ISSP. If we use a more specific question such as the one on satisfaction with working conditions included in the 2005 EWCS (the one we have discussed earlier in this section), the

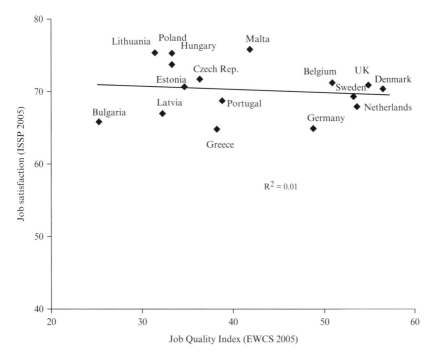

Source: Authors' analysis from EWCS 2005 micro-data and ISSP (2005).

Figure 6.12 ISSP index of job satisfaction vs. our comparative job quality index

results look much more reasonable (see Figure 6.13). Although the range of variation of this index is also considerably smaller than that of our index (from 53 to 80), and although there are some strange realignments (Portugal gets a higher value than France and Finland, for instance), the results look quite consistent with those of our index. The extent of correlation between our index and this working conditions satisfaction index is relatively high. Therefore, a more specific satisfaction question makes a considerably better index for comparative purposes, which makes it even more surprising the fact that it is the general job satisfaction approach which has become a standard in surveys and debates about job satisfaction from a comparative perspective. Still, even though the average scores of such a working conditions satisfaction index seem to approximate the country rankings of our multidimensional index moderately well, the problems of opacity and excessive simplicity mentioned earlier remain. A specific index of satisfaction with working conditions might be a useful

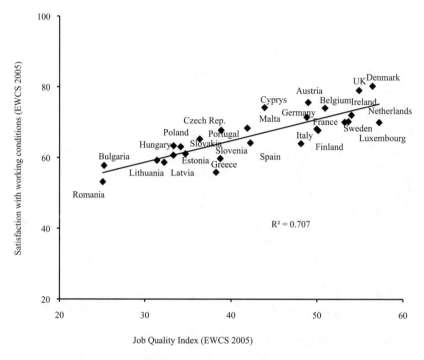

Source: Authors' analysis from EWCS 2005.

Figure 6.13   Satisfaction with working conditions vs. our comparative job quality index

piece of information for contrasting and externally validating the results of a multidimensional index as the one proposed here, but it can never be a valid substitute.

NOTES

1. Formally, the Pen's parade is simply the inverse of the cumulative distribution function.
2. The literature on inequality measures is vast and extensive. Though we know that, probably, the Gini index is not the best available measure (for instance, their decomposition possibilities are very limited), it is by far the most used and popular one in Economics and other Social Sciences.
3. This type of correction is used, for example, by the United Nations in the *Human Development Report 1990* (UNDP 1990).
4. See, for example, Cowell (2011) for a detailed review of the most popular indexes and their properties.

7. Conclusions

Generally in Social Sciences, but particularly in Economics, what cannot be measured hardly exists. This book has discussed the possibilities for developing a sound synthetic measure at the European Union of one of those virtually non-existing issues in current economic debates: job quality. Since the late 1990s, European policy makers have been speaking about the need to take job quality into account for the development of employment policies: but the lack of a widely accepted and respected measure of job quality (the lack of even a shared understanding of what job quality is) has kept this issue at a rhetorical level so far.

There are non-negligible reasons to take seriously the development of a good European job quality indicator. European full-time workers spend on average 42 hours a week in their jobs: obviously, whatever happens during this significant amount of their life will be very relevant for their overall well-being. Furthermore, job quality is strongly linked to many of the key goals of high-developed economies – sustainable employment rates, gender equality, productivity, etc., so, in order to adequately evaluate the performance and progress of European economies, it is necessary to track the distribution and evolution of job quality. All these concerns are heightened in the current context of crisis, which involves accelerated processes of change and transformation of employment structures and working conditions: we have detailed information of how the crisis is affecting employment in quantitative terms (many people are losing their jobs), but we know nearly nothing about its implications for the quality of jobs (are the conditions of those that remain at work also somehow affected?).

But despite all these good reasons for having a good and comparable measure of job quality at the EU level, there is no established standard in this matter. This does not mean that there are no proposals: in Chapter 4, we reviewed nearly 20 different existing proposals, at the EU level and beyond. But the lack of an agreed concept and set of standards on this issue means that the underlying assumptions, measures and to a lesser extent results of these different proposals often contradict each other. This is obviously a problem for the definitive establishment of job quality as an important element of European employment policy, besides the more

traditional concern about job quantities. Of course, it has to be acknowledged that measuring job quality is not an easy task: but it is not necessarily more difficult than other key concepts of social policy whose measure
has been standardized in recent times, such as employment and unemployment, poverty, inequality or even something as evasive as human development. Job quality is a complex issue, but it certainly *can* be measured, and
should be measured.

The first difficulty that must be addressed if we want to measure job
quality is to agree on what job quality is. In our survey of existing proposals of job quality indicators, we saw that those indicators often depart from
different concepts and assumptions: but perhaps most importantly, most
of these indicators lacked a clear definition and underlying model of what
job quality is. This has very negative implications for the coherence of the
measures proposed. For instance, some of the most important indicators
of job quality currently available (including the proposal of the EU itself)
include measures of job *quantity*, which betrays a conceptual confusion
that is obviously negative for the credibility and usefulness of these indicators. It is also quite common that these indicators include (as components
of job quality) measures of more general social issues such as social protection, education or poverty, all very important items in themselves and
surely related to job quality in some ways, but clearly not aspects of job
quality under any reasonable demarcation of the concept.[1] The lack of a
clear definition of the concept and demarcation of its scope tends, in fact,
to make the existing proposals of job quality indicators catch-all measures
of anything that is arguably related to work, employment and workers'
well-being, and yet normally lacking some of the most important aspects
of job quality identified by the specialized Social Sciences literature.

In this book, we proposed a model of job quality based on a review of the
existing literature on this issue, to serve as the basis for the development of
a new indicator presented in Chapters 5 and 6. The theoretical underpin-
ning of this model comes from a discussion (in Chapter 2) of three broad
approaches to measuring job quality that can be found in recent specialized literature: to use job satisfaction as a catch-all simple indicator of job
quality, to define job quality according to the answers of workers to a set
of predefined questions, and to draw from the Social Sciences literature
in order to identify (and model) job attributes that have an impact on
the well-being of workers. We opted for the latter approach because of
the problems associated to the first two alternatives, limitations that arise
from the difficulty of disentangling the effect of the real conditions of work
and the effect of (unrelated) subjective processes on the responses given by
workers to survey questions on job satisfaction or on what makes a good
job. The review of the existing Social Sciences literature on job quality

allowed us to identify six broad dimensions of job quality (pay, industrial democracy and participation, intrinsic quality of work, quality of the employment relation, health and safety and work–life balance), which we then operationalized into a set of components, sub-components and indicators following the guidelines of the literature review, constructing a nested multidimensional model of job quality which was put in practice in Chapters 5 and 6 of this book. For this purpose, we used the best existing European statistical source on job quality, the European Working Conditions Survey, which unfortunately does not cover the dimension of industrial democracy and participation, which therefore had to be left out of the empirical application of our model.

This index was constructed following the broad methodological guidelines presented in Chapter 3. Job quality is a multidimensional concept and, therefore, any overall indicator will have to be constructed by aggregating information on the different attributes (or dimensions) of work and employment. Ideally, such aggregation should be done at the individual level using a single source. An indicator constructed at the individual level allows the differentiation of results for specific groups of workers which might be of special interest for policy, such as women and men, older workers or the low-paid; also, a multidimensional index constructed at the individual level allows to take into account the interaction between the different components of job quality for specific workers and jobs (for instance, whether there is compensation or accumulation of good and bad attributes). Preferably, job quality indicators should be updated with some regularity so that they can be used to track changes over time, although the pace of change of job quality is not as fast as the pace of change in employment numbers, so it would be unnecessary to match the frantic rhythm of production of labour force statistics. Finally, an EU-level job quality indicator has to confront the important problem of comparability: because there are important structural and cultural differences across Europe, the definition of some of the dimensions of job quality may have to be adapted to national specificities, but if this is taken too far, the comparability itself can be compromised and therefore the usefulness of the whole effort jeopardized. In our own proposal presented in Chapter 5, we opted for full harmonization and comparability, drawing from a dedicated EU-level survey (the EWCS). But it has to be acknowledged that for many of the methodological dilemmas presented in Chapter 3, there are no easy or univocal solutions: depending on the specific objectives in each case, and crucially on the resources available, specific solutions will have to be identified. What is most important in this sense, both for the usefulness and for the credibility of the indicator, is that each of the methodological decisions taken was well-explained and documented.

According to the principles discussed in Chapters 2 and 3, in Chapter 4 we carried out an extensive review of the main indicators of job quality that can be found in recent Social Sciences literature and policy papers. Although some indices are clearly better than others, none of the existing proposals is totally satisfactory, as most indicators miss some key dimensions or are based on debatable methodological decisions. However, there has been rapid progress in recent years in this matter especially in the European context (most of the reviewed proposals originated in Europe), so there may soon be a proposal that eventually becomes an international standard of job quality measurement. To contribute to such aim, in Chapters 5 and 6 of this book we presented our own proposal of a job quality index for the European Union: although the limitations imposed by the dataset used for its construction (the EWCS) necessarily make it a preliminary proposal (until we have adequate statistical sources on this matter, any proposal will have to be partial and preliminary), we hope it can be a good starting point, or at least an illustration that reorients the debate to firmer grounds.

Chapter 5 presented a detailed account of the construction of this index, from the coding of the original EWCS variables to a homogeneous normative metric to the aggregation of its components into a single index. This index is based on a model which is directly derived from the literature review carried out in Chapter 2, taking into account the methodological guidelines discussed in Chapter 3 and trying to overcome the problems of existing proposals surveyed in Chapter 4. In our view, the main strengths of our proposal are the following: 1) the scope of the index is clearly and strictly delimited to those attributes of jobs which have a direct impact on the well-being of workers, leaving out other confounding elements which refer to the labour market rather than to jobs (such as level of unemployment) or to workers' expectations rather than their realities (such as job satisfaction); 2) the index has a clear and transparent structure, which in most cases can be traced back to the relevant literature in a particular field of studies of job quality, and which guided (though not unequivocally: there is some unavoidable arbitrariness in this) the allocation of weights and recoding of the original variables; 3) our measure is fully calculated at the individual level, which provides a great deal of flexibility to the analysis, which can be carried out for specific subgroups and which can take into account the existence of interactions between the different components of the index at the individual or job level; 4) it provides a clear and unambiguous evaluation of job quality that can be used for normative comparisons at any level (including by country), with the possibility of decomposing the overall scores in its components for gaining a clearer understanding.

Of course, our index is not without problems, and some of the decisions taken in its construction are relatively uncommon in this area and hence are open for discussion. In particular, two methodological characteristics of our index differentiate our proposal from previous ones: the procedures followed in the recoding of the original variables to a homogeneous metric and the method of aggregation of the dimensions into the overall index. In order to stick to a normative logic in our index and to avoid artificially homogeneizing the distribution of the different components of job quality, we opted for a normalization of the original variables based on justified reasoning rather than statistical transformation such as a Z-scores standardization. It could be argued that this introduces more arbitrariness in the index, but we believe it is a more transparent and adequate method for a normative index such as the one proposed here. With respect to the aggregation of components into the overall index, we used a geometric rather than arithmetic method of aggregation, because in our view its properties are more adequate for a normative index of job quality: it assumes a decreasing contribution of each component to the overall level of job quality (which is more coherent with current research on the determinants of welfare, which tend to find that increases starting from a low initial level contribute much more than increases starting from a high level) and it takes into account the interaction between the different dimensions, penalizing large discrepancies in the different dimensions rather than assuming that they can perfectly compensate each other. We believe these decisions are fundamentally sound and make our proposal stronger, but we understand that it is in the nature of scientific and policy research that anything can and indeed must be criticized. Our proposal being essentially illustrative, our main goal was to present a clear, well-justified and transparent index that can feed the necessary debate on a job quality indicator for the European Union.

But as the proverb goes, the proof of the pudding is in the eating, so in Chapter 6 we put our proposal into practice by analysing the distribution of job quality in Europe according to our index. The results obtained allow making two different kinds of reflections. From the perspective of the index itself, the results show that the proposed index works well in the context of a large number of countries with different levels of economic development. The ranking of countries is comparable with previous proposals (in particular, with the most ambitious and solid proposals, such as ETUI's job quality index), while offering some important advantages such as the transparency of the index, the possibility of deepening the results both in terms of the index itself (taking advantage of the complex nested structure of our index) and in terms of any subgroup of the population we are interested about (taking advantage of the fact that our index is calculated at the individual level). The fact that the dimensions and components of our index are anchored in different traditions in the Social Sciences studying the impact of jobs on workers' well-being brings further possibilities of interpreting and deepening in its results at different levels. Furthermore, the test of robustness included in the analysis proves than the results of the index are contingent neither to the specific weight given to the five dimensions, nor to the adoption of a geometrical average instead of an arithmetic average to aggregate the dimensions into a single index.

From the perspective of the results themselves, several findings arise. In the first place, our JQI ranks Scandinavian countries, Luxembourg and the UK at the top, Continental European countries in the middle, Southern Europe in the mid-bottom and Eastern Europe at the bottom. As mentioned, this ranking has proven to be remarkably robust to different weighting schemes and aggregation procedures, and is very similar to the rankings obtained not only by other job quality indices, but even by other evaluations of country economic and social performance (such as competitiveness or human development). In the second place, we showed how differences in job quality across Europe are mainly driven not by differences in the employment structure across countries but by the existence of large discrepancies in terms of job quality within the same types of jobs (broadly defined as the combination of occupations and sectors of activity) among the different European Union members. Obviously, structural differences also matter: for instance, construction jobs tend to be associated with tougher working conditions (as reflected by our index). But the identified differences between European countries in terms of job quality are mostly the result of differences in job quality as such, and only secondarily of differences in their economic structures: an important corollary of this is that the reduction of differences in job quality across the EU would benefit more from the development of specific policies aimed at improving the quality of jobs than from focusing on the economic growth and structural modernization of the currently worst performers. In the third place, we illustrated the usefulness of our proposal for addressing distributional issues. In this respect, it is worth highlighting the negative association between the average value and the inequality of the distribution of job quality; that is, countries with high average levels of job quality tend to exhibit a narrower dispersion in this variable and vice versa. But this relationship is not perfect, so when we jointly consider the mean and the dispersion of job quality – using a kind of social welfare function – some countries (such as Denmark or Sweden) climb up positions in the ranking, while others (such as Ireland or Spain) recede. In the fourth place, the individual construction of our index allowed us to study the distribution of job quality for specific subgroups of workers. This analysis shows that, other things being equal and after controlling for human capital endowments, occupation and sector of activity, both women and young workers enjoy on average lower levels of job quality in all dimensions, with the exception of health and safety and work–life balance in the case of women. In the fifth place, we focused our attention on the relationship at the individual level among the different dimensions of job quality. We showed not only that the different ingredients of job quality are mostly positively correlated (good and bad attributes tend to accumulate rather than compensate each other) but also that this positive association holds even after controlling for workers' human capital endowments, which casts (even more) doubts on the validity of the theory of wage compensating differentials, suggesting the existence of segmented labour markets across Europe. Finally, we studied the association between our index and two different versions of a simple index of job satisfaction (a general one which we could compare at the country level, and a specific index of satisfaction with working conditions which we could compare at the individual level): such comparison illustrates the advantages of using a multidimensional and objective approach as the one proposed here (in terms of the further complexity and transparency of the analysis) instead of the black box of using job satisfaction as a catch-all indicator of the quality of jobs.

The broad picture of the levels of job quality across the European Union that is painted by our index (which as we have seen, is not dissimilar to that of previous proposals) is remarkably consistent with the existing differences in economic development across Member States (in fact, the statistical correlation between the comparative version of our overall job quality index and per capita GDP at PPP at the country level is 0.94). To some extent, this result is almost tautologic, since as income grows, the gains in productivity are associated to increases in wages, which is one of the main dimensions of our index. But the gains in productivity are also used to improve other aspects of job quality: in fact, even if we eliminate wages from the equation (looking only at the non-pecuniary elements of job quality, what we called earlier an 'amenities' index), the correlation is still quite important (0.55), and a broad consistence remains if we look at specific dimensions (though the more detailed the analysis, the more idiosyncrasies we find in the results). This consistency, together with the consistency across different methods of normalization and aggregation of the job attributes and with the broad consistency between the country ranking derived from our proposal and previous ones, not only amounts to a reassuring validation of our index but also (in our view) to a vindication of the feasibility of measuring job quality for comparative policy purposes. Such consistency would never exist unless there is something out there, in the reality of European working life, which can be called job quality, which is distributed in a particular way across countries and workers, and which can be measured with a reasonable degree of validity and precision with methods such as those proposed here.

Therefore, job quality can be measured. But should it be measured? A high level of consistency between the results of our index and more traditional measures of economic performance such as per capita GDP could be used as an argument against the interest of measuring job quality (the highest the consistency, the lowest the added value of a new indicator). But that would be, of course, totally wrong. Only in the case of the wage dimension of job quality is the correlation with GDP as high as to suggest an unnecessary duplication of information: but as mentioned earlier, this was to be expected since GDP per capita is directly linked to the wage dimension of job quality (such dimension is aimed at capturing the access to resources granted by the compensation from work, a concept similar to that behind per capita GDP in PPP). An index of job quality must include wages as an important element (integrated within a multidimensional framework), even if that means that the country differences in the index tend to be dominated by differences in the standard of living because the differences in the other components are not so large. The strength of a multidimensional index is that it can be easily decomposed to go beyond its overall scores: as we have seen, when we look at the non-pecuniary attributes of job quality important differences arise, which means that for the same level of economic development some countries are providing much better jobs than others (even if the pay levels are on average relatively similar for equally developed economies). As we saw in Chapter 6, not only for the same level of economic development, but even for the same type of economic structure, there are significant differences in the levels of job quality across Europe. And perhaps most importantly, the added value of having a new index does not reside so much in the comparison of the average national scores (which is always limited and potentially misleading), but on the possibility of comparing the distribution and components of job quality across the different countries as we illustrated in Chapter 6.

So in our view, job quality can, and should, be measured for international comparative purposes. The European Union, the largest-scale real-life experiment of economic and social integration in history, is uniquely positioned to develop and give policy weight to such a measure. Such a measure could expand considerably the scope of EU employment policies, going beyond the traditional fixation with the number of people working and considering the conditions under which such work takes place. And it is quite likely that if the EU would do that with some degree of seriousness, it would inmediately become a de facto standard at a worldwide scale.

NOTE

1. For taking into account the potential interaction between job quality and some of these other elements of the social and institutional framework, we suggested in Chapter 3 to construct a side-index (a kind of *satellite* account) rather than including alien elements into the job quality index.

Appendix
Effect of sex, age and schooling years on the probability of considering a job attribute very important

Table A1   Effect of sex, age and schooling years on the probability of considering a job attribute very important (%) (2005)

	Job security				High income				Opportunities of advancement				Interest of the job			
	Female	Age	Age²	Schooling	Female	Age	Age²	Schooling	Female	Age	Age²	Schooling	Female	Age	Age²	Schooling
AUS	7.17	0.82	−0.01	−1.75						−1.29	0.01		5.06			1.82
WGER	−9.04				−5.35			−0.98	−4.93	−1.11	0.01		−7.35			2.72
EGER					−7.00		−0.01	−1.77								2.80
GB	−8.65	−1.35	0.01	−1.22	−6.25	−1.25	0.01	−1.01								2.76
US		1.12	−0.01	−3.56			−0.01	−3.55	−6.90	−1.96	0.02	0.91				1.23
HU							−0.01					−2.35				2.59
IR	−9.14					−1.05		−1.09	−10.79	−1.80	0.02	1.14	−8.37			2.77
NO	7.03	0.94		−2.71		0.75	−0.01	−0.72	2.96		−0.01					3.34
SW	17.57			−2.01		0.98	−0.01	−0.64		−1.13	0.01		12.13			2.19
CZ	16.24	1.57	−0.01			1.17	−0.02	−1.97				1.10				2.59
SL		1.05		1.00	−5.59	0.83	−0.01		−8.69	−1.14	0.01					2.86
BU		0.85	−0.01									3.30				3.02
RU							−0.01	−1.28		−1.72	0.01	1.13		−1.08		3.20
NZ				−2.06						−2.12	0.02					
CAN				−2.60									11.33			2.23

	C1	C2	C3	C4	C5	C6	C7	C8	C9	C10	C11	C12	C13	C14	C15	C16
PHI	-6.20			1.56	-7.56			1.02				2.86				2.02
ISR		0.83	-0.01			1.17	-0.01	-1.01					-6.68			1.05
JAP			-0.01		-8.64	1.16	-0.01	-1.10	-3.47							1.44
SPA				-0.59				-0.88					5.40			1.17
LAT					-6.08				5.46	-1.81	0.01			-2.15	0.02	2.64
FRA	5.70			-1.91	-6.93		-0.01	-0.60	-5.51			3.33	-5.04			1.27
CYP				1.34	-12.85			1.55	-7.85			1.32				2.27
POR							-0.01	-1.33								1.05
DEN	6.96			-1.24	-3.21				-2.81							2.11
S WZ				-1.28				-0.68		-0.88	0.01		-5.98			2.51
BEL		1.16	-0.01	-1.89				-2.01		0.88	-0.01	-1.27		1.29	-0.01	2.37
FIN	12.46			-0.88				-0.51	-3.77				6.48			1.04
MEX	-4.08			1.15		1.20	-0.01	0.67				1.19				1.20
TAI				0.64								0.81		-0.95		2.28
SA				0.89										-0.99		1.63
KOR	-4.93	1.48	-0.02	1.55	4.72		-0.01					1.84				1.94
DR	-4.70			1.36				1.21				1.93				1.09

Table A1 (continued)

	Work independently				Helpful to other people				Useful to society				Control over working time			
	Female	Age	Age²	Schooling	Female	Age	Age²	Schooling	Female	Age	Age²	Schooling	Female	Age	Age²	Schooling
AUS	3.93	0.58	-0.01	0.48	13.53			0.55	8.02			0.93	7.34	0.84	-0.01	
WGER	-9.16			1.65		-0.80	0.01			-0.90	0.01	0.90				0.65
EGER	-8.88			2.53					6.59	-0.87	0.01	1.15				
GB				1.02				1.38				1.46				
US		1.50	-0.01		8.52								-4.14		-0.01	-0.77
HU	-8.20	0.95	-0.01	1.82				1.93		0.85		1.44				0.68
IR	-11.70		-0.01	1.00				1.81				2.01		1.34	-0.01	
NO		1.74	-0.02	1.16	9.11				9.79					2.13	-0.02	0.75
SW		2.29	-0.02	3.12	16.75				9.90				4.75	1.97	-0.02	
CZ				1.70	9.99			1.60	8.18			1.82				
SL					6.27							0.83				1.23
BU			-0.01	1.63				1.02				1.46				
RU				2.30								0.89				1.38
NZ	-4.33				5.56			-0.73	7.16							
CAN				0.88	11.81				14.02				12.85			

260

PHI	-7.53		1.19	-5.46			2.26				1.88						1.07
ISR	-5.19		-0.90								1.58	0.80	-6.22				
JAP																	
SPA						0.01											
LAT			1.32	5.71	-1.00	0.01											
FRA	1.09	-0.01		7.97				4.22			1.56	0.81	7.78	1.60	-0.02		
CYP	-11.12		0.93				1.53						-6.61				
POR	-5.24		0.83				0.71						-5.80				-0.79
DEN	2.50	-0.02	1.04	12.93													0.68
SWZ	-13.16	1.18	-0.01	7.39		-0.01		5.05			0.71			1.70	-0.02		
BEL	-6.26	2.09	-0.02	0.88	1.37	-0.01			1.40	-0.01				1.43	-0.01		
FIN	1.97	-0.02		11.19	1.33	-0.01	-0.46	4.64			0.68			1.47	-0.02		0.68
MEX	-5.78							-5.67									
TAI	0.47	-0.01	0.84				1.38	3.27	0.77	-0.01	1.24		3.60	0.59	-0.01		0.68
SA						-0.01				-0.01							
KOR	1.31	-0.01	0.75				0.69		1.77	-0.01	0.89			1.19	-0.01		
DR	0.75	-0.01	0.54		-1.01	0.01	0.66			-0.01	1.21		-4.60				

Note: Marginal effects evaluated at means from a *probit* model. Only those results significantly different from 0 at least at 10% level are shown in the table.

Source: Authors' analysis from ISSP (2005).

References

Akerlof, G. (1980), 'A theory of social custom of which unemployment may be one consequence', *Quarterly Journal of Economics,* **94** (4), 749–75.

Anker, R., I. Chernyshev, P. Egger, F. Mehran and J. Ritter (2003), 'Measuring decent work with statistical indicator', *International Labour Review*, **142** (2), 147–78.

Atkinson, Anthony B. (2006), 'OECD letter from Tony Atkinson', paper released after the Joint Research Center–Centre for Research Long Learning/Organisation for Economic Co-operation and Development Workshop on Measuring Well-being and Societal Progress Milan, Italy, 19–21 June, accessed 15 November 2010 at http://crell.jrc.ec.europa.eu/Well-being/OECD%20Letter%20(well%20being).doc

Autor, D., L. F. Katz and M. S. Kearney (2006), 'The polarization of the US labour market', *American Economic Review. Papers and Proceedings*, **96** (2), 189–94.

Avirgan, T. (2009), *Survey of Job Quality Indicators for the European Parliament*, Brussels: Labour Asociados.

Avirgan, T., L. J. Bivens and S. Gammage (eds.) (2005), *Good Jobs, Bad Jobs, No Jobs: Labor Markets and Informal Work in Egypt, El Salvador, India, Russia, and South Africa*, Washington, DC: Economic Policy Institute.

Behrens, V. J. and R. M. Brackbill, (1993), 'Worker awareness of exposure: industries and occupations with low awareness', *American Journal of Industrial Medicine*, **23**, 695–701.

Bell, D. (1973), *The Coming of the Post-industrial Society*, New York: Basic Books.

Bescond, D., A. Châtaignier and F. Mehran (2003), 'Seven indicators to measure decent work: an international comparison', *International Labour Review*, **142** (2), 179–212.

Blauner, R. (1964), *Alienation and Freedom*, Chicago IL: Chicago University Press.

Bonhomme, S. and G. Jolivet (2009), 'The pervasive absence of compensating differentials', *Journal of Applied Econometrics*, **24** (5), 763–95.

Bonnet, F., J. B. Figueiredo and G. Standing (2003), 'A family of decent work indexes', *International Labour Review*, **142** (2), 213–38.

Botton, A. de (2004), *Status Anxiety*, London: Hamish Hamilton.

Braverman, H. (1974), *Labor and Monopoly Capital*, reprinted 1998, New York: Monthly Review Press.

Breaugh, J. A. (1985), 'The measurement of work autonomy', *Human Relations*, **38** (6), 551–70

Breaugh, J. A. (1999), 'Further investigation of the work autonomy scales: two studies', *Journal of Business and Psychology*, **13** (3), 357–73.

Bredgaard, T., F. Larsen and P. K. Madsen (2005), 'The flexible Danish labour market – a review', Centre for Labour Market Research (CARMA) research paper no. 31, Aalborg, Denmark.

Brisbois, R. (2003), 'How Canada stacks up: the quality of work – an international perspective', Canadian Policy Research Networks research paper no. 23.

Brown, C. (1980). 'Equalizing differences in the labor market', *Quarterly Journal of Economics*, **94** (1), 113–34.

Brown, D. and M. McIntosh (1998), 'If you're happy and you know it. . . Job satisfaction in the low wage service sector', London School of Economics Centre for Economic Performance paper, London.

Brown, D. A., J. Gardner, A. J. Oswald and J. Quian (2008), 'Does wage rank affect employees' well-being?', *Industrial Relations*, **47** (3), 355–89.

Bucardo, J., S. J. Semple, M. Fraga-Vallejo, W. Davila and T. L. Patterson (2004), 'A qualitative exploration of female sex work in Tijuana, Mexico', *Archives of Sexual Behavior*, **33** (4), 343–51.

Buunk, B. P. and F. X. Gibbons (1997): *Health, Coping, and Well-being: Perspectives from Social Comparison Theory,* Mahwah, NJ: Lawrence Erlbaum Associates.

Caprile, M. and J. Potrony, (2006), 'IQT: Objetivos y metodología', in *Anuario Sociolaboral de la UGT de Catalunya 2005*, Barcelona: UGT and CRESC, vol. II, pp. 53–63.

Chatani, K. (2008), *From corporate-centre security to flexicurity in Japan*, International Labour Organization employment working paper no. 17.

Chatzis, C. *et al. (*2004), 'Greek employee awareness of carcinogenic exposure', *Preventive Medicine*, **39** (4), 657–65.

Clark, A. E. (2005), 'What makes a good job? Evidence from OECD countries' in Stephen Bazen, Claudio Lucifora and Wiemer Saaverda (eds), *Job Quality and Employer Behaviour*, Basingstoke: Palgrave, pp. 11–30.

Clark, A. E. and A. J. Oswald (1996), 'Satisfaction and comparison income', *Journal of Public Economics*, **61** (3), 359–81.

Clark, A. E., Y. Georgellis and S. Peter (1999), 'Job satisfaction, wage changes and quits: evidence from Germany', *Research in Labor Economics*, **17**, 95–121.

Cornelissen, T. (2006), 'Job characteristics as determinants of job satisfaction and labour mobility', Fakultat der Universitat Hannover Diskussionspapiere der Wirtschaftswissenschaftlichen dp-334.

Cowell, F. R. (2001), *Measuring Inequality*, Oxford: Oxford University Press.

Coyle, D. (2001), *Paradoxes of Prosperity. Why the New Capitalism Benefits All*, New York and London: Texere.

Creedy, J. and G. Kalb (2005), 'Discrete hours labour supply modelling: Specification, estimation and simulation', *Journal of Economic Surveys*, **19** (5), 697–734.

Davoine, L., C. Erhel and M. Guergoat-Lariviere (2008), 'A Taxonomy of European Labour Markets using Quality Indicators', Centre d'études de l'Emploi.Rapport de Recherche no. 45.

De la Torre, A., A. Havenner, K. Adams and J. Ng (2010), 'Premium sex: Factors influencing the negotiated price of unprotected sex by female sex workers in Mexico', *Journal of Applied Economics*, **13** (1), 67–90.

Diener, E., E. M. Suh, R. E. Lucas and H. L. Smith (1999), 'Subjective well-being: three decades of progress', *Psychological Bulletin*, **125** (2), 276–302.

Doeringer, P. B. and M. J. Piore (1970), *Internal Labor Markets and Manpower Analysis*, Lexington, MA: D.C. Heath and Company.

Dolan, P., T. Peasgood and M. White (2008), 'Do we really know what makes us happy? A review of the economic literature on the factors associated with subjective well-being', *Journal of Economic Psychology*, **29** (1), 94–122.

Doogan, K. (2009), *New Capitalism? The Transformation of Work*, London: Polity Press.

Dorsey, S. and N. Walzer (1983), 'Workers' compensation, job hazard, and wages', *Industrial and Labour Relation Review*, **36** (4), pp. 642–54.

Duncan, G. J. and B. Holmlund (1983), 'Was Adam Smith right after all? Another test of the theory of compensating wage differentials', *Journal of Labor Economics*, **1** (4), 366–379.

Easterlin, R. A. (1974), 'Does economic growth improve the human lot? Some empirical evidence', in P.A. David and M. W. Reder (eds), *Nations and Households in Economic Growth: Essays in Honour of Moses Abramowitz*, New York: Academic Press, pp. 89–125.

Edgell, S. (2006), *The Sociology of Work: Continuity and Change in Paid and Unpaid Work*, London: Sage.

Ehrenreich, B. (2009), *Smile or Die. How Positive Thinking Fooled America and the World*, London: Granta Books.

Elias, P. (1997), 'Occupational classification (ISCO-88), concepts, methods, reliability, validity and cross-national comparability', OECD, Directorate for Employment, Labour and Social Affairs labour market and social policy occasional papers 20.

Elias, P. and M. Birch (1994), 'Establishment of community-wide occupational statistics, ISCO 88 (com) a guide for users', Institute for Employment Research University of Warwick, working paper.

Eurofound (2002), *Quality of work and employment in Europe: Issues and challenges*, Dublin: Eurofound.

Eurofound (2006), *Fifteen years of working conditions in the EU: charting the trends*, Dublin: Eurofound.

Eurofound (2009), Childcare services in Europe, Dublin: Eurofound.

European Commission (2001), 'Employment and social policy: a framework for investing in quality', communication from the Commission to the European Parliament, the Economic and Social Committee and the Committee of the Regions, COM(2001), **313**.

European Commission (2007), *Towards Common Principles of Flexicurity: More and Better Jobs through Flexibility and Security*, Brussels: European Commission.

European Commission (2008), *Employment in Europe 2008*, Brussels: European Commission.

European Council (2008), 'Council decision of 15 July 2008 on guidelines for the employment policies of the Member States', 2008/618/EC.

Fernández, R. and C. Nordman (2009), 'Are there pecuniary compensations for working conditions?', *Labour Economics*, **16** (2), 194–207.

Fernández-Macias, E. (2006), *The construction of income bands for the 4th European Working Conditions Survey*, Dublin: Eurofound.

Fernández-Macias, E. and M. Petrakos (2006), *Quality assurance in the 4th European working conditions survey*, Dublin: Eurofound.

Fernández-Macias, E. and J. Hurley (2008), *More and Better Jobs: Patterns of Employment Expansion in Europe (ERM Report 2008)*, Dublin: Eurofound.

Festinger, L. (1957), *A Theory of Cognitive Dissonance*, Palo Alto, CA: Stanford University Press.

Flanders Social and Economic Council (2009), 'Quality of work in Flanders 2004–2007', paper presented at the ETUI Conference 2009, 18–19 March, Brussels.

Frank, R. H. (1985), *Choosing the Right Pond: Human Behavior and the Quest for Status*, Oxford: Oxford University Press.

Frank, R. H. (2004), 'Human nature and economic policy: lessons for transition economies', *Journal of Socio-Economics*, **33**: 679–94.

Frank, R. H. (2008), *Microeconomics and Behaviour*, New York: McGraw-Hill.

Freeman, R. B. (1978), 'Job satisfaction as an economic variable', *American Economic Review. Papers and Proceedings*, **68** (2), 135–41.

Friedman, M. (1953), *Essays in Positive Economics*, Chicago IL: University of Chicago Press.

Gallie, D. (ed.) (2007), *Employment Regimes and the Quality of Work*, Oxford: Oxford University Press.

García Mainar, M. I. (1999), 'La satisfacción con el trabajo en España', *Documentación laboral*, **59**, 113–29.

Gertler, P., M. Shah and S. M. Bertozzi (2005), 'Risky business: the market for unprotected commercial sex', *Journal of Political Economy*, **113** (3), 518–50.

Ghai, D. (2003), 'Decent work: concept and indicators', *International Labour Review*, **142** (2), 113–45.

Golden, L. (2001), 'Flexible work schedules: what are we trading off to get them?' *Monthly Labour Review*, (March), 50–67.

Goos, M., A. Manning and A. Salomons (2009), 'The polarization of the European labor market', *American Economic Review*, **99** (2), 58–63.

Gordon, D. M., R. Edwards and M. Reich (1982), *Segmented Work, Divided Workers: The Historical Transformation of Labor in the United States*, New York: Cambridge University Press.

Green, F. (2006), *Demanding Work: The Paradox of Job Quality in the Affluent Economy*, Princeton, NJ: Princeton University Press.

Guest, D. (2002), 'Perspectives on the study of work–life balance', *Social Science Information*, **41**(2), 255–79.

Heery, E. and J. Salmon (eds.) (2000), *The Insecure Workforce*, London: Routledge.

Hirsch, F. (1977), *The Social Limits to Growth*, Cambridge, MA: Harvard University Press.

Hofinger, C. and G. Michenthaler (1998), 'Der Arbeitsklima-Index. Ein mikrobasiertes Meß-instrument für die Entwicklung der Arbeitswelt', *Diskurs Sozial*, **1**, 17–38.

Hull, F., S. Friedman and T. Rogers (1982), 'The effect of technology on alienation from work', *Work and Occupations*, **9** (1), 31–57.

Hurley, J. (2006), *Questionnaire translation process in the 4th European Working Conditions Survey*, Dublin: Eurofound.

International Social Survey Program (ISSP) (2005), 'Module on work orientation', accessed 15 November 2010 at www.issp.org.

Jackson, A. and P. Kumar, (1998), 'Measuring and monitoring the quality of jobs and the work environment in Canada', paper presented at the CSLS Conference on the State of Living Standards and the Quality of Life in Canada, 30–31, October Ottawa.

Jencks, C., L. Perman, and L. Rainwater (1988), 'What is a good job? A new measure of labor-market success', *American Journal of Sociology*, **93** (6), 322–57.

Jones, S. (1984), *The Economics of Conformism*, Oxford: Basil Blackwell.

Kalliath, T. and P. Brough (2008), 'Work–life balance: a review of the meaning of the balance construct', *Journal of Management & Organization,* **14** (3), 323–27.

Kohn, M. (1976), 'Occupational structure and alienation', *American Journal of Sociology*, **82** (1), 111–30.

Krueger, A. B., and L. H. Summers (1988), 'Efficiency wages and the inter-industry wage structure', *Econometrica*, **56** (2), 259–93.

Lambert, E. G., N. L. Hogan, and S. M. Barton (2001), 'The impact of job satisfaction on turnover intent: a test of a structural measurement model using a national sample of workers', *Social Science Journal*, **38** (2), 233–50.

Lancaster, K. J. (1966), 'A new approach to consumer theory', *Journal of Political Economy*, **74**, 132–57.

Lane, R. E. (2000), 'Diminishing returns to income, companionship and happiness', *Journal of Happiness Studies*, **1** (1), 103–19.

Lanfranchi, J., H. Ohlsson, and A. Skalli, (2002), 'Compensating wage differentials and shift work preferences', *Economics Letters*, **74** (3), 393–8.

Lara, E. and S. Rubio (2006), *Tenemos Buenos empleos? Impacto de las políticas económicas de El Salvador*, San Salvador: Fundación Nacional Para el Desarrollo and Global Policy Network.

Layard, R. (2004), 'Good jobs and bad jobs', CEP occasional paper no. 19.

Layard, R. (2005), *Happiness: Lessons from a New Science*, London: Penguin.

Leigh, J. P. (1995), 'Compensating wages, value of a statistical life, and inter-industry differentials', *Journal of Environmental Economics and Management*', **28** (1), 83–97.

Leschke, J. and A. Watt (2008), 'Job quality in Europe', ETUI-REHS working paper 2008.07.

Leschke, J., A. Watt and M. Finn (2008), 'Putting a number on job quality? Constructing a European job quality index', ETUI-REHS working paper 2008.03.

Mangione, T. W. and R. P. Quinn (1975), 'Job satisfaction, counter-productive behavior and drug use at work', *Journal of Applied Psychology*, **60**, 114–16.

Marmot, M. (2004), *Status Syndrome: How Your Social Standing Directly Affects Your Health and Life Expectancy*, London: Times Books.

Martin, A. and G. Psacharopoulos (1982), 'The reward for risk in the labour market: evidence from the United Kingdom and reconciliation with other studies', *Journal of Political Economy*, **90** (4), 827 53.

Marx, K. (1844), *Economic and Philosophic Manuscripts, Manuscritos: Economía y Filosofía*, reprinted 1968, Madrid: Alianza Editorial.

Mathios, A. (1989), 'Education, variation in earnings and non-monetary compensation', *Journal of Human Resources*, **24** (3), 456–68.

McGillivray, M. (2006), *Human Well-Being Concept and Measurement*, London: Palgrave Macmillan.

Melchior M. *et al.* (2007), 'Work stress precipitates depression and anxiety in young, working women and men', *Psychological Medicine*, **37** (8), 1119–29.

Merriam-Webster (2010), *Merriam-Webster Dictionary*, accessed at www. merriam-webster.com.

Michenthaler, G. (2006), 'The Austrian work climate index', paper presented at the European Working Conditions Seminar on Job Satisfaction, 9–10, November Helsinki.

Mill, J. S. (1848), *The Principles of Political Economy with Some of Their Applications to Social Philosophy,* edited by J. M. Robson (1965), and republished in *The Collected Works of John Stuart Mill, Volume II – (Books I–II)*, Toronto and London: University of Toronto Press and Routledge and Kegan Paul, accessed 15 November 2010 at http://oll. libertyfund.org/title/102/9741/72321.

Muñoz de Bustillo R. and E. Fernández Macías (2005), 'Job satisfaction as an indicator of the quality of work', *Journal of Socio-economics,* **34** (5), 656–73.

Mussmann, F. (2009), 'The German "good-work" index (DGB-Index Gute Arbeit)', paper presented at the ETUI Conference 2009, 18–19 March, Brussels.

Navarro, V. (1982), 'The labor process and health: A historical materialist interpretation', *International Journal of Health Services*, **12**(l), 5–29.

Organisation for Economic Co-operation and Development (OECD) (2008), *Handbook on Constructing Composite Indicators. Methodology and User Guide*, Paris: OECD.

Ose, S. O. (2005), 'Working conditions, compensation and absenteeism', *Journal of Health Economics*, **24** (1), 161–88.

Oswald, A. J. (1997), 'Happiness and economic performance', *Economic Journal*, **107** (445), 1815–31.

Oswald, A. J. and N. Powdthavee (2008), 'Does happiness adapt? A longitudinal study of disability with implications for economists and judges', *Journal of Public Economics*, **95** (5–6), 1061–77.

Parent-Thirion, A., E. Fernández-Macías, J. Hurley and G. Vermeylen, (2007), *Fourth European Working Conditions Survey*, Dublin: Eurofound.

Peck, J. (1996), *Work-Place: The Social Regulation of Labour Markets*, New York: Guilford Press.

Pen, Jan (1971), *Income Distribution*, Harmondsworth: Allen Lane.

Peña-Casas, R. and P. Pochet (2009), *Convergence and Divergence of Working Conditions in Europe: 1990–2005*, Dublin: Eurofound.

Preinfalk, H., G. Michenthaler, and H. Wasserbacher (2006), 'The Austrian work climate index', presentation to the Research Seminar of the European Foundation for the Improvement of Living and Working Conditions.

Purse, K. (2004), 'Work-related fatality risks and neoclassical compensating wage differentials', *Cambridge Journal of Economics*, **28** (4), 597–617.

Rao, V., I. Gupta, M. Lokshin, and S. Jana (2003), 'Sex workers and the cost of safe sex: the compensating differential for condom use among Calcutta prostitutes', *Journal of Development Economics*, **71** (2), 585–603.

Ritter, J. A. and R. Anker (2002), 'Good jobs, bad jobs: workers evaluations in five countries', *International Labour Review*, **141** (4), 231–58.

Robinson, J. C. (1991), *Toil and Toxic: Workplace Struggles and Political Strategies for Occupational Safety*, Berkeley, CA: University of California Press.

Rosen, S. (1986), 'The theory of equalizing differences', in O. Ashenfelter and R. Layard (eds), *Handbook of Labor Economics*, vol. I, Amsterdam: Elsevier Science Publishers pp. 641–92.

Sehnbruch, K. (2004), 'From the quantity to the quality of employment: an application of the capability approach to the Chilean labour market', Center for Latin American Studies working paper no. 9.

Sen, A. (1976), 'Real national income', *Review of Economic Studies*, **43** (1), 19–39.

Sen, A. (2000), *Development as Freedom*, Oxford: Oxford University Press.

Sennet, R. (2005), *The Culture of the New Capitalism*, Cambridge: Yale University Press.

Shepard, J. (1977), 'Technology, alienation, and job satisfaction', *Annual Review of Sociology*, **3**, 1–21.

Skalli, A., I. Theodossiou and E. Vasileiou (2008), 'Jobs as Lancaster goods: facets of job satisfaction and overall job satisfaction', *Journal of Socio-Economics*, **37** (5), 1906–20.

Smith, A. (1776), *An Inquiry into the Nature and Causes of the Wealth of Nations*, edited by A. S. Skinner and R. H. Campbell reprinted 1976 Oxford: Clarendon Press (1976).

Smith, M., B. Burchell, C. Fagan and C. O'Brian (2008), 'Job quality in Europe', *Industrial Relations Journal*, **39** (6), 586–603.

Solow, R. M. (1992), *The Labor Market as a Social Institution*, Oxford: Basil Blackwell.

Spector, P. E. (1997), *Job Satisfaction. Application, Assessment, Causes and Consequences*, London: Sage.

Tangian, A. (2005), 'A composite indicator of working conditions in the EU-15 for policy monitoring and analytical purposes', Hans Bockler Foundation WSI Diskussionspapier no. 135, Dusseldorf.

Tangian, A. (2007), 'Is work in Europe decent? A study based on the 4th European survey of working conditions 2005', Hans Bockler Foundation WSI Diskussionspapier no. 157, Dusseldorf.

Thaler, R. H. and S. Rosen (1976), 'The value of saving a life: evidence from the labor market', in N. E. Terleckyj (ed), *Household Production and Consumption*, Boston, MA National Bureau of Economic Research, pp. 265–302.

Tilly, C. (1996), 'The good, the bad, and the ugly: good and bad jobs in the United States at the millennium', Russell Sage Foundation working paper no. 103.

Toharia, L., M. Caprile and J. Potrony (2008), 'L'Indicador de Qualitat del Mercat de Treball (IQT) a Espanya', in *Anuari Sociolaboral de la UGT de Catalunya 2005*, Barcelona, Spain: UGT and CRESC, vol. II, pp. 42–51.

Union of Industrials and Employers' Confederations of Europe (UNICE) (2001), 'UNICE position paper on the commission communication "Employment and social policies: a framework for investing in quality"', accessed 15 November 2010 at http://www.businesseurope.eu.

United Nations Development Program (UNDP) (1990), *Human Development Report 1990. Concept and Measurement of Human Development*, Oxford: Oxford University Press.

Vallas, S. P. (1988), 'New technology, job content and worker alienation', *Work and Occupations*, **15** (2), 148–78.

Veblen, T. (1898), 'The instinct of workmanship and the irksomeness of labor', *American Journal of Sociology*, **4**(2), 187–201.

Veblen, T. (1899), *The Theory of the Leisure Class. An Economic Study in the Evolution of Institutions*, New York: Macmillan.

Veenhoven, R. (1991), 'Is happiness relative?', *Social Indicators Research*, **24**, 1–34.

Verba, S. (2007), 'Cross-national survey research: the problem of credibility', in I. Vallier (ed.), *Comparative Methods in Sociology. Essays on Trends and Applications*, Berkeley, CA: University of California Press, pp. 309–56.

Vinopal, J. (2009), 'The instrument for empirical surveying of subjectively perceived quality of life', paper presented at the conference Working

Conditions and Health and Safety Surveys in Europe: Stocktaking, Challenges and Perspectives, European Trade-Union Institute, Brussels 18–19 March.

Viscusi, W. K. (1979), *Employment Hazards: An Investigation of Market Performance*, Cambridge, MA: Cambridge University Press.

Viscusi, W. K. (1980), 'Union, labor market structure, and the welfare implications of the quality of work', *Journal of Labor Research*, **1** (1), 175–92.

Viscusi, W. K. and J. Aldy, (2003), 'The value of statistical life: a critical review of market estimates throughout the world', *Journal of Risk and Uncertainty*, **27** (1), 5–76.

Weber, M. (1905), *The Protestant Ethic and the Spirit of Capitalism*, London: Unwin Hyman (1930).

Wilkinson, C. (2001), *Fundamentals of Health at Work: the Social Dimensions*, London: Taylor and Francis.

Wilkinson, R. and K. Pickett (2010), *The Spirit Level: Why More Equal Societies Almost Always Do Better*, London: Penguin.

Witte, H. D. (1999), 'Job insecurity and psychological well being: review of the literature and exploration of some unresolved issues', *European Journal of Work and Organizational Psychology*, **8** (2), 155–77.

Wright, E. O. and R. E. Dwyer (2003), 'Patterns of job expansions in the USA: a comparison of the 1960s and 1990s', *Socio-Economic Review*, **1** (3), 289–325.

Zizzo, D. J. and A. J. Oswald (2001), 'Are people willing to pay to reduce others' incomes?', *Annales d'Economie et de Statistique*, **63–64**, 39–65.

Index